PLASTIC TULIPS

in the

WINTER

A Memoir

PLASTIC TULIPS

in the

WINTER

A Memoir

DENICE VICKERS

This work is written through the eyes and emotion of the author, the way she sees life. It may not be the way others saw it. Names, characters, places, and incidents either are the product of the author's imagination or are used fictitiously, and any resemblance to an actual person, living or dead, business establishment, events, or locales are entirely coincidental.

Copyright © 2014 Denice Vickers
All rights reserved.
ISBN: 0988751003
ISBN 13: 9780988751002
Library of Congress Control Number: 2012923747
CreateSpace Independent Publishing Platform
North Charleston, South Carolina

DEDICATION

I dedicate this book to all those who are searching for an answer in life.

To the hurting, broken, bruised and the tormented. I pray that in these pages you will find the answer.

To my husband, Steve, who I love and under God he is my breath.

To my children Stacy, Misty, Stephen and Denice, I love being your mother. To their partners in life, Brian, Duke, Ben and Hillary, I love you. To all twelve of my grandchildren, you have my heart. You all bring fullness and joy to my life.

To my sisters, Janice and Leeann, and my brother Charlie, thank you for allowing me to open the pages of our life.

In memory of Momma, whose hunger and cry for God became deep rooted in my own life.

In memory of Pam: my sister, my friend.

ACKNOWLEDGMENTS

I would like to acknowledge the following people, whose encouragement and support have been invaluable to me in the writing of this book:

First and foremost, my husband Steve and our children, Stacy, Misty, Stephen and Denice, who believed I had something to say and never lost faith in me.

Thanks to Janice, my sister who got tired of me asking her "Is the book good". She finally told me not to ask her again. Thanks for believing in me.

Thank you to James Thayer, who is an author of thirteen thriller novels and an attorney. James helped me as a teacher of writing. I learned so much from him. He never spoke down to me. He could have with his education and all his completed novels. But then again, I would have kicked him in the butt. Smile James.

I cannot leave out this group of people that helped in editing. It truly takes a team. Thank you to my husband Steve, my son Stephen, Rick & Irma Alexander, Betty Dillon, Migdalia Pabon and Sebrena Eutsey.

Irma was the best friend life could have given me through all of the editing, she believed in me.

PREFACE

I want to say a word to you before you begin this journey with me.

My struggles were personal. My failures and victories in this life are of my human experience. This book is written for you the reader. I do not have the desire to be polished in my work, nor do I crave the accolades of those who will surely find fault with my writing. I decided to say what I wish to say in a conversational tone as I tell you my story. If you have an open mind and are searching for answers to your life, please pull up a cushioned chair and footstool and let me tell you about my life. Would you like a cup of coffee or a glass of ice-cold sweet tea? Here we go…

Denice Vickers

~~ I ~~
DADDY'S KILLING MOMMA

SUMMER 2007

ASHES TO ASHES, DUST to dust. Momma always said she wanted a marching band with a choir singing, *"When The Saints GO Marching In."* She wanted it to be a time of celebration. There Janice and I stood. She was sixty and I was not far behind. How did the years pass so fast?

As Janice and I looked out over the ocean, the setting sun cast an orange hue across the water. All the sunbathers and the children playing had gone in for the evening. Our toes dug deep into the wet sand as the waves rushed over our feet. The breeze, filled with the salty air, blew against our faces. We stood side by side, looking in deep silence…and from the depth of my being I heard my soul cry, *"Momma, are we there yet?"*

SUMMER 1955, fifty-two years earlier.

"MOMMA ARE WE there yet?"

"Yes Denice, now stop your wiggling. We will soon be there and we are all going to have fun, *yea!*" Momma always said "Yea!" It was her way of turning everything into a celebration.

Daddy was driving our 1955 four-door, two-tone, white and teal Chevy Sedan. He had his usual pack of Winston cigarettes in his shirt pocket with one lit in his hand. He propped his elbow up on the car door and hung his arm out the window. I watched him wiggle his fingers as he let the wind pass through them.

His name was Charles Rady Perkins. He was six two, thin and very handsome. The men's Vitalis hair cream made his black wavy curls look shinny. Daddy was a Royal Cup Coffee salesman and his job was to keep all the A&P grocery stores stocked with coffee. Everybody liked him, especially the female cashiers.

"Hey Charlie," they would say in a slow southern drawl, and with all his charm, and he was a charmer, he threw them a wink and a smile.

"Hey ladies," he responded as he walked past them. He did all of this so fluidly, almost like a dance, as he strutted to the sound of his own voice.

Nellie May, my mom, sat in the front next to Daddy. She was five two, had a small waist, shapely hips, large breasts and beautiful legs that she liked to show off in her three inch high heel shoes. Her shoulder length hair was a soft auburn color, thick, long, and wavy. Her hourglass figure made her look like a Hollywood movie star. I do not believe she ever knew how beautiful she was. That day she had on one of Daddy's starched white shirts, unbuttoned, with the sleeves rolled up, and underneath was her one-piece leopard bathing suit that tied behind her neck. She was barefooted.

My big sister, Janice Faye, was sitting by the window behind Daddy. She was the responsible one. The wind blew her hair back away from her face; she seemed to be daydreaming about her next adventure. She was eight years old, long and lanky, with brown hair, brown eyes and buckteeth. Momma cut Janice's bangs crooked. She could never cut them straight. The more she tried to straighten them out, the more crooked and shorter they became. Janice's buckteeth, glasses and short crooked bangs, made her look weird in her school pictures.

Janice liked to stand on the stump in the front yard and sing opera to the passing cars. She was convinced that she could be a great opera singer. Janice always asked, "If I build a statue of myself, will it make me famous?" It made sense to me, why not?

Pamela Sue always sat in the middle, playing with her doll. She was six years old with bangs and long blonde curls that framed her face. She had dark brown eyes with dimples on both sides of her cheeks.

Our maid, Bessie, said about Pam, "That child's dimples are so deep, I's sure two angels poked her there to make their marks and announce to the world this child gonna be a girly girl, before she done entered this world." Bessie was prophetic; Pam would always be the girly girl of the family.

Pam loved combing her doll's hair, dressing them up and playing tea party with her make believe friend, Miss McCarty. She loved to be cuddled. She would say, "Hold me, Daddy, hold me?" Daddy would sweep her up and sit her in his lap while he sat in front of the TV.

I watched them from across the room, and wished Daddy would hold me. I just couldn't ask. I sucked my thumb while Pam was all curled up in his lap and I wondered, "What does it feel like to be held by Daddy?"

I can't think of any talent Pam had. She was just soft and lovable. I figure when you're that beautiful who needs talent? I just knew that she was my sister and I loved her.

I sat in the back seat, behind Momma, as we headed toward the beach. I was holding my little black Bible that I got at vacation Bible school. Momma said I could bring it to the beach.

My name is Denice Lynne Perkins. I was four and a half years old with dark brown eyes and jet-black hair cut in a pageboy. I was an all out tomboy and proud of it. My claim to fame was that I was the loudest burper on the street. I could spit farther than any boy in the neighborhood and say a whole sentence in one long belch. I could whoop any boy's tail. It was my routine every morning to find the fattest frog and put it in my pocket and pull him out, to speak to it throughout the day. The freckles on my nose spread across my face like the stars in the sky.

I always got sunburned so badly on my shoulders that I got huge bubble blisters. Momma called it that first good summer burn. We stayed brown as a biscuit for the rest of the summer.

We lived in Montgomery, Alabama, the Heart of Dixie, known as the Black Belt for its black soil. It is also known as the Bible belt. We could drive to Panama City Beach, Florida in three hours, spend the day in the sun and drive back that evening. It was always a blast! Momma took a picnic because she said it saved money. We had Golden Flake potato chips with peanut butter and banana sandwiches on white Wonder bread. The ice-cold sweet tea tasted so good. Once we arrived at the beach, Momma laid out a blanket and started to unpack our picnic.

Daddy wore his white bathing suit and white dress shirt, unbuttoned with the sleeves rolled up. He poured peroxide on his hair and then took Janice, Pam and me aside and said; "Now girls, don't call me Daddy today. Call me Uncle Charlie." He threw his head back and laughed.

"Why can't we call you Daddy?" I asked.

He said, "Well Denice, we are going to play a game today. I will walk up and down the beach and tell everybody that I am a lifeguard. I want to make sure that all the girls feel safe while they are swimming."

I could see the smile lines around his eyes as he spoke. I thought to myself; Daddy is really brave to be a lifeguard today. I just didn't understand why I couldn't call him Daddy.

Momma spent the day with us playing in the water and building sand castles in the sand. She always made sure that we kids had a good time. At the end of the day, as the sun went down, all that was left was the sound of the waves. We waited for Daddy to find his way back. Momma sat down in the wet sand, stretched out her legs and let the waves rush over her. With a calm look on her face, she turned to me and softly spoke. "This is my favorite time of the day. I feel such peace."

As she said the word peace, it seemed to stretch as it came out of her mouth, *peace*. It was so comforting and peaceful. I would feel the emotion of her words and experience this scene many times in my life. The breeze blowing through Momma's hair, the look of total tranquility on her face, and the sweet sound of her voice as she said, "I feel such peace." She loved the ocean.

Momma was a good, beautiful, godly woman. She loved her children with every part of her being. But there was trouble in our home and it was only a matter of time before the dam would break.

That night, after we took our baths, Momma went to work in the kitchen cooking dinner. She made fried pork chops, mashed potatoes, gravy and lima beans that had been slow cooking all day. Of course, every night, Momma's fresh homemade buttermilk biscuits completed the meal. Momma sliced up an onion and a tomato on a plate and placed it on the table. "Now girls, eat you a slice of onion with your meal — it's good for your health." She reached for a piece of onion to chew on as she returned to the oven.

Momma's mother taught her how to make biscuits. Passing down recipes and style of cooking to your daughters was the southern way. We stood around Momma in the kitchen to watch her cook. Momma took a big wooden dough bowl that her mother had given her and sat it on the counter. Holding the sifter in one hand and pouring the flour into the bowl with the other, she began telling us about her mother teaching her how to cook.

Momma reached up into the cabinet above her and pulled out a can of lard, without measuring ingredients, she added lard and buttermilk to her flour. She kneaded the mixture in the wooden bowl until it made a ball, adding sifted flour until it felt just right. "You don't want your biscuit ball to feel sticky, so you just keep adding flour." She said as she kneaded the biscuit ball.

She would form the biscuits in the palm of her hand, set them down on a greased flat pan and then slipped them into the hot oven. Within minutes, the aroma of fresh biscuits cooking filled the air as they began to rise. Mom walked over to the sink, washed the dough off her hands and began to sing.

The love of God, how rich and pure
How measureless and strong!
It shall forevermore endure—
The saints' and angels' song.

I felt her peace as she sang. She picked up a fork and turned the pork chops that were frying in a large black skillet. She kicked her leg up in the air, smiled, looked at us and said, "That's my exercise."

The popping sound of the grease and the smell of the pork chops made you want dinner to hurry up so you could sit down at Momma's spread. We loved just hanging out with her. Momma always spoke to us while she cooked.

"What do you girls want to be when you grow up? Y'all are so smart and beautiful. You can be anything you want to be. You can go anywhere you want to go. Just trust in God. God is the answer."

Momma always said, "God is the answer."

She looked at Janice and asked, "Janice what do you want to be when you grow up?"

Janice gave a quick response, "Momma I want to be a go-go dancer in a cage or a Heart Surgeon."

Momma never made us feel stupid when we spoke. She always made us feel that what we had to say was important. Nothing we said was ridiculous.

Let's look at this—two choices: A go-go dancer in a cage or a Heart Surgeon. It made sense to Pam and me. After all, this was Janice and it fit Janice just right. It was very common for Janice to get a frog or a turtle out of a ditch and cut it open just to see all the parts and how the heart worked. When she became a teenager, her favorite clothes to wear to parties were what we called the "shimmy dress". It was a strapless dress with layers of little string tassels all over it. She wore her hair ratted chin length with bangs, smoothed out into a bubble. Her black cat eye shape, rhinestone glasses, were the latest in fashion. Janice could shimmy and go-go the night away. She just never got her cage. Oh! Wait a minute, that's later. I think she did.

The three of us were still gathered around Momma listening to each other's dreams. Momma then turned to Pam.

"Pam, what do you want to be when you grow up?"

Pam pressed her hands together almost as if she was going to Pray and put them next to the right side of her check as she spoke, "I want to be a singer and sing love songs like *Let Me Go, Lover*" and "*Love Is a Many Splendored Thing.*" She was a romantic. Brenda Lee was one of her favorites. She sang "*Sweet Nothings.*" Pam would sit on the floor with her 45's, singing along, playing her favorite love songs on the record player.

A new boy named Elvis Presley hit the scene singing, "*That's All Right, Momma.*" He shook his hips and legs, which upset the adults.

They said, "It's vulgar, the way he shakes." The teens loved it. They screamed and yelled. Some girls just stood there and cried as he sang. He dressed different. The adults didn't like that either. They said, "It's just not proper." He wore longer jackets with color and shine. When teens had dances, some of the boys tried to dress like him.

We were too young then to be concerned about whether Elvis was vulgar when he shook his hips and legs. All I knew was love songs and songs to dance to, would play an important role in our life. He and others on the radio would take us through our teens and help us forget our troubles, even if only for a moment.

Momma asked me, "Denice, what are your dreams?" taking the pot of boiling potatoes over to the sink to drain them.

I followed her, "Momma I want to be a cowgirl or a Christian." She was not surprised. She held the lid to the pot as she drained the potatoes.

Her eyes lit up with delight as she turned, smiling, looking down at me and said, "A cowgirl or a Christian, huh? Well, why can't you be both?"

Momma spooned the drained potatoes into a mixing bowl, added milk, butter, salt, pepper and began mixing the ingredients together, all the while, listening to me.

As serious as I could be and with all the emotion I could muster up I said, "Momma, if I'm gonna to be a real cowgirl, I'm gonna have to kill me some Indians and I don't think Christians can do that."

Tilting her head down at me, smiling from ear to ear, she shook her thick hair as she threw her head back laughing out loud. She said, "Denice, you're a pistol ball and you're right about that, but somehow, I bet you'll find a way to be both. You, Denice, can be a cowgirl and a Christian." I shook my head in agreement.

She placed the mashed potatoes down on the dinner table next to the plate of pork chops. Janice pulled the hot biscuits out of the oven and placed them on a plate next to the butter dish. Dinner was ready.

That night, as I lay in bed, I imagined what it would be like to be a cowgirl. I thought about riding along side Roy Rogers and his horse, Trigger. Dale Evans, the best cowgirl ever, would be there too. She was my hero! I wondered what my horse would look like. Maybe white with brown spots? Visions of my adventures as a cowgirl danced in my head and I drifted off to sleep. I slept sound that night, dreaming the sweet dreams of a child, not knowing that tomorrow would be a day I would never forget. A day no child should ever have to remember.

I woke up, put on what I called my soldier shorts. They were red, white and blue with little soldiers all over them. I went to the kitchen to find Momma, dressed for work, making breakfast. Janice was pouring glasses of orange juice for everyone. Pam was sitting at the table coloring. I took my seat next to Pam and grabbed a crayon to color on the opposite page. Daddy walked into the kitchen wearing his black dress pants and starched white shirt. As part of his usual routine, he said good morning to everyone, poured himself a cup of black coffee and headed off to work.

While we ate our biscuits, sausage and eggs, our maid, Bessie came in through the backdoor. She said, "Well, Mrs. Perkins, it's a mighty nice day outsides. Makes me wants to get in my garden with my greens and cook me some up."

I liked Bessie a lot. She was a stout, full figured black woman. Her gray hair was pulled real tight flat on her head in a bun. Her chubby arms wrapped around me as she pulled me close; her love swallowed me up into her big bosoms. She always called me her Baby Girl.

She said, "You Momma's breakfast tastes so good that if you put it on top of you head, you tongue slap you brains out trying to get it." I could see that in my mind's eye. Momma grabbed her purse and rushed out the door to her job as a bookkeeper. After breakfast, Janice and Pam went to a friend's house down the street.

Bessie said to me, "You stay here with me Baby Girl.

I went outside to find a frog. There was a ditch by our house where you could find some of the biggest frogs you've ever seen. You had to be careful where you stepped because there were always broken Coca-Cola bottles in there and I was always bare-footed. Sitting in the ditch, as if waiting for me, there was the perfect sized frog for today. I bent over to pick him up; he tried to get away, I had gotten good at catching frogs, so it wasn't long before I had him in my hands. He looked me in the eyes and gave out a croak.

I said, "Mr. Herbert, where have you been?" We were meant to be buddies for the day. "Mr. Herbert, you will fit just right in my pocket." He seemed to like the name too, so I put him in my pocket and went about my morning.

Around lunchtime, I decided to go inside to see if Bessie would fix me something to eat. Daddy's car was in the driveway. This wasn't unusual, since he sometimes came home for his lunch break. I stepped inside and could hear Daddy talking to someone. It was a woman's voice. I knew it wasn't Momma. They were laughing. I walked into the living room and stood by the door. They didn't see me, but I saw them. Daddy was sitting on our brown sofa.

Our neighbor, Mrs. Maria, who lived a few doors down, was standing with one knee propped up on the sofa next to him. She had short black hair and was barefooted, was wearing white short shorts and a royal blue button up cotton shirt, tied in a knot under her breast. Teasingly, she grabbed a throw pillow and held it to Daddy's face as if to smother him. She stood up facing him, giggling with her legs slightly spread apart and her hands on her hips.

She said, "Charlie, now you stand up and slow dance with me, you bad boy." He grabbed her by the waist, pulled her down onto the sofa and started to tickle her.

I walked into the kitchen where Bessie was cleaning and asked," Bessie, why is that woman hugging on my Daddy?"

Bessie's eyes open wide turning the whites of her eyes into a complete circle. She leaned down and pushed my bangs away from my sweaty face as she whispered.

"Now hush you Child! You hush now. You don't needs to bother you self about that. You go outside, and you play. I call you in when you lunch is ready." Bessie opened the screen door and gave me a little push. "You stays outside until I call you in. You hear Baby Girl?"

I said, "But."

"No buts about it, now. You stay outside and you waits for me," she said.

"Yes, ma'am," I replied. I picked up a small rock, threw it and watched how far it went. I reached in my pocket and pulled out Mr. Herbert.

"Mr. Herbert, why was my Daddy tickling Mrs. Maria? Why was Bessie so upset?" Mr. Herbert let out a croak. I sighed. "I guess you don't know either, do you?"

I was drawing in the dirt with a stick when Bessie opened the screen door.

"Baby Girl, come on insides and clean you self up for lunch." When I sat down at the table, a sandwich was waiting for me. I ate my food as Bessie set the ironing board up in the living room.

She said to me, "After you finish eaten, you come lays you self on the couch for you nap and I gonna sing to you as I does my ironing, alright?"

"Yes, ma'am Bessie." I answered. I lay on the sofa, and Bessie turned on the fan to blow toward my face.

"Now you sleep honey child while I iron. You such a sweet baby girl," she said.

I realized that Daddy and Mrs. Maria were no longer in the house. It wasn't long before the sound of Bessie singing caused my thoughts to drift:

> *Up in the morning*
> *Out on the job*
> *I's work like's tha devil for my pay.*
> *But that lucky ol' sun has nothin' to do.*
> *But roll around heaven all day.*

It wasn't a black spiritual, but Bessie sang it like it was. Her voice had so much soul in it when she sang. I lay there sucking my thumb, picturing that lucky old sun just rolling around heaven all day.

Waking up from my nap, I heard Pam giggling with someone in her bedroom. I walked in to see. She was playing with her dolls. To my surprise, I saw she was playing with Fat Henrietta.

You have to understand why I called her Fat Henrietta. She was the neighborhood bully. If you had something she wanted, she took it. She knew and we knew, just by sitting on top of one of us, you were a goner. She had frizzy brown hair, red face as round as a basketball, covered with freckles and big lips that overtook her face. The voice that came out of that child sounded like angry thunder.

It was strange for Pam to be playing with her. I thought to myself, why not give those dolls a chance? Fat Henrietta saw me approaching them and in her slow thunderous voice asked me. "What do you want?"

I placed my hand on my hips, showed her attitude of my own, like, who's afraid of the Big Fat Henrietta? I spread my feet apart and stood firm. I was going to tell her what for. I had a deep alto voice of my own; I too could sound like thunder. Gritting my teeth and squinting my eyes, I told her, "I'm gonna play dolls with y'all."

Pam continued combing her doll's hair. Henrietta rose off the floor; she looked like a giant up against me; she was as big around as she was tall and twice my age. Her big red face began to turn redder, beat red, and tomato red; I knew that somebody was in trouble. Her response was that of a bear about to eat her live prey.

"NO YOU'RE NOT! GET OUT OF HERE!" she roared.

Her words came out as if she had a mouth full of mush, but what she was implying was that I was dead meat. Her face looked as if it were going to explode. She stepped toward me, her fist ready to pound me in the ground.

Pam jumped up from the floor and screamed, "Don't you dare hit my little sister!"

For a moment, by the tone in Pam's voice, I thought she was going to get rough. I had never seen Pam do that, but being that I liked a good fight, I was not going to wait around to see if Pam had it in her.

I hit Fat Henrietta, swinging my arms and legs, going to her like killing snakes. I was as fast as all get out. I began to belt out Elvis' song "Hound Dog". In my mind, I was going to beat her deader than a doornail. I was singing, swinging, kicking and hitting her and she was hitting back. I was getting ready to go into the next verse of hound dog, when she knocked me a good one across the face.

Momma says, "Some people act too big for their britches." I thought this was a good time to take her down a few notches. This was it, my big chance to use my secret weapon. I pulled Mr. Herbert out of my pocket; the juiciest, fattest frog and threw it right in the center of fat Henrietta's face. Her eyes grew wide as she gasped for breath. I doubled over laughing at the sight of that fat, slimy frog legs spread across her face, sliding down her cheek. It was a powerful feeling given to me at that moment.

She grabbed him and slung him across the room. Fat Henrietta screamed as she ran out the door. I ran behind her. I wanted to watch my enemy run. Our house was on a hill and I could see her running and screaming for a long way. Standing at the top of the hill, I hit my bare chest and gave out a loud Tarzan yell. "Ah-ah-AHHHH ah ah, HH-ahahahahah." I knew she could hear me as she ran. That was a good day. That was a fabulous day! It made me slap happy. I always did like the taste of victory, even at that age, and it never would change throughout my life.

It was around that time I had to stop putting frogs in my pocket. Momma walked in from work that day and Bessie complained, "Miss Nellie, I's washed and I's dries Denice's shorts, and as I folds them, I's found a dried up, dead, flat, frog in hers pocket. Miss Nellie, I just can't stands it. I just can't stands it. You got to do something with that child. It just ain't fitting for her to runs around with frogs in her pocket." That ended the days of frogs in my pocket. I was getting older. It was time.

Bessie then told her what I had seen that day when I walked in on Dad.

Momma said, "Bessie, you can go on home. I'll finish up the ironing myself."

I remember that night so clearly. The windows were open and there was a cool breeze blowing through the curtains. Momma was ironing. Janice was sitting on the sofa watching TV. The fan was blowing on her face. She was wearing her matching plaid short outfit. Pam and I were sitting on the floor. Pam had on a baby blue nightgown and was playing with her doll. I was playing with my plastic horse. I didn't have a shirt on but was still wearing my soldier shorts.

The front door opened. It was Daddy coming home from work. Momma placed the iron down on the ironing board. She was ready to blast him. I could almost see the smoke coming out of her nostrils.

"What were you doing today?" Momma asked in an accusing tone.

"What do you mean what was I doing? I was at work all day, Nellie. What do you think I was doing?" He shook his head and tightened his upper lip.

Momma screamed, "Don't you look at me and lie to my face! What was Maria doing in our house? Who does she think she is coming in my house?" Momma's body trembled as she stepped closer to him.

His eyes narrowed as he grit his teeth. He slammed his car keys down on the table and yelled, "I don't know what you're talking about, you stupid woman."

Momma shook her finger as she pointed at him and yelled, "Charles you're a liar!

What were y'all doing back there? Denice saw y'all. How could you Charles?"

Momma looked over at me and back at Daddy. We were scared of how bad this could get. Pam was crying.

He moved in toward Momma.

He said, "Nellie, you're just nuts. You're losing your mind woman. You're going crazy woman, you're just a nut case."

Momma hated when he said that. It always made her angrier. She demanded an answer, yelling at him, "Charles, what were you doing with her? I know you are in an affair with her. I better not see her face around my house or my children."

He walked over to the television to change the channel.

He said, "You're always thinking the worst. What is wrong with you, woman? It is all in your head." He looked at her, tapped himself on the forehead and said, "You're just a nut case. You're losing your mind. You're the stupidest woman around." He laughed, shaking his head as if she was the loser.

That did it. She threw the hot iron at him. The iron missed and knocked the lamp off the table next to the sofa. She walked up to him to blast him with threats.

"Charles, if that woman comes in my house again, I will go over to her back door and when she answers it, I will slap the living fire out of her."

Pam grabbed her doll and slid over into the corner. Holding her knees to her chest and burying her face into her baby doll, she continued crying.

Daddy grabbed Momma with both of his hands around her throat, lifted her body off the floor and dropped her. She stood back up and screamed, "Charles, don't you touch me."

He locked his jaw and his nostrils began to flare. He took a step closer toward her. His eyes narrowed, he slowly raised his hand in the air and with all his strength, slammed his open palm across her face. She took a hit. A red imprint of a large hand began to form on the side of her cheek.

She screamed out and then said, "Don't you hit me again Charles!"

He raised his hand in the air to give her another blow. She swung her arm out to protect her face. He grabbed her by the wrists and threw her against the wall. He threw her to the floor, straddled her and pounded her face, over and over. She was screaming for help. Momma screamed out, "Don't hit me, God, help me, Charles, don't you hit me, God help me." Then she yelled, "Oh, my children." I think at that moment she realized we were seeing all this.

Janice ran over and pulled me off the floor and onto the couch. She then began to plead with Momma and Daddy to stop fighting. "Momma, Daddy, please stop, stop before someone gets hurt." It didn't do any good. It was as if they didn't even know we were there.

Daddy was still hitting her. She tried returning the punches, but they seemed to have no affect on him. She got up from under him, grabbed my plastic horse next to her and threw it at his head. He dodged the toy; she ran to the kitchen. She came back through the doorway holding a butcher knife.

Pam was crying saying, "No Momma, no."

He folded his arms and pushed out his chest as he blurted out, "Oh, what are you going to do now, stab me?" The smirk on his face said it all.

"If that's what it takes." she yelled. Momma's hand went up in the air as she ran toward him with the knife and a blood-curdling scream.

He grabbed her wrist, and they began to wrestle with the knife. Pam covered her face.

Janice jumped between them and tried to push them apart; she looked at me and screamed, "Denice, Run, Denice! Run to the neighbors house, tell them Daddy's killing Momma!"

They were struggling with the knife between them; Janice tried to separate them. I ran into the kitchen and out the back screen door into the cold, dark night, running as fast as my four-year-old legs would carry me. The darkness scared me, but I was more afraid of not making it in time to save Momma! I could feel my heart beating out of my chest, sliding down into the ditch to cross over into the neighbors yard. I felt my bare feet land in the wet mud as it went between my toes. I remembered the broken coke bottles in the ditch, but it didn't matter. I had to save Momma. Climbing out of the ditch, I saw a back porch light on. I ran as fast as I could. I banged on the neighbor's door and yelled, "Call the police." A man answered the door.

Breathless I cried out. "Call the police! Call the police! Tell them Daddy's killing Momma!" Not for one-second did I worry about Momma hurting Daddy.

The police came, but by the time they arrived, the fight had already stopped. Momma and Daddy decided not to press charges. The officer instructed them before leaving.

"You two get your problems worked out and keep it quiet." This would prove to be a regular event for Janice, Pam and I.

The next morning I told Bessie about the police coming to our house.

She said, "Now you hush Baby Girl. You do not needs to talk about that. You come outside while I hangs the clothes on the line."

BESSIE WAS ALWAYS chatting with her friend Rosie, who rode the bus with her every day. They both wore the same blue cotton dresses that other maids wore on the bus. Rosie worked for Mrs. Angela next door. She was skinny and her legs looked like she was walking on toothpicks. I don't think she wore a bra because she looked like she had two fried eggs up under her dress. She wore her hair in two pigtails, but to me they looked like two Brillo Pads on top of her head. When she smiled she showed all her big teeth.

Rosie and Bessie spoke as if they were solving the world's problems under the clothesline. This was their meeting place.

Bessie would throw her hands up in the air laughing and her eyes would roll around like a ball in a pinball machine. She was so tickled listening to Rosie. Rosie talked none stop and danced around doing a happy jig on her toothpick legs.

I enjoyed lying in the grass, listening to them talk and laugh, while Rosie told her stories.

Rosie said, "Last night while my man was laying in that bed sleeping, and he was done still in his dirty work clothes. I thought to myself, if I could come up with some kind of spot remover, and pour it all over that man from head to toe and he just disappear. Well I be rich! I know a bunch of white women folks that would buy my spot remover."

Bessie laughed, "Rosie, now you talking trash. You'd better watch out thinking like that. When you does you trash talking, I's feel my stomach gonna bust wide open like a watermelon."

Rosie chatted about Sissy, "Sissy told me something dis morning on the bus."

She smiled really big as if she had a secret." She said, "You know she works for that Mrs. Wilson, who lives in that big old bankers house down the street. That Mr. Wilson, come home from the bar drunk and done beat his wife for the very last time."

Bessie said, "Watch out now Rosie!"

Rosie smiled and said, "He just a snake in the grass."

Bessie said, "What you say, look out now?"

Rosie kept talking, "The other night that Mrs. Wilson got Sissy to stays late."

Rosie now had Bessie's attention.

She acted out what she was saying. "Theys laid a big bed sheet on the floor, in front of the front door, and when that Mr. Wilson stumbled in drunk that Mrs. Wilson and Sissy, both of them, holding brooms in theys hands, knocked that fool down, on that there bed sheet, and theys ties him up."

Bessie screamed out, "No. You don't say?"

Rosie smiled showing all her big teeth, "Oh, yes I does say. She got Sissy to help her ties him up in that there bed sheet, and they done beat the living stew out of him with theys brooms."

Rosie said, "Sissy said that Mrs. Wilson done lost all her class. While she was beating that Mr. Wilson, she was hollering and beating and screaming out, *You have beaten me for the last time*" then said, "Sissy said she kicked him in his manhood."

Rosie screamed out laughing and jig dancing. Then she stopped and said, "Then theys put him in bed."

Rosie was just a smiling, swaying as she spoke.

Bessie was laughing, shaking her head, "You don't declare?"

When Rosie saw that Bessie was responding to her story, the more excited she got telling it. So she continued rattling on.

Sissy said he woke up the next morning, and he was a changed man. He told that Mrs. Wilson, that he was through drinking, cause he done got himself beat up at the bar and he was in terrible pain. That fool was black and blue all over. Sissy said that Mrs. Wilson said the clouds of joy were on her side, and they done found the cure for all men. Just ties them up and beat the living fool out of them.

Bessie screamed out laughing saying, "Rosie, hush you self."

Rosie still talking, "Sissy said she never did like that Mr. Wilson. She said he was just an old Cracker Jack Fool." Rosie was dancing the happy jig, slapping her legs and laughing. She began to twist one of her Brillo Pads hair buns and said, "I's gonna tells all the girls bout this on the bus today."

Bessie snapped a clothespin onto the line, shook her head and gave Rosie a warning, "You gonna get you self in trouble with you trash talking. Now Rosie, stops you trash talking, my Baby Girl don't needs to hear bout this." Bessie continued snapping clothes on the line.

Rosie grabbed the clothesline pole and began swinging herself around it. As she did she sang:

I's gonna tell everybody
I's gonna tell everybody
I's gonna tell everybody
Bout that Snake in the Grass

I's gonna tell everybody
I's gonna tell everybody
I's gonna tell everybody
Bout that Cracker Jack Fool

Bessie said, "Yeah, and you gonna gets us all in some heaping trouble, you better hush you self"

Top Left: Momma dancing; Top Right: Mom & Dad;
Bottom Left: The three of us; Middle: Dad in a hula skirt
dancing with another woman.

~ 2 ~
BRINGING IN THE CHEESE

MOMMA'S MAIDEN NAME WAS Nellie May Lindsey. She was a city girl raised in

Birmingham, Alabama. She was the youngest of nine children. Her Daddy was a tall, slim man who worked at the steel mill. He was a quiet man who believed in working hard to provide for his large family.

Her mother was a short round full figure of a woman. She was a happy, godly woman who was an avid reader. She walked to the library every morning and picked out a new book to read. Momma said she read romance novels. That may explain the nine children. Their front porch wrapped around their two-story house. She sat on the porch swing every afternoon, after she finished reading her library book, she would then read her Bible.

All the kids had their chores after school, and with that many children helping out, the big house was kept clean. At the end of the day, her mother cooked a meal, which always included home-made buttermilk biscuits or corn bread. Her Momma taught her to cook the southern way. There were flavorful dishes of Southern fried chicken, fried catfish, chicken and dumplings, fried okra, fried green tomatoes, candied yams, turnip greens and collard greens serving the liquid as "pot liquor" to dunk your cornbread in.

After dinner, all nine children cleaned off the table and washed the dishes. It was a happy home. Momma said her older brothers always teased her. They would say, "Nellie hesitated in the street." She would cry thinking they were saying she did something bad in the street. She was young and did not understand that hesitating meant she paused in the street. She thought they were saying she wet her pants in the street.

One of Momma's brother's became a street preacher. They called him Holy Hubert on the UCLA campus. Holy Hubert was a preacher in the late 1960s. He went to campus to preach the gospel of Christ to hippies, radical socialists and Satanists; many found Christ as a result of his life and ministry.

Mom's mom taught her that if you swear on a Bible, you'd better be telling the truth. It's dangerous to swear on a Bible. She said God would hold you to it even if it were a lie.

The older siblings got married and moved out on their own. Her parents decided to rent the upstairs of their home and use it as a boarding house. Momma, being the youngest, was the last child left in the house.

My Daddy was a country boy. His parents were cotton farmers in Holtville Alabama. They grew their own vegetables, raised hogs on their farm and picked cotton on another farm for extra money. Daddy started cotton picking at the age of five for a nickel a day until he was nine years old. He said that it was back breaking work. There was no indoor plumbing at the farm, just an outhouse. Daddy's mother gave birth to fifteen children. Ten of them were healthy, and five were stillbirths. To say raising a family in rural Alabama in the 1930's and 1940's was difficult would be an understatement. It was common to subsidize your income by making moonshine.

They had a saying, "If the Lord's willing and the creek don't rise I'll be there for the hoedown."

On Sundays, all the farmers hooked up their wagons and got together for a good ol' fashion hoedown. The local fiddler usually came. He was loved by the families and condemned by some churchmen. These churchmen only saw the idleness, liquor, the Devil's Box, people drinking, dancing and playing music. People brought their guitars and banjos. They sat on the porch playing their music and singing. It was a simple life for honest, hardworking people. Out in the yard was an iron pot over a fire, where they boiled sugarcane to produce cane syrup and pull candy. There was always plenty of moonshine.

All of this was going on during the middle of the Depression. It became very hard for families to feed all of their children. One day Daddy's father lined up all his children and told them that they couldn't afford them any longer. The oldest boys would need to leave. Daddy, at nine years old, had to leave. Daddy and a boy name Thorn from another farm hitched a ride on the back of a flour truck into the city. Thorn got his name from his Daddy, who said he was a thorn in his flesh. He already had nine children when Thorn was born and he didn't want nor need another mouth to feed.

For over a hundred miles, they worked their way, helping deliver fifty pound bags of flour to country grocery stores throughout the backwoods of Alabama. The night they arrived in Birmingham, they were dogged tired. Dad's older brother already lived in Birmingham, so he was able to stay with him until he could get out on his own.

Eight years later, Daddy was working at a grocery store as a bag boy. Momma walked in and their eyes met. It was love at first sight. Momma thought Dad was the most wonderful thing in the world. The only problem was, she was engaged and her fiancé was half way around the world fighting in the Korean War. Momma wrote him a letter saying that she was going to have to break off the engagement. A few months later, Momma and Daddy married. He was seventeen and she was eighteen.

Daddy got a job working at the US Steel mill for the next few years. He started lying and chasing women immediately. Her diamond ring was the first lie she caught him in. Momma's diamond fell out of its band. She took it to the jeweler to have the diamond set back in.

"Ma'am," the jeweler said. "I hate to tell you this but this is not a diamond. It's just a piece of glass."

Momma gasped and swayed on her feet with embarrassment. She felt faint; it hurt her. She didn't care that Daddy couldn't afford a diamond ring; she just couldn't believe that he would lie about it.

They had their first child, Janice. A year and a half year later came Pam and a year and a half after that I was born. After my birth, Momma's mother died. Between Daddy's lies, postpartum depression, and her mother's death, Momma just couldn't handle it all. At twenty-seven years of age, she would have the first of several nervous breakdowns.

NOVEMBER 1955 CHRISTMAS was around the corner. I loved that time of year. I loved the cold air, bundling up in my coat, riding downtown in our car with Momma and Daddy. We looked at all the homes decorated for Christmas. Christmas was a magic blanket that wrapped around me. It made me feel safe and secure for the moment.

Every year there was a Thanksgiving Day parade on Dexter Avenue in downtown Montgomery. It began in front of our State Capitol. The city set up the biggest Christmas tree that any tree farmer could grow. It was decorated with bright lights and huge red, blue, green and gold Christmas balls. Every intersection was strung with garlands, twinkling lights, and big gold bells hanging in the center. Large, five pointed stars were shinning bright as they hung from the street lamps that lined the downtown streets with red and gold ribbon wrapping the poles.

The crowds gathered on each side of the street waiting with excitement for the parade to begin. The First Baptist Church Choir in their green Christmas choir robes with a red satin collar stood on the steps of the capital. The choir director led them in Christmas carols. Everyone had bundled up with hats, coats and gloves. Some brought blankets to stay warm. Children sat on their Daddy's shoulders so that they could see the parade as it passed by. State buildings, office buildings, the small storefronts of jewelry stores, women's dress shops, men's suits, the Woolworth store, the Five and Dime General Store, the corner drug store and even the popular Chris's Hotdogs with its cigar and magazine stand left their doors and windows open so people could watch the parade.

The employees of the Belk's Department Store were always allowed to bring their children to work with them the day of the parade. The children stood inside where it was warm and they looked out from the storefront window. Momma said that they were drinking hot-cocoa and eating cookies and candy the bosses had catered in for them. They were pointing at the floats as they passed by. All the stores were decorated for Christmas, and everybody had the Christmas spirit.

We drove around looking for a parking place. Janice, Pam, and I were bouncing all over the back seat pointing out the decorations. We could hardly wait for Daddy to park. We were like race horses standing at the starting gate. Just park and let us out.

Momma said, "Now kids, what we're going to do is park our car and walk a few blocks. We want to stand on the side of the street about midway. That way when the candy is thrown from the floats, they will still have plenty of it left to throw our way."

It's funny how Daddy was such a kid at times. He always got excited and playful. This was one of those times. I guess, though, he couldn't be that way all the time because his stomach hurt him. Dad had bad stomach ulcers. He would get indigestion so bad that at times he had to lick straight baking soda from the palm of his hand and drink buttermilk from the jug to soothe the acid.

We found a place to park and made our way to Dexter Avenue. There were so many people there. We were able to find a spot big enough for the five of us. The parade was just starting.

The choir passed by and shortly after a group of clowns appeared. Some were juggling, honking horns and using noisemakers while on roller skates and driving miniature cars. The loud trumpets and beating drums of the Robert E. Lee High School marching band appeared. In the front rows, were the majorettes twirling their batons.

Pam jumped up and down saying, "I want to be a majorette someday."

Following close behind the marching band was a float with the high school homecoming queen. She was wearing a beautiful cobalt blue gown and giving a Queen's wave with her long white gloves. She waved with one hand and held the crown on her head with the other to keep it from falling off. The star football players were also on the float, throwing candy to the children in the crowd. The Lanier High School's marching band with their float and homecoming queen wearing a red gown and white gloves was next. Her tiara shined as brightly as a queen's. Right behind them were the Boy Scouts, Girl Scouts and Brownie troops.

I yelled, "Here comes my favorite part, the horses!" It was the Montgomery City Police officers riding on horseback.

"Momma, I wish I was on the lead horse. I love horses."

She looked at me smiling, "Oh Yes, don't their legs look strong, and notice how they hold their heads and tails high; they prance when they walk. Don't they Denice?"

I nodded, pointing I yelled, "Look over there; they look like cowboys." They were the local farmers who competed in the local rodeo.

There were several horses and with that came horse droppings in the street. I was sure they planned the parade around it. We watched to see, if a big smiling cheerleader or majorette would step into a pile of horse poop. We were overjoyed, and screamed in fits of laughter if it happened to the football team we weren't rooting for.

Santa Claus was the last float to come down the street in the parade.

I yelled, "Janice, Pam. Here comes Santa on his sleigh!"

The children in the crowd started calling, "Santa! Santa! Santa!" I jumped up and down, waving my hands and clapping for his entrance.

"Santa is coming! Here comes Santa Claus," I yelled. I felt it was my job to announce his coming.

His float looked like the North Pole covered in snow, and his sleigh was black and gold. A big red velvet bag overflowing with presents wrapped in every color with bows were sitting next to Santa Claus. He was smiling and waving. All around Santa's sleigh were toys for every girl and boy.

I wondered which ones were going to be mine on Christmas morning. Elves were dressed in red and green velvet shirts and pants. Their pointed hats and shoes had bells dangling from them as they waved throwing candy to everyone.

"My goodness he sees me. I think he recognizes me because he is waving." I threw both my hands up into the air and yelled as loud as I could.

"Santa, don't forget to come to 405 Nottingham Drive! Santa, I want a bicycle. I've been a very good girl this year!"

Pam and Janice were jumping up and down and caught the candy that Santa's elves were throwing from the float.

THE FOLLOWING WEEK, Bessie approached Momma. She began to speak while she fumbled with a white sheet of paper she had rolled up in her hand. Momma already knew what she was about to tell her. "Mrs. Perkins, I need to talk to you about something."

Momma could tell, by the way, she was fumbling with that piece of paper she was concerned about something. "What is it, Bessie?"

"Mrs. Perkins, I can't rides the bus tomorrow, I'm afraid I won't be able to comes to work."

There was a boycott in our town. A colored woman who worked in downtown Montgomery by the name of Rosa Parks refused to move to the back of the bus. It was required by city ordinance. She wouldn't give up her seat to a white man. Momma said Mrs. Parks was tired from a long day of work. In the newspaper, she was quoted as saying, under other circumstance; she would have given up her seat willingly to a child or elderly person. Momma said that this time Mrs. Parks had had enough of the treatment she and other coloreds received. She was arrested and put on trial.

"Bessie, don't you worry I will drive my car and pick you up."

Bessie responded, "Mrs. Perkins, I couldn't ask you to do that! You know those white folks won't like you giving me a ride in your car. And us black folks, we done join together saying we won't ride those buses till they treats us with respect."

Momma said, "Don't you worry about it. You need the work, and besides, I need you."

Bessie shook her head and said, "Thank you, Mrs. Perkins. You know, I does need the work, and my Lord's lookin' out for me. You just come gets me at the corner of my street. Everything will be just fine."

Momma loved Bessie and respected her as a hard-working woman. Momma told us Bessie had children of her own to feed. She didn't need to stay out of work. She treated Bessie as her equal. Momma never saw color. She just saw a hard-working woman.

The boycott lasted 381 days. It made it hard on Momma but like she said, she needed Bessie and Bessie needed to work. That night while Momma was cooking supper she told us, "It's wrong the way colored people are treated. It's not right. They're people just like us."

Janice said, "Momma, Peggy Jo said her Daddy said that coloreds don't love their children. He said that they don't have souls that'll go to heaven... Is that true Momma?"

I spoke up and said, "Peggy Jo said if a black person rubs up against you, their black color will rub off onto our white skin. I told Peggy Jo, "Bessie's color doesn't rub off on me."

Momma bent down and looked us directly in the eyes. "Girls, you listen to me! You listen to me good! Their blood is the same color as our blood. If they got a cut on their arm, they'd bleed red blood just like us. They do have souls and Jesus died for them, too. They love their children just as I love all of you. That Mrs. Parks shouldn't have to give up her seat to any man. She is a woman just like me. That is wrong; I tell you! It is wrong and don't y'all ever forget it."

A few days later we were downtown with Momma shopping. We were picking out dresses to wear to church on Christmas. We heard the sound of glass breaking. We ran to Momma for security without even checking to see what it was. "Oh, my lands!" Momma said, as she faced the source of the noise.

"Dear God!" The shopkeeper said as she ran to the front. She shouted, "Someone threw a brick and busted the window out."

Momma's eyes grew wide on her face. She gathered us up like a mother hen would gather her baby chicks. She said, "Come on, girls we need to get out of here."

Momma grabbed my hand and said, "Janice, Pam, let's go, now." Immediately, my arm flew out in front of me and jerked my body into motion toward the store entrance. There was broken glass everywhere.

"Careful where you step girls," Momma cried out.

The big storefront window was now just a hole next to the door. People were screaming, shouting, and acting crazy. Janice and Pam were walking swiftly behind us trying to keep up the pace.

"Momma, what's going on?" I asked. It was obvious by her voice that she was frightened. "Keep quiet Denice."

"Why did someone throw a brick through Miss Mitchell's window?" Janice asked.

"Hush, Janice, keep walking."

None of this was making sense to us. What's happening? The smell of smoke filled the air. Dozens of people were running to their cars, trying to get away, while others were doing the vandalizing. Our hearts were racing, while Momma was trying to get us to safety.

"Girls, get in the car now," Momma told us to lock the car doors.

There was so much noise all around. Pam started to cry. It was strange. Just a few seconds ago we were picking out dresses, and now we were in the middle of a war zone. Quickly, we were in our seats and the car door was shut. Momma started the car and pulled out of the parking spot.

She cried out, "God help us!"

People were everywhere. Buildings and storefronts had broken windows with fires burning inside them. Cars and buses flipped upside down and on fire. People were running in the streets not knowing which direction to go. Some in fear were falling to the ground while others screamed for their lives. We had to drive slowly to keep from running over people in the street. Three men where standing yelling over a young black boy lying in the street.

One-man shouted threats, "I'll burn your black ass. Get your ass up boy."

Another man shouted, "Boy, I'll shoot you graveyard dead if you don't get out of my sight."

The third man yelled, "You better run, I'm gonna make you a black grease spot on this street."

The young black boy took off running down a dirt road, in fear of his life. I hope he made it home safe. Bricks were being thrown into storefront windows. Buildings and cars were being set on fire. The police had fire hoses, hosing down people trying to stop the riot.

We drove a few blocks and then right in front of us there was an old black man with children in the back seat of his car. Four white college age boys began to rock his car back and forth, trying to flip it over with them inside. The boys were laughing at the frightened passengers.

Momma jumped out of our car, pointed her finger at the boys, gritted her teeth, stomped her foot and yelled, *"Don't you dare!"*

They stopped what they were doing and looked up at Momma. Their eyes were wide; they glanced left and right. They knew they had been caught, like a kid getting caught with his hand in the cookie jar. They looked at each other and ran off.

She told the black man, "Mister get your kids home to safety."

The old black man's body was shaking as he tried to protect his children. There were two young boys and a little girl about my age in the back seat. Tears running down their faces, their arms around each other, holding tight, so the white boys couldn't get them. The four white boys had been laughing as they tried to flip the car. Why would someone do something like that? Why would they scare these people?

I was proud of my mother at that moment. Not that I wasn't proud of her before, but I think it just brought to mind what kind of person she was. She always stood up for what was right. That is where I got my guts, from my Momma.

That night I lay awake listening to the peaceful sounds that filled the house. My mind kept replaying the images of that day's events. Images and sounds I couldn't understand.

I was five years old, and my life was changing before my eyes. Momma and Daddy were always fighting. There were people full of anger and hatred everywhere I looked. People were hurting each other in the streets. Is this what life is like? Where are the heroes? Where are Roy Rogers, Dale Evans and Superman when you need them? Momma always says, "God is the answer." Where is God in all of this? Why won't He stop all the fighting? If He is the answer, then what is the question? These thoughts and questions swirled around inside my head until I slipped into sleep.

CHRISTMAS CAME AND WENT. Winter turned to spring. Spring turned to summer and we traded in our coats, scarves and boots for tank tops, shorts and bare feet. The summer was ours again. We were like the "Little Rascals." The neighborhoods very own "Spanky and Our Gang." I guess Janice, being the oldest, was our "Spanky". She was the one in charge of all the neighborhood kids. They always followed whatever we were doing. We took cardboard boxes, flattened them out to slide down the steep hill that our house was built on.

Our big white dog had one brown side to his face. We went and got him for free at the dog pound and named him Lucky. If we had not bought him that day, he would have been put to sleep. So he was lucky to have a home. Lucky was always right there, chasing us as we flew down the hill on the cardboard box. We even put him on a flat box, and he went flying down the hill. I don't think he knew he was a dog. He did whatever we did.

We liked picking red and black berries and sprinkling them with some milk and sugar. Of course we had our lemonade stands. Daddy saw us one day and decided to get involved in the selling part of it.

He said, "What you want to do is water down your lemonade so you can make, twice, the money!" Being kids, we tired of it quickly and wanted to move on to the next fun thing to do. He wanted us to keep it going.

I loved putting on my metal roller skates and skating down our steep driveway. The problem was, I was going so fast that I didn't know how to stop. I always ended up with my rear-end torn up on the landing. I came up with a great plan. I'd use the pillow off my bed and fasten it to my hinny with Daddy's black belt. That way, at top speed, I could sit down to stop. It worked just fine.

After dark, the fun kept going. We loved playing "Hide and Seek" with all the neighborhood kids. I was a good hider. We also liked catching fireflies. They were called lightning bugs because their tails lit up. We snapped their tail while still lit. We placed it on our finger and said, look at my diamond ring. Sometimes we put them in a Mason jar with grass and holes in the lid. Later in the night, while lying in bed, we'd give that jar a little shake and those fireflies lit right up. The three of us lay there watching them all lit up and flying around in the jar.

One afternoon, Janice said, "Today we need to do something different. Why don't we have a church service in the garage? Denice, you run around the neighborhood and tell all the kids to come. Pam and I will set chairs out."

Momma always said I had a built-in intercom system. I could talk real loud. I was bold too. Janice always sent me to gather everybody. It wasn't long before the kids began to show up. Janice did the preaching, and Pam did the singing. I passed a paper plate around to take up the offering. No one had any money, but we still passed the plate because that made it like a real church service. Janice preached with a lot of enthusiasm, she said, *"Now, if any of you dirty rotten sinners want to get saved from your dirty rotten sin, then come down for this altar call and repent."*

Johnny, who was known as slow in the head, might have thought it was a real church. He stood up and ran over toward Janice. He was crying and slobbering all over her.

Janice put her hand on his head and yelled, *"GET SAVED YOU DIRTY ROTTEN SINNER."* We all clapped for Johnny.

Pam just kept singing, *"Let Me Go Lover"* as loud as she could as she stood on two stacked Coca Cola crates. It wasn't a church song, but it was one of her favorite love songs.

I believe God looked down on that poor boy and did something in him, even if we were kids.

IT WAS A HOT and humid summer with no air-conditioner in the house. We did have an attic fan in the hallway and the screen doors were left open to let in cool air. Daddy had a tan year round. On Saturdays, he cut the grass in his shorts and didn't wear a shirt so that he could stay cool.

Momma took us to church every now and then, but most of the time we stayed home on Sundays. She didn't trust Daddy being home alone. He loved to listen to gospel singers and country music on the radio and he played his favorite records. Hank Williams, was one of his favorites, a man who had lived in Montgomery, Alabama, and eventually was buried there.

I remember watching Daddy slow dance around the living room, bare-chested in his white shorts. This day, he was slow dancing alone and singing out loud as Hank sang, *"Your cheatin heart will tell on you..."* He smiled as he danced and sang. He swayed to the music.

Hank sang, *"I'm so lonesome I could cry,"* Daddy had a look on his face as if he could feel Hank's lonesomeness in that moment.

I sat on the sofa sucking my thumb watching him perform with Hank, *"Hey, good lookin, whatcha got cookin, How 'bout cookin somethin up with me"* Daddy danced his way towards Momma, who was in the kitchen cooking. He danced her into the living room. They laughed together as he spun her around. She kicked her legs up as she danced. Momma had a cute pair of shorts, with a sleeveless button up plaid shirt. She was smiling, enjoying every minute of his attention. She was barefooted, her wooden spoon still in her hand. Momma was a good dancer. It was a good day.

One time Daddy went to church with us. It was Easter Sunday. Momma had new dresses made for each of us girls. We even got to pick out our own fabric.

Momma said, "Denice, this looks just like you. Red and white dotted Swiss." It was a full dress with a large white collar. I felt pretty in red, and it was my favorite color.

The choir director walked up to the podium and with a firm voice said, "Everyone, take your song books from the back of the pews and turn to page two fifty-nine, we will sing, "Bringing In The Sheaves". We will sing the first two verses and then the chorus."

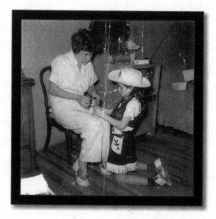

Daddy was sitting next to me. I thought it would be a great opportunity to lay my head down on his lap and suck my thumb. I lay there listening to Daddy when I noticed he was not singing the right words. Even though everybody was singing, Dad had a proud look on his face as he sang. I think he just made up songs as he sang them. The song went:

Bringing in the sheaves
Bringing in the sheaves
Here we come rejoicing
Bringing in the sheaves

Daddy was singing:

Bringing in the cheese
Bringing in the cheese
Here Columbus, Georgia
Bringing in the cheese

Mom helping me dress my cowgirl doll.

I remember thinking, why doesn't daddy sing the right words to the song? I noticed he was smiling as he held the songbook upside down. Daddy didn't seem to care. He just kept smiling as he sat tall and straight singing out loud with confidence. I could hear him above everybody.

3
DUCK AND COVER

AUGUST 1957

I WAS GETTING OLDER and without realizing it, I was changing into a girly girl. We no longer needed Bessie since I was starting school. I missed her, but I was excited about going to school and meeting new friends.

Momma took us shopping for school clothes. I found the neatest petticoat. The bottom of it had a tube that you blew up with air like a balloon. It made my skirt stand out and it made it look like I had on several petticoats. To complete the outfit, I wore white majorette boots with a tassel on the front of them. I could not wait to get to school. There I was, in my brown corduroy full skirt, blow up petticoat and majorette boots.

The school bell rang as the teacher took her yardstick, tapped it on her desk and told everyone to go to his or her seat. I was the first one to sit down. When I did, there was a loud pop. The tub in the petticoat burst. The full skirt and petticoat flew over my head and everyone laughed. I pulled my skirt down from over my face, laughing with them. It didn't embarrass me at all. The teacher made me stay after school for causing so much commotion.

Halloween was quickly approaching and I got to help the teacher decorate the classroom. Janice, Pam and I made our own costumes out of Momma's old bed sheets. Every year I chose to be an Indian princess. I cut holes in the sheet for my head and arms and then cut strings to make fringe all around the base of the sleeves and dress and made a belt and headband with the rest of the left over sheet. We had glue and glitter with mixed colors to design a tepee and stick horses on the dress and headband. My hair, in long braids, was just the right touch. I was convinced that everyone thought I was a real Indian princess. I was hoping my Brownie socks didn't give me away. Once it turned dark outside, all the neighborhood kids ran door to door with brown grocery bags, while the parents stayed home and gave out candy.

I always got in trouble for talking and laughing in class. The punishment was to draw a circle on the blackboard, stick my nose in it, and try to stand still for a long time. I was so tickled at the fact my nose was stuck in a circle on the blackboard that I could not stop laughing, which also made the kids in class laugh. I guess I did always act like I had ants in my pants. My teacher got so frustrated with me that I had to go sit in the hallway on a bar stool with a sign hung around my neck that said "BABY" and a large orange cone shaped hat on my head that read "DUNCE." I didn't even know what dunce meant.

Pam's class was walking by on their way to lunch, along with some other classes. I sat on the stool in the hallway waving to everyone as they passed by. When she saw me, she ran up and started crying, "I'm going in that room and tell your teacher she can't do this to you."

I assured her it was fun getting to see all my friends as they went to lunch. She moved on to the lunchroom with her class. Pam told Momma about it, and Momma asked if it bothered me? I told her I enjoyed it.

Momma thought it was funny and said, "Denice, you wake up happy and go to bed happy. You are tough as nails. You should not disturb the class though." She liked my free spirit. She never wanted me to change.

Much to my surprise, I found out I was my teacher's favorite student. It was typical for me to be told I had to stay after school for talking in class. All the children went home after the bell rang except me. She would say, "Now Denice come sit in this desk by me while I grade papers."

She would go to the teachers' lounge and get us both a Coca-Cola. While she graded papers, I sat and talked her ears off, rattling on and on. I talked about anything and everything. She nodded her head and smiled as I spoke. I guess I kept her company.

Once a week when the school siren went off, we scrambled to get under our desk; we kneeled down, our heads ducked and our arms wrapped around our neck. This was called Duck and Cover.

The day the teacher yelled for the first time, "DUCK AND COVER."

Billy wet his pants and Mary Catherine cried out, "I want my Mommy!"

Many people built bomb shelters in their backyards and stocked them with food, radios batteries and flashlights. They feared the Russians were coming. We were shown films of people running for cover, adults getting under their office desks, and children in their classrooms getting under desks. The teacher told us we would never know if the siren was real or practice. We always took it very serious. She said it was important to learn to duck and cover in the event of a nuclear war.

WE HAD A COUSIN, who was in his late twenties, he was in the military and stationed at Gunter. He, his wife and his three little girls would come into town from Birmingham to go over to Gunter Air Force Base to buy groceries in the commissary. They came to visit a number of times that year. He always walked in the door, and after a visit with Momma and Daddy, said, "I'm going outside to swing, and I'm going to take someone to swing with me." He looked at Janice, Pam and me, and would say, "I pick Pam because she is the most beautiful and has the most beautiful brown eyes."

He took Pam by the hand and led her outside. She would always look back at us like she didn't want to go with him. You know, with a sad expression. I didn't care that he always picked Pam. I didn't want him to swing me anyway. I thought he was gross. The fat that hung over his white thin belt and his ugly white patent shoes made him look as cool as an old wrinkled man in a Speedo.

Pam said to me, "It's not that good being beautiful, Denice."

I just thought she wanted to make sure my feelings weren't hurt. Thank goodness he was transferred and we did not have to see his face again for years.

The three of us slept in the same bed. Pam was always in the middle. She took us through the same routine every night.

"Janice," Pam whispered, in her trembling voice, "Can I put my arm through your arm?"

Janice always said, "Yes, Pam." Pam sounded so scared.

Then she asked, "Denice can I put my arm through your arm?" I answered her, "Yes, Pam."

Again she asked, "Janice, can I put my leg on top of your leg?" Janice said, "Yes, Pam."

"Denice, can I put my leg on top of your leg?" "Yes, Pam."

She had both of her arms and legs wrapped on and through ours. That was how we slept, so that Pam felt safe.

We laid in the dark all wrapped up with each other, Pam whispered, "I'm scared!"

I whispered back, "What are you scared of?"

She would say, "I'm scared of being placed in a coffin and buried under the ground."

I responded, "That's stupid. Don't think like that."

Janice spoke up, "Y'all' stop it, don't say that Pam, let's go to sleep."

Pam was so scared. The same thing happened every night. Some nights Pam didn't ask us, we just let her wrap herself around us.

Momma and Daddy took us to a funeral in the country. I don't remember who the little girl was. There was a little blonde girl in a coffin.

Pam cried, she said, "She looks just like me."

That year just was not a good year for Pam. She cried a lot and said she was afraid of the dark.

Pam failed the third grade, so that made her only one grade ahead of me. Her grades just dropped suddenly. The last day of school Janice walked in on Pam and found her crying in her bed. She was sobbing like her whole world was falling apart.

Janice sat on the side of the bed with her, "What's wrong Pam?"

Pam looked up from her tears and said, "I failed this school year and everyone will know when I repeat the third grade. I don't want to go back to school next year. I don't want everybody pointing at me saying I failed." She continued to cry.

Janice put her arm around her. "I'm going to tell you a secret. If you do it, it will change your life." Janice always had good advice to give.

Pam looked up at Janice. "Pam, if you will act as if you are somebody, then everyone will think you are somebody, and that will make you be somebody."

Next year, just walk in that third grade classroom and act like it does not bother you one bit, and that you already know everything the other kids are going to learn this year, and that's the way they will see you as smart."

Pam spoke through her tears "Okay, I will."

She trusted Janice and decided right then to hold her head high and act important, act as if it did not bother her to repeat the third grade. It worked. God knows I'm telling you the truth.

Years later, as three adult women sitting in a booth having dinner in a restaurant talking about our childhood, Pam repeated those words to Janice. She said, "You will never know what that meant to me. I have never forgotten those words and that moment you came into my room."

4
PLASTIC TULIPS

DADDY HAD WORK TO do at one of the grocery stores he stocked in Florala, Alabama. He took the family so we could have a vacation for three days while he worked. We checked in to Nelson's motel on Lake Jackson. The paint was peeling from the windowsills, but the room was clean and tidy. There was the primary kitchenette, sink and yellow Formica counter, with a small gas stove and refrigerator. There was a coffee maker and toaster on the counter. The room had an odor somewhat like mothballs and there was no air conditioner. We didn't care. There was a double bed and two single beds with quilts on them.

Janice said, "Look Mom, it has a kitchenette. We can make banana and peanut butter sandwiches, and there is a stove so you can make a jug of sweet tea." Janice always tried to help Momma think happy thoughts to make her laugh.

Pam and I started jumping up and down, dancing around looking in every nook and cranny of the motel room. We felt it was perfect. We rushed through the luggage to find our swimsuits and hurried to get down to the lake. Normally Momma would be singing and looking for her bathing suit. She was appearing to be having one of her bad days. On bad days, Momma was quiet.

Daddy said, "I have to go to one of my stores to do some stocking. I'll be back at lunchtime."

Janice, in her older sister way, said, "Come on, let's get our swimming suits on and go down to the lake so Momma can get some sleep." We put on our swimsuits and ran out the door in search of fun things to do.

There was a big old oak tree with a thick rope hanging from one of its limbs. The rope had a huge knot on the end. You would grab hold of the rope with both hands. You held on tight, got a good running start, jumped up onto the knot, wrapped your legs tight around the rope and leapt out over the lake. The key was letting go of the rope at the right moment. If you waited too long, you would plop down on the ground, let go too soon and you would drop in the shallow water. Either way, you looked ridiculous. I was determined to swing out the farthest. We entertained ourselves swinging out over the water for the rest of the morning.

Janice looked up and said, "Denice, Pam, let's go. Daddy is back. I just heard him whistle for us to come eat lunch."

Letting go of the rope, I ran back up to the motel room feeling very proud of my rope swinging accomplishments. I stepped into the room, to the familiar smell of propane gas. A knot formed in the pit of my stomach.

Daddy ran to the bathroom and tried to open the door, but it was locked. He kicked the door, until it broke off the doorjamb. He yelled, "NELLIE, WHAT HAVE YOU DONE? YOU STUPID, STUPID WOMAN!" Momma was lying in a tub of water. Her shorts and top were wet. Daddy was still yelling at her.

Momma opened her eyes, moaned, rocking her head back and forth saying, "No, No, No."

Suddenly, all of the fun of the morning vanished and from inside of me came fear and darkness. Daddy reached over to the space heater and turned off the gas. He jerked down the towels she had hung over the window. He opened it to get fresh air into the room.

He lifted Momma's limp body out of the tub, gritting his teeth in anger.

"You stupid, stupid woman." He said, as he laid her on the floor where towels had been stuffed around the doorjamb.

All Momma could say was, "No", shaking her head back and forth "No, No, No," She did not want to be rescued. She was convinced death would be better. She had waited for death but death did not come that day.

Daddy said, "Kids let's pack up and go home. I'm going to put your Momma back into the hospital." At times like this, I always got a knot in my stomach. It was a sense of having no control. I felt helpless. I hated that feeling.

The doctors said it was another nervous breakdown. The psychiatrist put Momma on antidepressants and sleeping pills. She wasn't home several days when Daddy found her again in bed with pills spilt on the floor. She overdosed on sleeping pills. Daddy walked over to the bed and began to shake her yelling, "WOMAN, YOU ARE JUST A NUT CASE, LOOK AT YOU, YOU STUPID WOMAN!" He picked up the phone and called an ambulance.

The ambulance sped up our driveway, with its lights flashing, horn blowing, and sirens loud. It scared Janice, Pam and me. The two ambulance drivers came running into the house and straight to Mom. Janice, Pam and I watched as they wheeled Momma out of the house on a gurney. We followed them outside. Momma squeezed the sheet tight under her chin as she held her head to the side in shame. They shut the double doors on the back of the ambulance.

Daddy yelled as loud as he could, so that mom could hear him, "THIS TIME I HOPE YOU DIE!"

The two ambulance drivers looked at Daddy and then looked at each other. Looking back at him, one was biting his lip as if he were holding back his tongue. The other one's eyes narrowed and he balled his fist up tight as if he wanted to beat the living hell out of Daddy. They got into the ambulance and drove away with Momma in the back of the ambulance. I hated she was alone and at that moment. I hated Daddy for saying that to Momma.

I always thought it was Daddy's fault Momma had nerve problems. I didn't realize that she was crying out for help. The voices that seem to be inside her head were shouting so loud she could not hear the soft voice of God.

The next day Daddy took us up to the hospital to see Momma. He stood at the nurses' station and instructed us to go in her room. I wanted Daddy to come with us, so I waited a second, watching him.

"Hey ladies," he said, with a smile and a strut. "How are you pretty girls doing? Are the doctors treating y'all good today?"

They began to giggle, shifting their hips in their white nurses' uniforms. His eyes lit up when he talked to women, and his left eyebrow always rose when he flirted. Daddy's tall and lean frame, black curly greased hair, one curl falling forward, melted the women every time. He stood in the hallway talking to the nurses as he leaned against the counter. He did this little thing with his cigarette. He played with his cigarette as he smoked, rolled it between the tips of his fingers, and then took a long slow drag.

I looked back at him, one last time, and then followed Janice and Pam in to see Momma.

A nurse walked in after reading Momma's chart. I looked at her and wondered how she found a uniform that size. She was a fat woman. She had white stockings and a white cap sitting on her frizzy bleached blonde head. She looked like a giant marshmallow. Holding the clipboard in her hand, she pointed at Momma and in a deep husky voice asked, "How could you do this to your children?" I looked at her and thought, she wasn't just fat, she was mean too! I wanted to find a needle and pop that marshmallow.

Momma's eyes were full of fear and anguish. She lowered her chin and placed her hands over her face in shame at the nurses' harsh words.

She turned her face toward us and said, "You just don't know." She moaned in her pain. "You just don't know, you just don't know."

There was a look of nothingness, hopelessness, and despair on her face. Her face appeared aged and worn.

She cried out, "God help me, help me!"

The three of us just looked at her. We were little children. We loved our Momma. I did not understand why God did not help. The crumbling earth of the path was giving way under her steps. She heard voices that came from within her mind.

She cried out, "God help me," as she was sinking. God was watching. He heard her cry.

The psychiatrist changed Momma's antidepressants, which we called her nerve pills. Momma wouldn't stay on them. She didn't like the way they made her feel. Doctors today might have diagnosed her with a chemical imbalance. To what degree I don't know, I just know it was more than depression. Psychiatrists didn't have enough information back then. If it seemed that you were crazy, you were put into a mental institution or you were just diagnosed as depressed. She received shock treatments. These were electrical shocks to the brain. It seemed to help for a short time, but then she got depressed again. She worked hard at not acting depressed. We always knew when mom went in for shock treatment. She would come home calm, quiet and not smiling. Janice, Pam and I loved on her, and told her everything was going to be all right.

Now that I am grown, I am so sorry that I can't reach back in time, to help that young woman and her little children. God was watching. He knew. Momma always said, "God is the answer." I just didn't know how and when.

49

It wasn't long after all this that Momma found out she was pregnant. Nine months later she gave birth to my little sister, Leeann. I was nine years old and no longer a baby. Mom would declare; *"My children are a blessing and are everything that is right in my life."* She always made declarations out loud for us to hear.

Momma's declarations began to establish her foundation. Pushing out the hopelessness, she was making a choice to pay attention to the stones God laid in her path for her next step. She was beginning to recognize the difference between the voices on the outside and the still, small voice within. Momma made her declarations out loud, to stabilize her emotions.

Leeann became our doll. She had curly, light brown hair and was born with a personality that lit up a room. We dressed her up and played with her as if she were our toy doll. Janice, Pam and I made up a song we sang to her called, *"The No, No, Jazz."* Leeann would shake her head real fast saying no as we laughed and sang to her. We loved her.

Leeann, at the age of three, loved dressing up in one of Momma's negligees, dragging it on the floor and running around the house. We put eye shadow, lipstick and a string of feathers around her neck. She looked just like a little princess. At a very young age, she showed interest in cooking and decorating.

Mom's depression caused fights between her and Dad. Dad was doing his own thing as he ran around town. Momma worked hard, making sure that our lives were safe and full of fun. I think she did this because there was so much turmoil in our home. She began to have more good days than bad.

Friday nights, she made homemade fudge with pecans and hot chocolate. We put blankets down on the living room floor with the lights out to watch Shock Theater. It was the last television show before the station went off the air for the evening. *Frankenstein, The*

Hand, Dracula and *The Mummy* were some of the scary movies. *We* all got scared. Pam, of course, sat in the middle, with the covers over her head. If it got the slightest bit scary she would say, "Tell me when the scary part is over." I loved those Friday nights.

Momma demanded that we showed respect to Daddy, but it was hard to respect him when he lied so much. One day I was in the back seat of our car with Daddy. He was driving a man from our neighborhood around town saying, "Yes, you see these two houses? I own over one hundred homes like them and rent them out."

It wasn't true. He was very a convincing liar. Mother and Daddy were doing well financially together. We lived in a middle class neighborhood. He didn't need to lie. I think Daddy lied so much that he believed his own lies.

One night I overheard Momma, "Charles, you better stop going out into the woods to that barn. You are going to get caught at those cockfights."

Daddy just laughed at her. "Nellie, you are just a nut case."

I remember hearing Daddy in the kitchen saying he was invited to a KKK meeting. Momma warned him about going. "Those men running around in white hooded robes are just a bunch of jack-legs." Jackleg was Momma's curse word.

Momma demanded that we showed respect to adults, "Yes, ma'am and no ma'am. Yes sir and no sir." We were to respect people in authority. This included presidents, teachers and police. We couldn't cuss and most slang words would get us into trouble. Dadgum and shoot were words out of the question for us to use. Momma would say, "You can't say that word."

We would say back to her, "But Momma that's not cussing." She would retort, "It's a slang word, I'm not going to have it."

Good morals were necessary to keep our minds and body clean, which meant no petting or going any further or looking at things you shouldn't. It was called being a good girl. A bad girl would smoke, drink and run with the wrong crowd. It was also wrong to wear a neckline that was too revealing, kiss or make out with boys and of course, have sex.

It was easy to know who the good girls were and who the bad girls were. If someone said, "She's a bad girl," you knew what that meant. There was a saying: bad company corrupts good manners. If any of our girlfriends appeared loose, acting like a "bad girl", Momma always said, "I don't have a good feeling about her. I don't want you to hang around her."

We said, "But Momma, she's a good girl." Momma was usually right. She said, "Whatever is true, honest and of a good report, think on these things. Live a life acceptable in the sight of the Lord."

WE SOLD OUR HOUSE on the hill and bought a larger new home. It was a one-story brick house with green shutters that had a front porch with four white columns. The living room had a big picture window and the den was open to the kitchen. There was a bar dividing the two rooms and sliding glass doors that opened to a big back yard. Janice, being the oldest, got to have her own bedroom. Pam and I shared a room with twin beds, but Pam never slept in her bed. She slept with Janice.

I helped Daddy plant St. Augustine grass and twenty-four baby pine trees all in the front and back yard that summer. There were already three huge oak trees in the front yard that had Spanish moss hanging from them.

Winter came and one Saturday morning, Daddy woke me and said, "Denice get your coat on and come outside." It was so cold that morning; the ground was covered with frost. It was a dark, damp, cloudy, gloomy day. I went outside, and Daddy handed me a handful of plastic tulips in every color.

"Here," as he handed them to me. "Help me plant these tulips."

I began to stick different colored plastic tulips into the ground. Daddy bent over doing the same. We were working side by side.

I asked, "Daddy why are we planting plastic tulips in the winter?" I continued sticking them in the ground waiting for his response. I was cold.

He said, "Because Denice, as people drive by and see our tulips; they will wonder how we can grow tulips in the winter. We will be the only ones that can grow them."

I remember thinking, but these aren't real, they're plastic. Why would we try to fool people and make them think we can grow tulips in the winter? It seemed to make sense to him.

Janice, Pam and I stood behind the curtains watching cars drive slowly by. Some people got out of their cars to touch them, to see if they were real. Planting plastic tulips in the winter was just another thing Daddy did, that seemed odd. To be the only one that can grow tulips in the neighborhood, in the winter seemed to be important to him. I remember looking at him as he talked about it with joy. I always noticed the smile wrinkles by his eyes. Daddy was fun, but he lived in his own world.

I loved Friday nights when we would hook up with our friends at the roller skating rink. We took our own boot-skates that we had gotten for Christmas. We wore boy Levi jeans, we pegged from the knee down to the ankle on the sewing machine. They were heavily starched and ironed with a seam down the front. Pam always got into the back seat between Janice and me. She would say, "Y'all hold me up. I don't want to wrinkle my pants." She kept her legs straight, without sitting.

We just let her lean on us. Janice and I were used to her perfectionism. Pam's hair and makeup always had to be perfect. She leaned on us all the way to the skating rink, supporting herself on her elbows. We knew we were helping Pam to keep her pants from wrinkling. The skating rink was next to a black neighborhood we called the projects. Black children stood watching the white kids go to the rink. I never looked over at them. Only one time, my eyes came on a black girl about my age. She spoke to me as our eyes met.

She asked, "What's it like to skate in there?"

I couldn't answer her. I thought if I did, it would be bragging. I was ashamed. I was ashamed I could not say, come in and see for yourself. I never understood why blacks weren't allowed to eat in the same restaurants with white folk. Why buildings had separate bathrooms, White restrooms and Colored restrooms and separate drinking fountains with signs above them that read *"White"* and *"Colored"*. The whites had a real fountain and the colored had a dirty sink or water hose. Even the whites' sign was professional that said, *"Whites only."* The coloreds were on a piece of paper with a black marker that read, *"Coloreds."* It didn't need to say the word, *"Only"* because white folk were not going to drink after a colored and get their diseases. At least that is what they said. How stupid, is stupid? I am ashamed of that. I hope, I am not judged by the blacks, for this ignorant time I lived in.

In the summer time, I didn't like to wear a shirt outside to play. It was too hot. Janice and Pam had already gone to Momma and complained.

"Momma, you've got to talk to Denice. She needs to start wearing a bra. She's embarrassing us."

Momma had a talk with me. I did not want to hear it, but I gave in because my boobs were hurting, and I was beginning to think I did not need to whoop boys anymore, because they were cute.

Momma told us that girls who have breasts at a young age are sexually active. Whenever I saw a young girl with breasts, I thought she was doing things she should not be doing. Momma had said so and I believed her. I overheard some older girls at the skating rink talking about what boys like—big boobs. That's what boys like.

The owner of the rink had hired a young teenager whose jobs were to skate around, blow his whistle, control speeding skaters, play the records and announce the next skate. Couples skate was going to be announced. I now knew what boys liked, so I went into the bathroom and stuffed my bra with toilet paper. I went into the bathroom flat chested and came out like Dolly Parton. It didn't bother me. My goal was to get a boy my age to ask me to skate in the couples skate. It worked. I saw him skating toward me and he asked me, "Do you want to skate?"

I smiled at him and said, "Yes."

He then asked, "Where did you get those?" He looked at my large breasts through my shirt.

"In the bathroom," I responded with confidence. He said, "Oh," shaking his head, as if that's the usual place to get them. We held hands and skated off to the music.

Momma was still cutting Janice's bangs too short and even tried to give her a home perm, which turned out to be one big frizz. That's about the time Janice put her foot down and took over the responsibility of her own appearance.

Every Saturday morning we danced in the living room to the television show, American Bandstand with Dick Clark as the host. We stood in front of the TV and screamed at our teen idols, whoever it was at that moment. It was really cool viewing the bandstand teens dancing together. The hairstyles and clothes were important to us. We watched to see what styles looked best while dancing.

Janice and Pam's girlfriends slept over Saturday nights. Janice was the life of the party. She was a mixture of Carol Burnett and Ann Landers. She looked and acted a lot like Carol Burnett and provided sound advice like Ann Landers. I was a year and a half younger than Pam, but they still let me into Janice's bedroom to hang out with them.

We listened on the record player to Pat Boone's *"April Love"*, Elvis Presley's *"Jailhouse Rock"*, The Platters' *"Smoke Gets In Your Eyes"*, Connie Frances *"Where The Boys Are"*, and the Everly Brothers *"All I Have To Do Is Dream"*. Dreaming together was what we did. Boys were always the subjects of discussion. Janice gave us her "Ann Landers" advice. Her best advice went like this: "Now this is very important. Before you enter a room, you tell yourself that in that room, all those people are waiting for you. The party can't get started until you arrive. You open the door of that room, walk in with confidence, with an attitude, I'm here, let's party."

A few weeks later we were at a YMCA football game when Janice noticed they didn't have a cheerleading squad. The other football team did. She had never been a cheerleader, and she couldn't cheer. She asked permission to form a squad and be the coach. They said yes. We put up posters announcing tryouts, over a hundred girls showed up. Pam and I became cheerleaders along with ten other girls. Of course it helped that Janice, our sister, was the judge for tryouts. My cheering looked more like a dance, with the swinging of the hips, not with the sharp moves of the hands as required in cheerleading.

On a bet that Janice would not jump into a ditch, which was about a ten-foot drop, she jumped. Our Cheerleading coach, who didn't know how to cheer and didn't know any cheers, was leading us with a cast on her broken leg, hopping around on crutches. We made up our cheers, and they had nothing to do with football. This was my favorite one:

> **Bobby socks**
> **Knee socks**
> **Nylon hose**
> **Sorry boys, that's as far as we go . . . . Yea!**

The other football team had cheerleaders with real uniforms, knew real cheers and had a real coach. At half time, they marched out to the center of the field with their cute uniforms and ponytails, with matching ribbons in their hair. You could see on their faces an uppity attitude. They did their cheer. We walked out in our home-made uniforms that Pam and Janice designed. We did our cheer that had nothing to do with football. The boys on the sidelines cheered when we finished. We didn't have store bought uniforms or know cheers, but we had something the other girls didn't have. We had confidence!

Pam was now in the sixth grade and very popular. On Valentine's Day she was given seven boxes of candy. She walked out of class carrying all those boxes with her books. Her male teacher sang out loud Little Richard's song, *"The Girl Can't Help It"*. She was embarrassed to have so many boxes of candy.

Pam saw me, "Here Denice carry some of these."

I looked at her, "Okay, but you have to share."

As we walked home, I asked her, "Pam why do so many boys like you?"

She said, "Oh, I don't know."

I said, "Well, everybody says you are beautiful."

She looked at me and said, "It's not that great being beautiful, Denice. Some girls don't like me for it."

Kicking the dirt with my shoe as I walked I said, "Well that's stupid as dirt."

Pam quickly told me to stop kicking the dirt and said, "You are just as beautiful, Denice, but you are too loud. Try to calm down some. You laugh and talk too much.

I responded, "Nope, I like me. I just can't be quiet like you. It would bore me to death. You are so proper, but as for me, I'm just me and I like me."

She laughed as she said, "Well, get on with yourself, you are walking too slow."

That night we had a party at our house. A boy from Pam's class showed up. His name was Tommy Vickers. It seemed all the boys had a crush on Pam, and Tommy was no exception. I thought he was the cutest boy I had ever seen. He had brown hair, which he wore in a flattop with bleach on the front.

Boys used Butch wax to make the front of their hair stand up; they called it training their hair. Dark pants or jeans and a plaid shirt were the fashion. The girls wore their hair long. Bobby pins or curlers were used to give our hair just the right look. We wore dresses or full skirts with a motif on them such as a poodle with a leash, fitted blouses tucked in at the waist, pedal pushers and jeans with bobby socks and white buckskin lace up shoes. Everyone showed up in style, looking good and ready to dance. Girls usually danced together and boys just stood around and watched the girls. They were still not sure of themselves, not about dancing, nor even how to have a conversation with one of us.

Janice, being the leader, said, "Now we are going to play spin the bottle."

She began explained the rules of the game. Everyone sat on the floor forming a circle, each take turns spinning the bottle, trying to make it spin fast and as long as possible. When the bottle stopped spinning, you and the person it pointed to would then go into Janice's bedroom to kiss one time.

It was Tommy's turn to spin the bottle. My eyes were focused on the bottle. Spinning round and round it went. It stopped. It was pointing at me. I had never been kissed. This is my destiny. I'm going to be kissed by the handsomest boy in the room. I looked over at him; he crossed his arms and had a frown on his face. He wanted it to be Pam or some other girl, not little Denice. I didn't care. This was my moment. I was about to be kissed.

We walked into the dark room, lit only by the soft glow of the streetlight shining through the long white sheer curtains. My heart was beating out of my chest. Tommy walked over to the window and stood with his hands in his pockets gazing out into the darkness. I walked over and stood beside him. He turned as if to leave the room.

Speaking up in a soft voice, "Tommy, aren't you going to kiss me?

He had his hands in his pockets as he looked down and said, "Yeah."

Then he kissed me. It was quick and to the point, but it was perfect for me. I thought I went straight to Heaven. Tommy turned around to join the party. I followed him.

The boys' left and the girls stayed for a pajama party. On the record player Bobby Vee was singing one of my favorites, "*Take Good Care of My Baby.*" With our baby-doll pajamas on, we lay across the bed, some girls on the floor, brushing and putting curlers in each other's hair; trying makeup on as we reminisced about the night and of course talked about boys. Our favorite Big Bam radio disk jockey played the latest tunes and we danced the night away to songs like Dion's No.1 hit song, *"Run Around Sue."* We told stories to each other, laughed and sang along with the radio. My head was still in the clouds from my first kiss.

I told the girls, "Tommy Vickers is the cutest boy in the whole wide world."

Janice said, "Denice, if you think Tommy Vickers is cute, you should see his older brother Steve Vickers." He was in junior high school with her.

I said, "Oh no, no one could ever be as cute as Tommy." What I didn't know, it would be Steve Vickers that would one day take my breath away.

~5~
THE GREEN THREAD

I T WAS CHRISTMAS. DADDY was going all out that year. He went to TG&Y and came home with strings of colored lights for the front yard. Lights covered the outside of the house, roof, windows and doors. He bought two silver metal Christmas trees with rotating colored spotlights that changed the color of the silver trees to red, blue, green and yellow. Daddy placed one in the living room, in front of the big picture window. The second one went in the bedroom on the end of the house that faced the front. It made Christmas wonderful.

Still fighting, police continued coming with their blue lights flashing to our house to break up the fights. Momma always screamed for Janice to call the police. She was afraid Daddy would kill her.

We didn't live very long in our new house; Momma and Daddy decided to rent it out to other people. I didn't know why, I just knew we were moving. I guess they thought they could make money by renting it out. It seemed Daddy was getting less and less interested in where we lived; he just provided a roof over our head. They rented the new house and bought a small, older home that was shaped like a box. It was a one story, red brick house that had been painted white and the white paint was chipping off the brick, it had a living room, two bedrooms and one bath. We put our dining room table and hutch in the small breakfast area. The address was 203 Bradley

Drive. It was in walking distance to Capital Heights Junior High and Robert E. Lee High School.

That summer, I walked everyday to Capital Heights Junior High School to hang out in the gym. I loved playing basketball. In one of the rooms was a record player and records. I met girls my age, the ones that I would be going to school with after the summer. We spent hours dancing together. The popular dances were the *"Freddy"*, *"Hully-Gully,"* *"Locomotion"*, *"Mashed Potatoes"*, *"Monster Mash"*, *"The Monkey"*, *"Pony"*, *"Watusi"* and the most popular was the *"Twist"*. These dances had songs that went along with the dance. American Band Stand kept us up on the latest fad.

Mrs. Hogan, who worked at the office in the gym, asked me, "Denice, a nursing home called me today and asked if we had any young people who could come and visit the elderly. Do you think you could get together a group of girls and dance for them?" I told her I wanted to, but I had to check with mom.

That night at the dinner table I was wiggling in my seat, "Momma can I go to a nursing home and dance for old people? Mrs. Hogan said she would take us. She said for us to wear skirts or dresses."

Momma said, "Of course you can. Some of them never have visitors. Those elderly people are all alone." She shook her head and said, "I will never live in a nursing home."

She took me shopping that night to find just the right skirt and blouse. I found what I had in my mind to wear, a white full pleated skirt that was right above my knees and a royal blue and white checkered short sleeve cotton blouse. I smiled at my reflection in the mirror. I washed and rolled my long hair with sponge curlers and slept in them so that my hair looked just right for the performance.

The girls and I loaded up the two cars Mrs. Hogan had for our trip across town. There were eight of us. We had practiced our dances the day before and we were ready. I suggested that on a couple of the dances we form a big circle and dance facing each other so that the old people could see our dance moves. We arrived and were escorted by one of the nurses to the dining hall. Everyone, except the bedridden ones, was in the dining hall. Their lunches had been cleared. There were smiles from a few of the nurses and patients. They had been waiting for us.

One man, in a wheelchair, was singing to himself; another, using a metal walker, walked in small perfect circles near the fireplace. There were two round tables decorated with tablecloths made of paper. One table had paper plates, napkins and a birthday cake. It was for everyone who had a birthday that month. The other table had small wrapped gifts, which had been donated.

I was in charge of setting up the record player. I searched around the room for a wall plug and the best place to set up things. I noticed a lovely woman as I started the music and began to dance. Her white hair loosely pulled in a ponytail, not on the back of her head, but in a pom-pom on top of her head. Her big blue eyes and rosy cheeks made the fullness in her face shine like the moon. The peach cotton dress, with its ecru lace collar, swayed as she walked around the room with her walker. She was on a mission. She was heading to the cake table.

I continued to dance to the music but kept a watchful eye on this lovely soul. The next song on the record player began to play as I led the girls in the best dance to the song. She and her walker crept in slow motion, onward to her mission. Soon a commotion began. She made it to the table, but it wasn't the cake she was after, it was the presents. She began stuffing them all down the top of her dress. One woman, holding a baby doll in her arms, as if it were a real baby, began to cry because she wasn't going to get a present.

Someone screamed out, "Mrs. Lottie's doing it again. She's stealing all the presents."

A little old man, whose wheelchair was parked next to the table, woke up from his sleep and started hitting the side of Mrs. Lottie's walker with his black cane. Nurse Lilly, a feisty black woman who was the caregiver, grabbed his cane and said. "Mr. Jenkins, don't do that. You are going to hit Mrs. Lottie's leg and hurt her."

Another woke from her sleep and screamed out, "BINGO."

Mr. Jenkins yelled out, "She ain't got the sense she was born with."

Nurse Lilly placed her hand on Mr. Jenkins shoulder to correct him, "Mr. Jenkins, don't be mean about Mrs. Lottie." She began to calm everyone down.

"Now we are going to be kind to each other today. Mrs. Lottie, it's not just your birthday alone. We must share."

We stopped dancing to see and listen to what was going on. I looked at Mrs. Lottie. The nurse began to pull all the gifts out from under her clothes. She looked like a little girl with her Mother straightening her clothes. The other nurse took her by the arm and slowly sat her down as she sat beside Mrs. Lottie's walker.

"Now, you sit down right here in this comfortable chair and we will let you pass the gifts out to everyone. It's going to be everybody's birthday today."

Mrs. Lottie had an enormous smile. She had been picked to pass out all the presents. Everyone calmed down, although there were some who never woke up during the entire commotion.

One elderly woman raised her hand and said, "If it is going to be my birthday I need to call my son. He doesn't know it's my birthday and he needs to come to my party."

Nurse Lilly assured her, "Mrs. Ellis don't you worry about that. We will make sure when he comes to visit you on Saturday that he sees you had a party and received a present." That seemed to be fine enough with her.

We danced two more songs, showing them our dance moves. Mrs. Hogan turned and smiled at us, "Well girls, I think it is time to go."

Gathering up the record player and records, I took one last look at my white haired friend, Mrs. Lottie. She looked straight at me with the sweetest smile, as if to say, thank you for coming to my party. It was a sweet moment for my memories.

IT WASN'T LONG after we moved into the house on Bradley Drive, when Momma found out she was pregnant again. Daddy told her to go have an abortion. That was out of the question for Momma. She gave birth to my brother Charlie, named after Daddy. We had another baby doll to play with and love. He was the sweetest little boy. At the same time Momma was pregnant with Charlie, the neighbor on the hill, Maria was pregnant. She was the one I walked in on in the living room with Daddy. She gave birth to a boy. It was her third child.

It seemed we couldn't get away from that woman. Mother became more suspicious and tormented by Daddy's actions. She looked for evidence to prove her suspicions. She looked for a lipstick smudge, the smell of perfume or a number in his wallet, maybe a receipt from a hotel. Unfaithful, liar, deceiver, and con artist were the words that kept Momma licking the ground in her torment. She was in pain.

One night she went outside and searched Daddy's car. She stormed in the house with a small green thread. It could not have been more than an inch and a half long. I knew, in her mind, it belonged to the other woman, perhaps to her skirt, dress or blouse while they were doing something they should not be doing in the car. By the time he returned from the grocery store with his carton of cigarettes, she had worked herself into a frantic state. Momma was pacing the living room floor. Every few minutes she looked out the window, lifting the side of the curtain and drawing it back to see if he was pulling into the driveway. She stood with her arms crossed, holding the green thread, ready to let Daddy have it.

He walked through the door holding a bag and his keys.

Throwing her hand up in front of his face, she screamed. "WHAT IS THIS? WHAT IS THIS?"

Daddy looked and said, "What do you think it is, you fool? It's a green thread." He walked passed her as he pushed her arm away.

We all looked at the green thread, as she held it between her thumb and forefinger.

Why did she have to find that green thread?

She followed him screaming to the top of her lungs. "What was she doing in your car?"

Daddy got mad and threw Momma across the room, hitting her in the face. The fussing, screaming, and hitting began. That's all it took. Daddy had her on the floor, straddling her as he pushed her and slapped her face, back and forth. He was pushing her body so hard; it was as if he wanted her to fade away into the floor,

We begged him, "Daddy, please quit, please Daddy, don't hit Momma."

It was common for Momma to wake up the next day and have to go to work with one or two black eyes and have to explain how she tripped and fell into a doorknob.

THE 1960s

IT WAS AN uneasy time in the world. Change was coming, but not without agony. George Wallace's 1963 Inaugural Address was on January 14, 1963, following his election as Governor of Alabama.

Wallace, at this time in his career, was a segregationist. He challenged the attempts of the federal government to enforce laws prohibiting segregation in Alabama's public schools. His speech was most famous for the phrase "segregation now, segregation tomorrow, segregation forever." It was the rallying cry for those opposed to integration and the Civil Rights Movement. Wallace, later in life, apologized for his unabashed racism and segregationist policies.

In an attempt to halt desegregation by the enrollment of black students, Wallace stood in front of Foster Auditorium at the University of Alabama on June 11, 1963. This became known as the "*Stand in the Schoolhouse Door*". Federal marshals and the Alabama Army National Guard forced him to step aside. He wanted to preserve segregation.

In his speech he said, "The President, John F. Kennedy wants us to surrender this state to Martin Luther King and his pro-Communists who have instituted these demonstrations."

Our local newspaper, The Montgomery Advertiser, read like this, "An African American group called "*Freedom Riders*" sparked a riot in downtown Montgomery. A crowd of white men, women and children threw stones through the windows at the Negro First Baptist Church while Dr. Martin Luther King, Jr., a black civil rights leader and Pastor of Dexter Avenue Baptist Church in Montgomery was speaking."

On August 28, 1963, that black preacher, Dr. King delivered a speech, "*I HAVE A DREAM*" in Washington D.C.

That speech was so powerful children heard their parents talking about it. I heard it on television that night. I did not understand all that was said and what would have to take place in the world for his dream to come true. I did recognize the right to have a dream, freedom, and that he wanted his four little children to live in a nation where they weren't judged by the color of their skin but the content of their character. That made sense to me.

The Montgomery Advertiser reported Negro Freedom Riders were assaulted with clubs by a group of KKK as they arrived in Montgomery on their bus. This was happening in my own hometown. On September 15, 1963, a bomb from a passing car blasted a crowded Negro church, the Sixteenth Street Baptist Church, killing four little black girls. Riots followed with two young Negro youth shot and killed. Gasoline was thrown into five businesses established by Negros, and burned to the ground. This was an attack by the Ku Klux Klan. Momma said the Ku Klux Klan were a bunch of rednecks filled with hate running around in white hooded robes.

Sitting in my seventh grade class on November 22, 1963, the principal came over the loud speaker and announced, "The President of the United States has just been shot in Dallas, Texas as he, his wife Jackie and the governor of Texas were riding in a convertible "in the parade." That's all that was stated.

The kids in my class didn't know how to respond and most began to cry, others just walked down the halls quietly. The assassination was played over and over the TV. We sat and Walter Cronkite reported it.

Our school principal called for a meeting in the auditorium with the student body, teachers, and all. He walked up to the microphone, tapped on it a few times, and then began to speak. "Students, our school has been chosen to have two colored students to join us this year. These two students were picked because they are honor students and come from very good homes. I expect you to be kind and respectful to them. They are not here to cause trouble, they just want to attend class and I will not stand for troublemakers. Anyone who causes trouble will immediately be expelled from school. Is this understood?"

Everyone responded, "Yes sir."

He said, "You may now go back to your classes." He walked away from the microphone, no one was smiling; a few were whispering back and forth. It was not to be taken lightly.

The next day a Negro boy walked into my history class and took a seat. Some kids just didn't look at him, but I did! He was wearing a pair of dark jeans with a white tee shirt and dark blue jean jacket. His jacket had writing on it with a permanent black marker. He had written words and sayings all over it, nothing bad, just songs and teen sayings that were cool. The main thing I noticed was that on the front pocket of his jacket he wrote, Pocket of Love. I think he was trying to express that he was a teenager just like us. He wasn't nerdy or anything as I had expected since he was an honor student. He noticed I was reading his jacket, so when our eyes met I said, "Hey."

He said hey, back. I thought he was brave.

I'm sure it was lonely at school for him and the girl. Everyone pretended they weren't even there. White teens didn't know what to say to a black teen. Do they talk about the same things white teens talk about? Do they like the same music? Is there anything we would have in common? Only a few had ever even talked to a black kid, just those white kids who lived on a farm and played with the children of the hired help. City kids had no contact with Blacks, except for the maids that worked in their homes. Things were changing.

ONE-DAY JANICE and Pam came to me in my bedroom. "Denice, Pam, and I are going to tell Momma we don't want Daddy to live with us anymore. We want her to tell Daddy to leave. We just want Momma to raise us. Are you coming with us?" I said, "Yes."

Momma came home from work before Daddy, and we did it. Janice looked at Momma and said, "Momma we want you to divorce Daddy."

Pam spoke up, "We're teenagers, and it is embarrassing when the police cars come with their blue lights flashing outside our house. We are tired of all the fighting."

Janice said, "Momma, we want just you to raise us. We can have a happy home without him."

Momma lifted her eyes looking directly at us, she asked, "Are y'all sure?"

We all answered her, "Yes ma'am." That's all she needed to hear.

Just then we heard Daddy's car pull up into the driveway. Momma looked at us and we looked at her. His car door shut, then the front door opened and Daddy walked in. We stood beside Momma in the living room. Momma spoke firmly, her mind made up and her children backing her.

She said, "Charles, get your clothes and get out. It's over."

He didn't even respond with an argument. He just walked into the bedroom and began to jerk the hangers from the closet. Momma began to empty his drawers out, throwing his clothes on the floor. Dad did not say a word. It was obvious he wanted to go anyway. He took his clothes and walked out of our lives for good.

I felt a ton of weight lifted off of me as he walked out the door.

They had been married twenty-two years. Divorce was not easy; even if there were problems in the marriage people stayed together. They worked it out or remained unhappy. You were looked down on when you came from a divorced home. It was not socially acceptable thing to do, only low class people divorced. We didn't care. We needed to have peace in our home.

Now, it was Momma and her five kids. Momma had been telling the other woman's spouse that his wife, Maria, was in an affair with Daddy. But he didn't believe her. One night he called. He said, "Nellie, do you think you could go with me? I think I see Maria and Charles's cars parked in a motel parking lot."

She said, "Sure I'll go with you."

All of us kids went to catch our daddy with the other woman. It was Maria and Daddy together in that motel room. Both divorces came quickly. Daddy and his girlfriend Maria married. She gave up her two older children, that were in elementary school and she kept the baby. Finally, all the suspicion was over. Daddy could not tell Momma it was all in her head anymore. He could no longer say she was a nut case. We could get on with our lives.

A FATHERLESS CHILD grows up thinking all things are possible, but nothing is safe. There was no man in the house to do repairs, so I learned to rig things at an early age. Cardboard taped over the window to cover up the empty space where glass once was, helped block out the cold air. The crack in the kitchen sink soon became a big hole that was the size of a cereal bowl. Old rags stuffed in the hole held water in the sink long enough to wash the dishes. A pot placed in the cabinet under the sink caught the water. Remembering to empty the pot full of water was necessary.

I took the vacuum cleaner apart many times to repair it. It eventually stopped. I had to sweep the carpet with a broom. The plastic knob to change the channels on the television set broke off. We rigged it with a dinner fork from the kitchen, bending the fork to wedge its teeth between the parts where the knob once fit. Something that would be odd to others became standard to us.

The crazy thing was that our friends adjusted to our home as we did. If the fork went missing from the TV, he or she would say,

"Where's the TV fork?" It would have been stuck back in the drawer with the other forks, but it was easy to spot, it was the bent one. Candles took the places of electricity if mom couldn't pay the power bill that month. We did not apologize or explain to our friends. They just accepted whatever we accepted to be normal. That was a powerful lesson.

Momma could not afford to buy meat, fruits and vegetables. Coffee and breakfast food became our breakfast and dinner. We could eat a balanced meal at school for thirty-five cents. We saved the newspaper and stacked it by the toilet to replace toilet paper, learning to rub the paper together to make it soft so it would flush.

At night, I could hear Momma's heartbreaking cry coming from her bedroom. I was too old to have a thumb in my mouth, but it felt comforting, so I sucked my thumb. I heard her cry out, "God help me! God help me; God help me!" I felt bad for her. She seemed alone in her tears. Why didn't God help her? Did he know that she was calling out to him for help?

Momma always said, "I would not give up my children for the world. My children are everything good in my life. If I had to beg, borrow or steal to feed my children. I would do it."

After Daddy left we felt safe and secure with Mom, no matter how hard things got. I guess Mom saw we needed her. It made her stronger. We knew she would be there for us. She never asked for help nor expected it from anyone but God. She believed in pulling yourself together and doing it, not being lazy, working hard and trusting God was her way. I guess some people just give up on life when hard times come. That was not Momma's nature. If you are knocked down, you get back up. You get back up stronger, and you do what is right in the sight of God. If I had to describe Mom in one word, I guess it would be, strong.

We woke up each morning to the smell of coffee brewing and fresh biscuits baking in the oven and the popping sound of bacon frying in the black skillet. Momma would shout out singing, making the song sound like a military call.

Get up, Get up. Get up in the morning
Get up, Get up. Get up in the morning
Oh - Can't get them, up
Oh - Can't get them up
Oh - Can't them up in the morning

"Girls rise and shine. You do not want to be late for school. Breakfast is ready."

We were getting older, and of course we were typical teens, cutting, dyeing and rolling each other's hair. We took our girlfriends' tubes of leftover lipstick that they were throwing away. We dug out the lipstick that was left in the tube, put it on a stainless steel soup-spoon and held it over the fire of the top burner on the stove. We then rolled an empty lipstick tube all the way down pouring melted lipstick into it. We then placed the tube on a plate, in the refrigerator, standing it straight up. Once it dried solid, we had a new tube of lipstick. Mixing a little red and a little pink together, we would come up with our own shades.

We got one pair of shoes at the start of the year. We called them our school shoes. They had to last all year, at least until summer, and then we went barefoot. Penny loafers were the shoes to wear. I was always rough on my shoes and about midway through the year I had to take a needle and thread to sew the side seams that had burst loose. Momma took us to Gaylord's and bought us new coats for school. They looked like mink coats to us, but they were acrylic. Janice picked a leopard coat, which matched her wild streak. Pam picked a black one. Her blonde hair showed off as if she were

Marilyn Monroe. The solid white mink was waiting on the rack. My long jet-black hair hanging down against it would work just right. We felt we looked like Hollywood movie stars in our acrylic mink coats.

Nobody ever locked his or her doors at night. It was a cold winter night and the door flew open while we were asleep. I guess it was not shut tight. The house was freezing when we awoke. Momma hurried to shut the door and start breakfast. I put on my white fur coat to get warm and stood by the wall heater. The synthetic fur on the back of the coat melted. I cried, not because the coat melted, but because it cost Momma hard, working money.

I was always trying to do things around the house to help. One afternoon, after school, I went home to wax the linoleum kitchen floor and breakfast area. I moved the china hutch and the cabinet doors flew open and every piece of china fell out.

I screamed, "No, this can't be happening." Kneeling down, picking up broken pieces in my hand, I called Momma at her work.

"Momma, I was going to surprise you and wax the kitchen floor. When I moved the hutch, the china fell out and broke." Momma was silent for a moment.

"How many pieces broke?" She asked.

I answered, "All of it."

She began to cry and said. "Oh God, can't I have anything?" I began to cry, holding the phone up to my ear listening to Momma cry too.

In a soft voice she said, "Denice, it's okay, you didn't mean to do it." I cried as I swept up all the broken china and threw it in the trash. Being only thirteen, I should not have tried to move that heavy hutch by myself. We would not have matching dishes forever again.

IT WAS AN AGE for trying new things with friends. A girlfriend of mine named Susan smoked cigarettes. I tried one and of course Momma found out. She beat the tar out of me.

As she spanked my legs, she was crying out, "Dad-gum your hide, Denice, you are better than this. I won't have it. Do you hear me? I won't have it. You are better than this!"

The next morning I was getting dressed for school, still in my slip she said, "There you are again" she spanked me one more time.

I never smoked again. Momma's belief in my goodness and me not wanting her to think less of me, made me want to do right. You know, it's a blessing when a parent speaks goodness over a child. If a child were constantly told they're no good, then why would anyone think they would turn out differently? The odds are against them already. Momma's words were powerful in our lives. Momma said I was better than that.

CHRISTMAS WAS DIFFERENT now that Daddy was gone. We didn't have the money to get a beautiful tree, but we learned if you picked a cheaper one, with a bad side to it, turned it toward the corner of the room; it worked just fine. Our tree was always falling over and even though we rigged it with a string to the curtain rod, it still fell.

Momma just laughed and said, "It wouldn't be Christmas if the tree did not fall."

We woke up to the smell of turkey cooking in the oven and Krispy Kreme donuts for breakfast. Our friends began showing up as early as they could to get away from their own homes. Momma was in the kitchen singing, cooking, making her dressing and fruit salad.

Everyone knew that at our house, you were welcome for Christmas lunch.

She always said she wanted us to be free spirits. Be whom God made us. She did not believe in putting on airs. She sat listening and watching us as we acted out our stories, laughing with us. Freedom of expression was a gift she gave to us, even to our friends. We were never too silly or too loud when we spoke. She threw in what she called her, "two cents worth." We all laughed at the other's latest adventures late into the night and Momma kept a fresh pot of coffee always ready. Momma made sure any teenager that walked through our doors felt welcome and that she was a listening ear for them. It was mostly boys between the ages of sixteen to twenty years old showing up. They always said they wished they could talk to their parents the way we all talked to Momma.

Mom started reading the Bible every morning at the breakfast table. We always laughed. It seemed always to fall open to the passage, *"Children, obey your parents"*.

"Momma we know that one."

She would laugh and say, "That's right, obey your parents."

Janice was in the tenth grade at Lee High school. Pam and I were in the seventh and eighth at Capital Heights Junior High School. Momma had so many responsibilities as a single parent with five children.

Every year at the start of the school year there were Cheerleading tryouts with a week of Cheerleading clinic. The tryouts were on Friday. Pam convinced her girlfriend Sandra to attend a cheerleading clinic. Every afternoon after the clinic, Sandra and Pam worked on the cheers in the backyard. Pam spent most of her time helping Sandra get better. Tryout Friday came. College cheerleaders were the judges. The gym was packed girls filled with anticipation and excitement. Once everyone had cheered, the judges began to call out the numbers of the girls picked. Pam's number was not called out, Sandra's was.

Pam knew she helped a girl who could not cheer and turned her into a great cheerleader. While she was helping her learn the sharp moves with her hands and jumps, Pam didn't get practice in for herself. She was happy for Sandra, jumping up and down in the bleachers screaming, "YOU DID IT SANDRA!" Pam was a proud friend and trainer.

We settled into the school year, and we lived for the weekends. Miss Durham's history class was on the second floor of the school. She had never married. That made her an old maid in our eyes. She was around fifty years old. It was hard to tell for sure. She must have been six feet tall and built like a linebacker. Her hairy upper lip made it hard to concentrate on what she was saying not to mention the black mole by the corner of her lip. I always looked at her lip while she was talking and wondered why she did not shave it. She could at least pluck that one black hair out of the middle of that mole.

I know I should have been listening to what was being taught in class, but I could not concentrate. I was always thinking of boys or thinking about what I was going to do the coming weekend. I lived for the weekends.

Miss Durham had a big stomach and always wore full dresses with a tiny belt. The problem was her stomach being big; the belt rode up under her breast. She didn't have a waist. The good thing was the belt did give a separation between her breast and stomach. Otherwise, it would have looked like she had no boobs or that they were down to her waist. I was sure she had never had sex. I heard women who get old without a man in their lives, get mean. She had a reputation of being mean to everyone, or maybe she just stayed in a bad mood all the time.

I heard Johnny Boyd and Mark McCray talking to each other at their desks. I sat across from Johnny. Johnny sat behind Mark.

He leaned over Mark's shoulder, "Mark, you know," as he pointed toward Miss Durham, "If she just got laid she would get a permanent smile on her face." Mark continued playing the drums on his desk with two pencils, which was something he was always doing because he was a drummer in a garage band.

He said, "Yep, but who would volunteer to put that smile there, King Kong?" Johnny slapped him on the back as they both laughed. I pretended I didn't hear them.

Miss Durham hit the bell on her desk with her ruler. "Everyone stop your talking. Pull your history books out. Turn to page 216. Tomorrow you are taking a test on Andrew Jackson and the Battle of New Orleans. This grade, for many, will determine if you are going to fail my class this semester, so I guess you..." The speaker made a loud squeaking sound and the school secretary in her high-pitched slow southern voice said, "Miss Durham, could you please send Denice Perkins over to the gym. Mrs. Hogan wants to talk with her."

Miss Durham stopped in the middle of her sentence "Denice, take your books with you just in case the bell rings while you are there." Then she continued to threaten everyone.

I walked in Mrs. Hogan's office, to my surprise, there sat Pam. Mrs. Hogan smiled at me and said, "Denice take a seat."

Pam had a look of fear on her face. She did not know what was going on. She was sitting all proper. I plopped myself down in the chair next to her. I was sure there was nothing to worry about because Mrs. Hogan was always a friend to the students.

She said, "Pam and Denice, I am going to tell you something, but it can't leave this room." There was a moment of silence as we sat side-by-side waiting for her next words. The student body had voted for seventh, eighth and ninth grade Miss Charming that morning. They would be presented Friday night at the Valentine School dance.

She sighed as she looked at us. "Pam, Denice, you were both voted as Miss Charming at your grade level."

Pam was smiling. I was not shocked that Pam got it. I guess I was a little surprised that I did. I have some girlfriends I thought might get it. I did hang out with the popular group.

She continued, "However", we are unable to let y'all have it due to your grades. You must have a B average. The runner-ups will be announced as the winners. They must never know that you won." She went on to say, "Normally we do not give out this information. I felt you two girls should understand why it is very necessary you pull your grades up." She said, "Now girls I trust you do not repeat this for it would rob the other girls that are going to be announced this afternoon as Miss Charming."

We were speechless. It didn't seem fair, and everybody knows whoever gets it is considered the most popular girl in that grade.

She then asked, "Girls do we understand each other?"

"Yes, ma'am", we both responded.

She said, "You can go back to your classes now."

We walked out of the gym doors toward the front door of the school. Pam buried her face in her hands as we walked. Tears were running down her cheeks as she tried to wipe them away before we went back to class. I tried to comfort her and make her laugh.

I said, "What's important is we know! Look at us, Miss Charming." I danced around in a circle throwing my hands up in the air dancing forward then backwards shaking my hinny as it turned into an Indian war dance. I said, "Come on, join me in the victory dance, I'm charming and I know it, it is a good thing, I'm a charmer."

Pam was still wiping away her tears. "Stop it, Denice".

"Ah, Pam, let's, celebrate our, win." I said trying to comfort her.

"Denice, you don't get it. We did not win. It just seems we can't have anything."

I stopped dancing as I looked, at her and said, "I know it's not fair, but what do grades have to do with being charming!"

She looked at me, "Denice, don't forget, we can't tell anyone."

"I know, don't be so sassy, I still know I am Miss Charming. I know they voted for me and that is all that matters."

"Well not to me, I want to walk out and have the roses placed in my hands by the most popular boy in the class." She said.

"I know," as I pictured that for a minute.

I said, "Let's enjoy the fact of knowing who the real Miss Charming winners are, we will fake it. I will go congratulate the winner that will be crowned Miss Charming and as I look at that crown on her head, I will stare at it and say to me, she is borrowing my crown, and I'm ok with it. The way I look at it, I was the student body's choice. I didn't loose. Pam, I will walk those halls smiling giving my queen's wave laughing, talking to everyone."

We did tell Momma that night. She didn't think it was fair. Pam pulled her grades up and made homecoming queen that year. That seemed to smooth out the feeling she had of things just never working out for her. I don't understand why things like that didn't bug me. I guess I felt as long as I knew that I was picked, that was good enough for me.

I hung out with all the girls: Beth, Debbie, Melissa, Barbara, Carol, Emily and Nancy. They were all the popular girls. I never learned how to study. That was the year I met Robin and KT.

6
CARPENTER'S DREAM

NOTHING SMELLS BETTER THAN freshly cut Saint Augustine grass. Keeping it cut is a hard job. If you do not keep it cut, it gets too high and then the lawnmower will keep cutting out. You then have to choke and crank the motor repeatedly. It then gets over heated and you have to wait until the motor cools off. I had just gotten home from school and noticed the grass was getting high. In the South, homes have large front and back yards.

I was cutting the front yard in shorts and bare-footed. Robin walked by on her way home from school. I recognized her from school. She stopped. She was watching me, hands on her hips.

She says, "I can't believe my eyes. Cute Denice Perkins is cutting the grass."

I turned the lawn mower off, wiping the sweat off my forehead with my T-shirt and replied, "Well, Robin, it's like this, if I don't do it; it won't get done. You are looking at the chief cook and the bottle washer. I have to do it all."

Robin lived around the corner in some apartments with her mom, who was divorced. She was tall like me, thin, and had with boxy hips. I say boxy because she didn't have a rear-end that stuck out. I worked at sticking mine out when I walked, but Robin had nothing back there to stick out. Her honey-colored hair had blonde streaks in it and was cut into a short bob style. Her big blue eyes were as blue as the ocean, along with a smile that took over her face. Robin did not know what it was like to have a yard to cut.

"It looks like fun, can I try it?" she asked.

My first thought was, is this girl crazy? I stepped away from the lawn mower and said, "Sure!" I figure if she is crazy enough to want to, let her at it.

I went in the house, fixed me a glass of ice-cold sweet tea in a mason jar and sat on the step of the front porch watching her. I expected her to know how to start a lawn mower. She tried to crank it without putting her foot on the mower to steady it, which made it jump as she pulled the cord. Of course, it did not start. I sat my glass down, walked over to her, put my foot on the mower, leaned forward to choke it and pulled the cord. Immediately it cranked.

I slapped her on the shoulder, "Now knock yourself out."

Returning to the mason jar of sweet tea, I sat back down with the theory that this is too good to be true, but I can dig this. She cuts the grass while I sit on the porch letting the cool breeze blow through my hair.

Robin and I became best friends. We were inseparable. Robin's friend KT also began to hang out with us. KT had silky, vanilla colored hair to her shoulders. She had small green eyes and a pretty face with a smile that was slightly crooked. Her skin was tan and smooth like butter. KT had the biggest boobs I had ever seen on a girl my age. I always thought she was chubby. Now that I think about it, she was not fat; it was just those huge boobs. I didn't know how they got that big because I knew she was not having sex.

Robin beat her boobs and yelled to the top of her lungs, "Grow, Grow." It didn't work! I told her if she continued to hit them, she would stunt them for sure.

KT said, "Rub them with cocoa butter."

I knew all the cocoa butter in the world was not going to make mine grow. I ordered a gadget from a magazine; I think the inventor's name was Mark. It was a pink plastic gadget that looked like a pair of false teeth the size of our hands, with a thick spring in the middle. You put it between the palms of your hands, elbows out and up and then you press it repeatedly between the palms of your hand. The magazine article read, "Guaranteed to increase your bust size two sizes in a matter of weeks."

Robin and I did it every day while chanting, "I must. I must. I must increase my bust." It did not work. It just made our armpits sore. We called it Mark. Eventually we gave up on Mark. I threw it in the trash because, I was afraid some boy would come over to see me, and there Mark would be, sitting on the table. Momma had given me the money for Mark, but she didn't mind me throwing him away.

Every day we walked home from school together and the same two boys would check us out when we passed them. I guess Jimmy got tired of us ignoring him, so this day after we passed them he yelled out, "Denice Perkins is a carpenter's dream, flat as a board." That did it! He was dead meat.

I was hot mad. I was going to be ready for him the next time I saw him. The plan came to me as I was eating a two-cent piece of hard candy named Mary Jane. Mary Jane would be a good name to use, since we did not know anybody at school by that name. The next day we passed each other he began to yell, "Denice Perkins is a carpenter's dream, flat as a board," that was all I needed.

I swung around, looked him straight in the face, pointing my finger at him, and yelled "Jimmy Port, everybody is talking about you and Mary Jane. I defended you, but if you don't shut your big fat mouth, tomorrow I am going to get on the school intercom system. I will tell the whole school that you and Mary Jane did do what they are all talking about!"

His face turned pale white as he began to stutter, "Whoa, whoa, what do you mean? Who is Mary Jane? What are they saying?"

"Jimmy, you know exactly who I am talking about, you know precisely what you did with her and you better walk softly because I have my eyes on you. If you call me a carpenter's dream one more time, I will stop protecting you and you'll wish you had me on your side. Jimmy, you mess with me and I'll fry your fish."

He said, "Okay, just don't go on the intercom. Tell everybody it's not true. I didn't do anything with Mary Jane."

I looked at Jimmy shaking my finger at him as I said; "It's looking very bad for you. Don't sweat it. I'll do my best to stop all the talking. But boy, you better walk softly and stay on my good side. Remember this Jimmy, I'm the mouth of the South and all I need is an intercom." That took care of Jimmy. Anyway, how could he know I was a carpenter's dream? I wore the most padded bra JC Penny's made.

On weekends, Robin spent the night with me. We were always up to something. A lot of the boys we knew had motorcycles. One Saturday, four boys drove up on theirs. They were cute guys that went to school with me. I wasn't into any of them, just friends. While we stood talking, I noticed the red motorcycle still had the keys in it. I whispered to Robin that I was going inside to get them all a drink.

A few minutes later I came out with four mason jars of sweet tea. They sat down on the front porch to drink their tea, and I jumped on that red motorcycle with Robin jumping on the back. We peeled off as I yelled out into the wind, "Bye boys".

I drove down the road as fast as it would go. The only problem was that I didn't know to watch out for gravel. We turned a corner too fast. Robin went flying in the air. She could have killed me for that. Her knees and elbows were bleeding, gravel stuck in them. What the heck, we had fun.

Robin, KT and I made a good threesome. Robin confessed she never kissed a boy. I knew KT hadn't. Neither one of them had dated. We had fun talking girl talk, and I just absolutely knew Robin needed to get over the fear of kissing. I did not have a lot of experience—just the kiss from Tommy Vickers the night I was in the fifth grade; when we played spin-the-bottle. That kiss lasted me for two years. I was sure that one kiss had made me a seasoned veteran.

We were planning on going to a dance, and I knew a particular boy was going to give us a ride home.

I instructed Robin, "When he walks us to the door, I'm going to go straight in, leaving you with him. If he starts to kiss you, don't panic." I explained to her just what to do.

Everything happened just as we planned. I walked into the house, turned the radio up loud and began to do the twist in the living room with Chubby Checker's, *"Let's Twist Again"*. I sang along knowing Robin was getting her first kiss. Robin came running in, jumping up and down with excitement and joined Chubby Checker and me doing *the Twist.*

~⟶ 7 ⟵~
COPS, CARS AND BOYS

W E CONTINUED TO HAVE theme parties on the weekend. Luau and beatnik parties were our favorite. We called to invite everyone. We assigned who would bring what snacks and drinks. That way Momma did not have to pay for the food. We had plenty of 45s for our record player. Janice and Pam decorated the house according to the topic. Janice was good at getting everybody to come. Whenever there was a party at our house it was standing room only. We kept the front door open so people could come and go. They came, bringing their favorite records to dance to, rock, psychedelic, folk rock and pop. We danced to all of them.

This was a time Girls at school wore A-line dresses, A-line skirts with twin sweater sets and bouffant dresses with the top tight and the skirt of the dress puffed out. Teachers measured the length of your skirt or dress. Anything shorter than three inches above the knee, you were sent to the principal's office and then home to change clothes.

Some teens still pushed the limits and after school began to wear miniskirts, colored tights, leather boots, fake eyelashes and dark eye makeup. Every girl wore heavy eye makeup. They wore their hair in many different ways—to their shoulder or in a beehive. That's where you tease your hair and pile it high on your head.

Pam wore her hair "teased", smoothed out into a bubble with no bangs, and sometimes she wore a satin ribbon in her hair. She now bleached her hair blonde. I called it the Marilyn Monroe blonde. Pam was a romantic; the color fit her personality. When Pam smiled, boys stopped in their tracks. Her brown eyes and dimples got them every time. Pam was the heartthrob of all the teenage boys at school. She looked a lot like the actress Sandra Dee. Pam was five feet-two inches tall, and had stopped growing at five-five. She had a cute figure and was growing breasts; she did not need a padded bra.

I was already taller than her. I was five-six and on my way to five-seven and a half. My hair was dyed jet-black, teased and smoothed out to my shoulders with a side bang. Some years I grew it down to the middle of my back. I was tall and lanky.

Janice and I were in a race with our height. She was my same height and would top off at the same height as me. Her hair was dark brown and she never dyed it. It was short with bangs that she rolled tight and then teased and smooth out into a bubble. Her rhinestone glasses were the latest style, and she knew she looked good, skinny legs and all.

The guys wore paisley and madras plaid shirts and khaki pants. The mod fashion, pop art movement affected everyone's appearance except the preppy youth from the upper class who stuck to the college look. Rock bands had their velvet trousers and wore high collared Regency Jackets. Boys started wearing their hair long.

Another look was the beatnik look, which was a black beret and black slacks for the boys and tights and with dark glasses for the girls. Flat shoes for the girls and sandals for the guys were just the right look. For the house party, girls and boys wore blue jeans or shorts.

AT THESE THEME PARTIES the twist was the most popular dance. Pam and Janice danced together at least once during the night. Janice always danced her way over to Pam, who was always standing with a group of guys. Janice grabbed Pam by the hand, she only said "Come on."

Pam knew precisely what that meant. They began to do the Bop to a fast song. Girls loved to dance together. "*The Loco Motion*" started playing. Boys lined up on one side of the room with girls on the other. Everyone loved to do the "*Stroll*". Toward the end of the night, teens had coupled up with the lights dimmed. Girls wrapped their arms around the back of the boys' neck as the guys wrapped their arms around the girl's waist. They slow danced cheek to cheek to Elvis "*Are You Lonesome Tonight.*"

Janice was crazy about Mitchell. She wore his jacket. People referred to them as "*jacketed*", meaning they were going steady. Some girls wore the boys' ID bracelet or his class ring. Sometimes the boy gave his girl a necklace with a heart on it to tag her as belonging to him. Going steady with someone was cool. The last few songs of the night ended with slow songs, followed by making out in each other's arms. There was a lot of kissing going on.

Pam did not have one serious boy she liked. She had many. She was not hurting for their attention. She did favor a boy named Chuck. He was a gentleman and they were more like brother and sister. If a boy didn't just knock her off her feet, she just kept him as a friend.

My boyfriend at the party was Donnie, who was thirteen. I had known him since I was in the fourth grade. He was a good skater. He rode a Honda 50, which I thought was cool. Off and on, I wore Donny's ring on a chain around my neck, saying I was going steady with him, but I broke up often with him, too.

There was a boy at the skating rink called Blaine, who was eighteen; his twin brother was named Braxton. I decided to go steady with Blaine because he would not put any pressure on me to do anything I did not want to do. Blaine had a car; he could pick me up for dates. We loved to go to the YMCA dances. One thing I liked about him was he was a great dancer. Blaine was tall and slim with dark blonde hair and wore the Clark Kent black frame glasses. That was a cool look. He wore a plaid button shirt with his navy pants and his burgundy penny loafers.

Blaine tried to kiss me every now and then, but I told him, "Stop trying to kiss me. It is never going to happen." He would just laugh at me and shake his head. He was willing to date me without a kiss. I liked that about him.

The Y dances were on Friday and Saturday nights. Robin, KT and I stopped going to the skating rink and went to the Y dances. Everybody was hanging out at the dances. There was always a local band playing and our favorite DJ from the Big Bam Radio station in town would be the MC. A two-dollar door fee was charged, and the room would be packed with teens. It was "outta sight". The lights were low, but you still could see everybody. Some nights they had a battle of the bands. Some nights it was a local DJ playing records while it was live on the radio. No matter what, it always was a big party!

There was no drinking and there was always a cop in the doorway to make sure that no alcohol was brought in. No hoodlums could come in that might want to start a fight with the other boys. There were a few adults inside, usually the YMCA manager, who stood against the wall and watched.

The weekends when there were no dances, there was always a way to find out where the crowd was going to be. Word would get around to hook up at the Montgomery Drive In Theater. It was fifty cents per person and some nights, a dollar a car load. Teens always hid in the trunks. Once parked, someone in the car got out and opened the trunk to let them out. Teens went from car to car, talking and sitting on the hoods of their cars watching the movie.

You could always tell which car had a couple necking in the back seat—the windows were fogged up. Two movies played each night with an intermission between them. You could go to the concession stand to order hot dogs, hamburgers, potato chips and candy. You could place your order over the speaker that hung next to the car window. Push a button and someone would respond, "Can I take your order?" A teenager came out holding a tray, wearing a white paper boat shaped hat with a little red stripe around the edge. It was usually a friend from school. It was a way to get them out to the car for a few minutes. You could also get a spiral shaped mosquito repellent to burn on the dashboard of your vehicle.

One Friday night, a carload of my girlfriends, I was the driver, heard there was to be a bonfire at the gravel pits. Even though I was only fourteen and didn't have a driver's license, Momma said I could use her green Falcon. We packed as many girls in the car as could get in. Word had already spread that Tommy Miser and Johnny Banks, known as JB, one of the Hoods, were going to drag race. Tommy Miser had just gotten a new 1965 Ford Galaxy 500 XL red and white convertible for his high school graduation to take to college the next year.

JB pulled up beside him at the Treasure Isle, the local hamburger hang out. JB drove a souped-up 1954 Ford Custom he and his buddies worked on all the time. He could really burn rubber. JB always wanted to prove his car was the fastest and it usually was. The time and place had been set and we went to watch.

Pam was with Chuck at "The Lights". That's the local area to park your car, listen to the radio, and look at the moon and city lights. It's the name the teens gave it. Couples sat and listened to the radio looking at the stars.

Janice was crazy about Mitchell, but Bryan was her best guy friend to hang out with. She always had time for him, and he did love to be at our house since he didn't have any brothers or sisters. Bryan thought of us as his little sisters; he looked out for Janice, Pam and me. Bryan and Bobby came by that night looking for Janice and Pam.

"Where's Pam, Janice?" Bobby asked.

"She's with Chuck at "The Lights", Janice said.

"She needs to be with us, not Chuck. Let's go kidnap her," Bobby said.

The three of them jumped into Bryan's car and off they went to kidnap Pam. Bryan was driving with Janice, who sitting between them in the front seat. They drove out into the dark countryside until they reached "The Lights". They spotted Chuck's car.

Chuck had been a friend of Pam's whom she met at the skating rink. He was one of the teens who would blow his whistle to slow the skaters' speed down. He was a cool guy with brown, curly hair and green eyes. One of his shoes had a thick built-up heel, around four inches, because one leg was shorter than the other. His boot skate was built-up too. It never seemed to be an issue for him; he was charming, and girls liked him.

"Bryan" Janice whispered as she instructed, "Pull up beside his car but turn your lights off first and turn the music down low."

Bobby flashed a flashlight in Chuck's eyes. Chuck turned to see who was pulling up beside them. He was surprised. He looked like he saw a ghost.

"Hey, man. What's going on? Who is out there?" Chuck yelled.

Usually it's the cops flashing their flashlights in the car windows to break up two people making out, but Chuck could tell it wasn't the cops. He heard the three of them laughing and whispering to each other. Bobby opened the car door and let Janice out as he jumped into the back seat. Janice ran around Chuck's car to the side Pam was sitting on.

Breathing heavily, Janice leaned in through the window, "Pam, Momma said we were to come get you and bring you home. She wants to talk to you."

Pam looked at Chuck, "Sorry, got to go."

She opened the car door, slid out and ran with Janice over to Bryan's car as she jumped into the back seat with Bobby. Bobby was a heartthrob around town and was always sweet on Pam, but she just saw him as a friend. All the girls were starry eyed over him with his football player physique, and blonde hair that hung down over his fair skin and blue eyes. He was drop-dead gorgeous and crazy fun.

Janice jumped in the front seat and turned the radio up as they drove away spinning their tires in the dirt. The music was blasting and the three of them were laughing. Pam still did not have a clue what was going on.

"What does Momma want to talk to me about? Am I in trouble?" Pam asked.

"We've kidnapped you." Janice said as she turned to sit sideways, resting her arm on the seat to look back at Pam.

"What do you mean? Momma doesn't want to talk to me?" she asked.

Bobby looked over at Pam. "You don't need to be with Chuck." Throwing his arm around Pam's neck he pulled her close to him.

She laughed, looking over at Bobby pushing him away. "Stop it, Bobby."

Smiling at Pam, he continued, "We wanted you to hang out with us tonight, so we kidnapped you."

Pam giggled at Bobby as Bryan and Janice were laughing and talking to each other.

She said, "Boy is Chuck going to freak out when he finds out what y'all were up to."

Bobby leaned his head out the window and gave a howl as if he were a wolf, then said, "He'll get over it, don't sweat it. Let's go to Treasure Isle and see what's happening."

It was not long after they arrived at Treasure Isle that they found out about the drag race happening at the gravel pits. They were walking back to Bryan's car when Chuck pulled in and saw Janice and Pam sitting in the car. Bryan and Bobby jumped in the car, handed Pam and Janice their cokes and drove away as they were still shutting the car doors. Bryan peeled out of Treasure Isle as he made tire tracks. Chuck pulled his car up behind their car, chasing them, getting close to their bumper.

Bobby mooned Chuck, pulling his pants down and sticking his naked behind out the window. Pam and Janice let out a high-pitched yell, turning their faces away not to be grossed out. Chuck was mad.

Pam was laughing, she said, "Y'all, I feel really bad about us being so mean to Chuck, he doesn't deserve this."

Janice looked back at Pam, "Pam, don't be silly, we girls just want to have fun. We don't need to be with our boyfriends all the time."

"Yeah, you are right," Pam answered.

Chuck drove to our house and sat with Momma the rest of the evening, waiting for Pam and Janice to come home.

They drove to the gravel pits while listening to the Big Bam Radio Show. Our favorite DJ said, "For all you young lovers out there tonight, here's a new song by Jimmy Glimmer & the Fireballs, "Sugar Shack."

Singing and moving in their seat to the beat, they headed for the gravel pit. It was a dark, tree-line dirt road that came to an open field. There was a bonfire. A crowd had already gathered around the bonfire. Cars lined the road on both sides with their headlights on facing each other, lighting the strip for the drag race. Girls and boys were sitting on top of the car hoods, in convertibles with tops down, or just standing on their cars. You did not dare stand in front in case one of the cars dragging got out of control.

I was with Robin, KT, Beth, Fran and Emily. We had heard about the drag race through some of our friends.

JB was a hood. He was not that tall, but he carried himself as if he were. He had brown eyes, brown wavy hair with side burns. His skin was not smooth; he had acne on his face. He was always under his car working on it, so I guess the grease affected his skin.

The hoods came from an area of town that was mostly low income. They were called hoodlums or greasers. They were tough acting guys. They respected their girls and demanded respect be shown to them. There were always a few that carried a knife stuck down inside of their motorcycle boots or high top Converse shoes. Some had tattoos on their arm. They dressed in dark blue jeans and wore a dark blue jean jacket with a white tee shirt. Their hair was kept long on top with short sides and side burns. It was greased and combed back. Some allowed a curl to fall forward. That was where the name greaser came from. A black comb was kept in the back pocket of their blue jeans and they drank beer and smoked cigarettes.

JB was known as the toughest hood. He was usually there to fight someone, to prove he was still the main man, the leader of the pack. It was usually one of our guys he wanted to pound in the face or at least rake him over. The hoods stuck together. When a hood ratted on another hood, they were ousted until he could prove to the main hood he could be trusted again.

You could always tell our guys from the hoods. They stuck out like a cocker spaniel among pit bulls, with their khaki pants, penny loafers and madras shirts. They weren't afraid of the hoods. They thought of them as a joke and the hoods felt the same way about them. The fact was the hoods didn't get the same opportunities. Their fathers, if they had one at home, were usually blue-collar workers.

Our guy's fathers were white-collar workers. Janice, Pam and I crossed over to the Hoods as friends. We all went to school together. We had hung out with them at the skating rink, and some had been to our house to hang out. They usually referred to their momma's as the old lady, but with our mom they showed respect. She corrected them quickly and if they said, "Yeah", to her, she would say, "Don't say, 'Yeah', to me, son. You say, yes ma'am."

The hoods looked out for the three of us. If we were out with our guys, and one of the hoods saw us, we knew by the wink of an eye that we had our own private security around without our guys even realizing it.

The two cars began to race their engines. JB's girl was standing in front of the cars ready to drop the flags, red scarf in one hand and yellow in the other, that had come from two girl's ponytails. The cops showed up with their blue lights flashing. Everyone jumped in their cars and scattered. It was all part of the night's fun. The police were our friends. They just came to break it up. They did not even chase a car. Over the police car speaker came, "Everybody break it up, go home." Everyone went back to the Treasure Isle to regroup.

On Saturday afternoon, it was a regular routine for all us girls to meet at Eastbrook Shopping Center. We'd hang out and look at the latest fashions in the stores. Some Saturdays a local band played outside the central store of the shopping center.

Now, it is the southern way to go bare-footed. If you had a big date for that night you were bare-footed in short-shorts, make-up on with curlers in your hair so you would look good that night. Your hair length determined the size of the curlers. For long hair to your shoulders, Pam, Janice and I, found that rolling your hair on orange juice cans with both ends cut out worked great. The larger the curlers, the less curl you would get and for the "flip" hairstyle it worked perfect.

Pierced ears were cool. There was not anywhere to go to get them pierced unless you went to a doctor or a tattoo place. I wanted my ears pierced. Pam assured me she could do it. She took an ice cube out of an ice tray and held it tightly on my ear. I gritted my teeth as she stuck the needle through my earlobe. She was screaming as she pushed it through.

I yelled out, "Pam, stop your screaming,"

She said, "I can't do the other one", still screaming and laughing. With the needle, stuck in my earlobe, I said with a firm tone, "Pam, don't you do this."

She screamed while rolling around on the bed. "No, I can't."

I told her, "I can't walk around with one pierced ear. I will hold an ice cube on the other ear. You pull that needle out and put the earring in."

She calmed down, sat up and said, "Okay, here goes."

Screaming, she pulled the needle out, put the earring in and then screamed the whole time she was pushing the needle through my ice-cold ear lobe. I was the one in pain, but she was doing enough screaming for the both of us. My ears were now pierced.

Pam had enjoyed it so much she did Janice's. Janice and I both held Pam down to pierce her ears. We all screamed at the same time.

MOMMA'S NERVES HAD gotten so much better since Daddy was out of the house. She no longer wanted to die. She wanted to live for her children. She had a hysterectomy and was taking hormone pills that really helped her. During dinner, Momma always brought up the topic of Daddy and Maria and what they did to us. I always got a sour stomach when I heard that. I didn't want to hear it, but it was always on her mind.

Isn't it something, when a mate cheats on the other one, the children feel they are cheated on also? We tried to lift her spirits, make her laugh and change the subject.

The psychiatrist told Momma, "Nellie, it's like you have this pain and you keep it in your pocket. You pull it out every day and rehearse the hurt repeatedly. You have to pull it out and throw it away." He was right, but that was hard for her to hear. He also told her, "You take life too seriously and should have some fun of your own. Have an affair with a man." That made Momma furious. She never went back to see him. She never respected psychiatrists again.

It was not uncommon for Momma to come home from work on a Friday and tell us on the spur of the moment, "Let's drive to Panama City and spend the weekend on the beach." We grabbed our beach towels, bathing suits, makeup and curlers. Momma packed the food to make tomato and onion sandwiches, and peanut butter and bananas for sandwiches, and always Golden Flake potato chips. Our friends were always invited, that is, all that would fit in the car. Driving late at night, Momma would sometimes stop to pick up hitchhikers. They were usually soldiers on three-day passes and by the time we arrived at the beach the hitchhiker felt like family.

We had our radio, beach blankets, and towels. We were ready for two days in the sun. The beach songs playing on the radio were *"Help Me Rhonda, Surf City"* and while we were still at war *"Solider Boy"* were hits on the radio. I had on a red and white polka dot bikini to go with the song *"Polka Dot Bikini."* Boys walking up and down the beach strip would always stop and talk to us. Before we knew it, we had a large group around us and it turned into a beach party.

Daddy never called. I only remember his calling one Friday to say "Denice, Saturday I will pick up Leeann, Charlie and you and take y'all for ice cream." I sat by the window and waited all day. He never showed up. I never looked for him or expected anything from him again!

Blaine was the great dancer that had a twin brother, but there was also a guy named Donnie I liked. Donnie invited me over to his house for dinner with his parents. I was always breaking up with Blaine, switching back and forth between the two guys. Donnie lived in a neighborhood with new homes on the street. I knew Daddy and his new wife Maria lived across the street from Donnie.

I told Donnie I was going to walk over there for a few minutes to see Daddy. I knocked on the door. Maria answered the door

"Hello, Denice." She was in short-shorts and was barefooted.

I said, "I want to see my Daddy."

She responded, "Come on in. I will get him for you." She walked with a bounce like she didn't have a care in the world.

Twisting her hair with her finger, she called out to him "Charles, it's Denice. She's come to see yah."

While waiting on Daddy, I looked around to see how they were living. I saw all new furniture. They had a sofa with matching lamps that sat on two shiny wooden end tables, and a matching coffee table. There was an oil painting hanging on the wall above the sofa. There was a green recliner for Daddy. I also noticed a brand new stereo cabinet that had a record player and radio combined. A silk flower arrangement sat on top of the stereo. Above the color television were two brass wall sconces that held pale peach silk flowers. Daddy walked in with a big grin on his face. He was barefooted and bare-chested with his white shorts on.

"Hey."

I spoke up nervously, "I was over here in the neighborhood and thought I would just drop by and visit for a minute."

"Well, have a seat," he said.

Daddy had his gospel quartet music playing on his record player. It was the Blackwood Brothers.

I said, "I just wanted to say hey. I'm having dinner with a friend of mine in the neighborhood. I knew you lived here and just wanted to see you. Daddy, I can't stay, I better go." I left.

I almost felt as if I were betraying Momma by being there. I wanted to leave. It was too uncomfortable for me. I was sad. I guess you could say I was upset. I needed to get back over to Donnie's and forget about it.

Walking back to Donnie's house, I thought about how everything at our house was broken-down and nothing matched. Not even the dishes matched. One thing I knew, I would not want to live with them if my life depended on it. I would rather be with Momma and struggle. I would rather eat eggs every day of my life and continue wiping my rear end with newspapers than to leave my Momma.

One thing about Momma, we always knew we could depend on her. I felt secure in my bed at night. I knew in the dark Momma's very soul was crying out to God for help, for her and her children. I never told Momma that I went to see him that day. I knew it would hurt her to know about the new house and all the pretty things. I could not change that I was his child, but I was proud to say, I was my mother's daughter.

~8~
YOUR DADDY'S DEAD

I NEVER LIKED MOMMA to be home alone. We were running around town on the weekends, doing what teenagers do. She was with Leeann and Charlie, but they were little. She needed to have an adult conversation. It was not unusual for me to come home from a date and find our guy friends sitting with Momma eating biscuits and drinking coffee. The power was often turned off because there was not enough money to pay the bills. That made it harder for Mom to come up with the past bill money and the turn on fee. We just lit candles and our friends thought it was cool, talking and laughing by candlelight. Mom taught us how to roll with the punches.

Momma let us date much too young. I see that now. We were not guided toward getting an education. College was out of the question. We lived day to day, trying to survive.

I always played sports. If I had a volleyball or basketball game after school, I had to rush home to clean the house or cut the grass before Momma got home from work. There was no time to study. Momma came home tired. She quickly changed into comfortable clothes and began to cook dinner. She was always talking to us about right and wrong, keeping ourselves pure, seeing people for who they really were and not who they portrayed themselves to be, having mercy on people, being kind and not judgmental, and always being respectful to others. The most valuable lesson she gave us was to know who you are and to like yourself as a person. Mom gave us another gift without knowing it; I call it, a gift of self-expression. She communicated with us and wanted to hear our thoughts on any subject. She would share her thoughts and let us all have our own opinion. We were not corrected. We were directed. It worked.

Momma made a choice every day to be happy and not feel depressed. I learned that choice is a powerful weapon. The Bible states, *"This day I call heaven and earth as witnesses against you, that I have set before you, life and death, blessings and curses. Now choose life, so that you and your children may live."* Deuteronomy 30:19 No one is defeated until he gives up. I will say now looking back, I wish mom had taken and stayed on antidepressants. It would have helped her and it would have been easier on us kids. Mom was taught against taking pills. As an adult I realize now, that just as a woman can go through female hormone deficiency, your brain has brain hormones that it is suppose to put out, but if it doesn't, an antidepressant will give it to you. In the same manor those female hormones do. The struggle would have left.

In the future I will mix and mingle with highly educated people and be impressed with their accomplishments, but I never felt inferior. Momma taught us the meaning of life and it was instilled so deep within us. Life has its way of forming who we are and who we become. Some of the most educated people I have met swim in shallow waters. I still meet people who are wet behind their ears and do not even know it. They think their education has made them smart. I listen to people talk and see that what they are talking about is something they have head knowledge on, but have never proven it in their own life. Sometimes I feel like saying, excuse me you are wet behind the ears. Who would a solider rather be train by, a man that has taken all the classes on how to fight and go into battle but never was willing to use what he learned just wants to talk about it? Or would you listen to the man that has been to war and made it home? Which one would you have questions for? One prepared for war, the other prepared and went to war. The substance of the man came from going to war. Life is a great teacher if you will allow it to be, it will dry you off. It will be your teacher if you will be its student. *Life is beautiful.*

JANICE AND MITCHELL were always together. When you saw Janice, you saw Mitchell. They never wanted to be apart. Janice went to Momma and said she wanted to get married. In Alabama, two sixteen year olds could not marry, but in the state of Mississippi, if each teenager had one parent's permission, they could legally marry.

Momma and Mitchell's Daddy, Harris, a divorcee, took the two teens to Mississippi to get married. Momma and Harris talked and enjoyed each other's company, on the three-hour trip to Mississippi and three-hour drive home. They began dating and it was not long before they were married. We were excited for Momma.

He was tall with broad shoulders, dark eyes and black wavy hair. Harris was a good man, a gentle man. Momma met him when he was a recovering alcoholic. She knew nothing about alcoholics. She had never been around alcohol. He had not been dry long when they met and not long after the wedding, he started back to his drinking. Harris decided to move into a boarding house so that we would not see him drunk.

In the meantime Mom's father, who lived in Birmingham, died. The nine adult children split the inheritance money. It was not a lot. It was enough to pay a rehab for six weeks, to get Harris dried out.

We thought that a rehab would fix his problem. Harris moved back into the house. Momma took the rest of the money and rented a small office space for her and Harris to open an accounting firm. Harris had an accounting background just like her. He just never showed up for work and Momma lost her entire investment. Harris wanted to stay dry, but he was hooked and we did not know how to help him.

Some days when I walked in the door after school, Harris would be reading his Bible. He was always a gentleman with me. He played with Leeann and Charlie, putting a coat hanger around his head and walking like Frankenstein, chasing them around the house. They ran screaming and laughing. He got a kick out of calling Charlie "Sally", but being that Charlie was so little he took Harris seriously and would start crying. He would shake his head and say, "Not name Sally, name Charlie." Charlie was such a handsome little boy with green eyes and blonde curls.

Harris was in and out of the boarding house. When he was not drinking, he came over for dinner. He loved Momma and would flirt with her saying, "Look at her, is she the cutest woman you've ever seen?" Momma had never gotten that kind of attention from Daddy. Harris continued his flirtatious remarks and Momma, while cooking would giggle and dance.

We heard Daddy and Maria had gotten a divorce. Their love affair lasted for years, but their marriage didn't last one year.

NINETEEN SIXTY-FOUR, it was a great time to be alive! I was fourteen. The Beatles were taking the USA by storm. I remember the night they were on the Ed Sullivan Show. We started screaming just as they began to sing. They affected style, with their tight fitted suites, to their zip up ankle boots and their head of hair.

It was also the year the cigarette boxes had a warning printed on them: Smoking can be hazardous to your health. It had not previously occurred to the US government to give the warning that smoking led to cancer and lung problems.

In school, it was a requirement that everyone take physical education. We were all in the gym lined up in rows with white T-shirts and our red PE shorts. Our teacher was facing the front, with her back to the class, leading us in exercises. I was always joking around wanting to have fun. As she led us in jumping jacks, I led the class in dance moves—the *Twist,* the *Monkey* and the *Jerk.* They all followed me. She was facing forward and thought we were following her. She turned around just as I was caught up in my dance.

She said, "Denice, Robin, I think the principal would love to discuss the subject of leadership with you and how the paddle feels on your behind." She pointed toward the gym doors and said, "Go to the office."

I felt bad that Robin was getting punished with me for something I started. We sat in the office waiting for the principal when the office phone rang. The school secretary answered it. Robin and I sat there whispering back and forth, conspiring on how we were going to explain to the principal why the whole class was dancing instead of following the teacher in jumping jacks? The secretary put the phone on hold, walked over to the school microphone system and pushed a button on the gym speaker. I looked up from Robin to hear the secretary say, "Please send Denice Perkins to the office."

I cleared my throat. I spoke up. "I'm right here."

She looked surprised to see me sitting there. She said, "Denice step into the principal's office. There is a phone call for you. It's your mom."

I picked up the phone, "Momma what is it?"

"It's your Daddy. He's dead. I will be there in a minute to pick you up," she said in a solemn voice. I stepped out of the office and told Robin. She put her arm around my shoulder to comfort me. I wasn't crying but I was a little shocked of the news. While standing out front of the school waiting for Momma, I tried to decide who I wanted it to be. I thought, I love Harris, but his alcohol problem has just made life harder for us. Daddy only shows up every now and then with a different woman to show off and to remind us kids that we are no good.

I wasn't sure which one I wanted to be dead. Momma drove up; I got in the car and asked, "Momma who's dead, Harris or Daddy?"

"It's Harris. Since he didn't come for breakfast this morning, I decided to go check on him at the boarding house. He did not answer the door. I looked through his bedroom window and saw him lying in bed. But when I knocked on the window, he still didn't wake up. The boarding house manager let me in. Harris was sleeping on his side, covered up with his blanket as always. He looked like he was sleeping, but he was gone."

A few days later the autopsy indicated he died of alcohol and sleeping pill overdose. It was an accidental overdose. They had been married about a year when he passed, and it had been a hard year for Momma not knowing how to help him. Now he was gone. It had been a problem, I felt relieved. One thing I realized is that life goes on and the world continues to change.

The world was changing around us as Momma dealt with life and her children. Pam was now dating William. He was four years older and played bass guitar in a popular local band. William was six feet tall with blonde-hair. Girls liked boys in rock bands and Pam was no exception. I have never seen her crazy, head over heels over any boy, but she was over this boy. His band played every weekend at various locations in town and college campuses near by. They had already cut their first album. It was a big deal because most of the local bands never made it that far.

It was not but a few months after she started dating William that Pam walked into the kitchen and said, "Momma, I'm quitting school and marrying William. He has to sign up for the Navy."

The next day at school all the cliques were buzzing. I knew what they were saying and thinking. I went to, Pam, "Please don't get married, please." I begged.

I said to her, "Well, Janice might have gotten married and now you, but I'm telling you, I'm not going to get married until I'm at least twenty-one."

She said, "Denice, you're going to eat those words. You're going to fall in love and you'll want to get married, too."

I folded my arms as I shook my head, "Not me. I'm not falling in love." Yet, here I was, the most boy-crazy teenager around.

Momma was not happy about it, but she saw in Pam the same determination Janice had had. Pam's boyfriend had joined the Navy, and she did not want him to transfer out of state without taking her with him. Momma, Pam, and William went down to the courthouse and they got married. William was twenty years old, and Pam was only sixteen. They could get married with the consent of one parent of the teen. Pam wore a two-piece cream-colored suit with a pair of cream high heels. Momma bought Pam flowers to hold in her hands.

In the South girls marry right out of high school unless they are going to college. Southerners have always married much younger than in the Northern States. We were living at a time when our young boys were not given a choice but were sent off to war. They married the girl they loved before they left to fight in the war. People felt that if they were old enough to fight on the battlefield they were old enough to be married. Most of them just wanted someone to write home to, someone who would be waiting for them when they returned.

Janice's marriage did not last but about two years. She found herself divorced and with a baby boy. Men were always attracted to Janice. She was Miss Personality, always up to something, always pushing the limits and always the leader of the pack. Janice said she felt like the black sheep of us girls. She really wasn't. She just had a wild hair about her.

A new song was playing on the radio, "*Mustang Sally*." Janice had a new man in her life, which had a red Mustang. They married and had two boys over the next few years. That made three sons for her. Like I told you, Janice made men believe in themselves, so her husband did very well while he was married to her. We loved him. He was a great guy.

ON FEBRUARY 8, 1965 the United States started bombing North Vietnam. Many of our guy friends were going to war. Janice's best friend Bryan was one of the ones going. We hated the war. Every day eighteen year olds were being sent to the front line to fight and every day we were getting reports of our friends we grew up with, were never coming home. Missing in action became a general term for us teens to hear.

It wasn't long after Brian left, that we got word a hand grenade went off and the shrapnel tore right into Bryan's stomach. He stayed in a hospital overseas for a time.

IT WAS A CRAZY TIME; music continued to speak to us. Local radio stations put on

Rock concerts. They brought in the biggest singers and bands. I always found a way to get on the front row, I screamed, danced, and got all dreamy over the performers. I was good at sneaking back stage, pretending I was with the band, with my long black hair and dressed to kill. The cops who guarded the backstage always believed me when I said I was with the band, and they just let me go backstage with the performers. Robin and KT followed.

I was always finding time to get a bucket of paint and paint the living room or bedroom. I called Momma one day and asked her if I could take a crowbar and knock out a closet to enlarge the living room and of course she let me. I can't imagine letting one of my children do that, but it sure made me a do it yourself kind of person.

I thought my life was looking up when Riley William Richmond III asked me on a date. He was eighteen and a hunk. He was tall, blonde, dressed to kill and walked with his arms out away from his body to show off his pumped up physique from weight lifting. I was fifteen.

Riley went to Sidney Lanier High School. Sidney Lanier High School was where the upper class went to school. You could always distinguish which boys and girls went to Sidney Lanier because they spoke with a very slow Southern drawl. They had what we called, "Old Money". Old money was when your great-grandparents and grandparents made money in their lifetime and passed it down generation-to-generation, whose families enjoyed the privilege of living off money they hadn't made.

Riley and I went on a double date. It was obvious that the couple in the back seat was going to spend the night petting and necking. I was furious. Even though I dated young, I had always maintained high morals and standards. The more they petted and played back seat bingo, the angrier I got. We were parked at the drive-in movie. I was determined to watch the movie. My date kept staring at me. I knew that he wanted to make out. I could see him out the corner of my eye while I watched the movie. His arm went up and over the back of my neck, dropping his hand over my shoulder with his hand dangling right over my right breast. I realized then the only reason he asked me out was to make out.

I moved his hand away from my breast and I asked, "Do you have a problem?"

He responded in his Southern drawl. "Are you going to watch the movie?"

I answered him with a question. "Riley, when you called me tonight, what did you say when you got me on the phone?"

He looked at me and spoke with a stern voice, "I asked you if you wanted to go out tonight?"

"Where did you say you were going to take me?" I asked. I was fuming.

He said, "I told you, to the movies." He spoke slowly as if he were spreading butter with this tongue.

We all grew up in the same town and just because you lived at another section of town and came from old money, didn't mean you had to draw out your words like that.

I responded with words sharp and to the point, "If you wanted to take me out to make out, why didn't you just call me up and say, 'Hello Denice, do you want to go make out tonight?'"

He looked toward the floorboard. His shoulders slumped. He wasn't used to a girl standing up for herself. "Well, you wouldn't have gone out."

"You are exactly right, Riley. I think you need to lift weights less and eat more brain food." His mouth turned down and his hands were tight on the steering wheel. He cranked the car and the couple in the back seat was now lying down, never realizing we had just left the drive-in.

I knew I was being mean, but I also knew guys talk in the locker-room and I wanted word out by him, "She doesn't play."

I opened the car door; turned around, and said, "Don't bother walking me to the door. There is no need in you trying to be a gentleman now." Riley burned rubber as he drove away trying to prove himself a man.

I went in the house and told mom, "I found out the only reason Riley asked me out was to make out. That is why I came home early. He was not all that girls say he is."

She laughed and said, "Denice you are pistol ball! I'm proud of you."

A few months passed. I just did not want to go steady with one boy and end up wasting my youth not dating different boys. I sat with Momma as we drank our coffee one night, talking.

"Momma, my teenage life is going to pass me by. I think I want to start dating boys and not need to be in love with them. I'm going to start dating boys just for friendship. I have decided I will date boys and not wait to look for that perfect guy. I just cannot find a guy that knocks me off my feet. I'm beginning to think I will never meet my match."

Momma said, "You should just get out there and date. Have fun Denice."

Momma was still battling depression. She had so much on her shoulders and very little support both emotionally and financially. It was important to her that I was enjoying life. I began to go on dates just for fun with every boy who asked.

Pam had moved in with her husband's parents in Florida. She got a job working in a department store while her husband was out to sea. The Vietnam War was still raging. Pam missed the family and she asked Momma if I could come visit. Momma put me on a Greyhound bus. I arrived at the bus station in sunny Florida. Pam was there waiting for my arrival. We enjoyed our visit together, catching up on everybody in the family. We talked about the move Janice, her husband and three sons had made to Miami, Florida. Now that Pam was married, she was going to give me her expert advice on life and boys. She wanted to make sure that I made good choices.

Right before she put me on a Greyhound bus to go home, she gave me some last minute advice. "If a man tries to sit beside you on the bus just get up and move to another seat. Do not go to the back of the bus. Stay toward the front because the back of the bus is where the coloreds sit or the bus driver will move you." The racial situation was changing, but very slowly.

I looked at her, laughed and said, "Pam, don't sweat it, I'll be fine."

She was taking this mothering job too seriously. The look of concern on her face said it all. I shook my head "Okay, I got it."

I had a new philosophy. I was just going to date every boy and keep my morals. A good-looking boy who was a student at Auburn University asked me out on a date. Jim was a very good looker with sandy color hair and blue eyes, his friends called him "Hunter" He was all into deer hunting, his dad owned a hunting lodge. He drove a green MGB sports car. He was built like a football player and dressed like a college student, khaki pants and pullover V-neck sweater with a white tee shirt underneath. He picked me up in his convertible and we drove downtown to the theater.

Most guys took dates to a drive in theater because it was cheaper. I could tell he was somewhat disturbed with me because I was not falling all over him as we walked in. Guys like him are used to girls clinging to their arm. I knew he had a reputation for being a good catch. I guess I was bored. We had nothing in common. I wasn't the clinging kind of girl. After the movie, we got into his sports car and all he could talk about were his sexual conquests with other girls. I think he was feeling me out. I was turned off by his conversation. I thought he was as dumb as a load of bricks. If he thought I was being impressed, he was wrong. I listened to the point I had had enough. I just am not the girl that will sit and listen to trash talk and keep my mouth shut.

I spoke up, "I think your bragging is gross and immature and I am certainly not that kind of girl. I was hoping there was more to you than this, but I was wrong."

He only responded, "Well, I'll take you home. There is certainly nothing further for us to do tonight."

I responded, "You're right, there isn't anything else for us to do together." He took me home. As far as I was concerned he could flake off the earth. I considered him to have a big head. He was small potatoes to me. Here I was again, another guy taking me home early because I put him in his place. My dating life was more frustrating than I had hoped for. I just wanted to have fun, not deal with all these jerks looking for a good time girl. Look, I was fun and could carry a good conversation and laugh about everything but funny is funny and stupid is stupid.

Finally, a great guy asked me out. It was a Thursday night and the phone rang. It was Matthew Folsom.

He said, "Denice, this is Matthew Folsom. I was wondering if you would like to go out tomorrow night. I thought we would go see Doctor Zhivago at the drive-in theater."

I answered, "Yes, that sounds great. I've been wanting to see it."

He said, "I'll pick you up around seven."

Mathew was tall, slim, tanned, brown eyes, and black hair. He was Hollywood gorgeous. We started dating. He had all the good manners a girl could want and he sure wasn't hard on the eyes. We laughed and talked about everything. We had a lot in common. We ran with the same group of friends and knew many of the same people. After about the fifth date he kissed me; I knew it was going to happen and I had already decided ahead of time to let him kiss me. I wanted to see if I felt any electricity. It was like kissing a wall. I did not feel anything, I did not know what kind of guy it was going to take to thrill me and knock me off my feet, but so far I had not met him. Matthew brought me gifts and was such a gentleman, but he did not leave me any dating room for other boys. He asked me out for the weekend at the start of each week.

Friday nights I was with him and then Robin, KT and I would spend Saturday nights at my house staying up late to watch Shock Theater and eating Momma's fudge. Everybody else was moving in the fast lane, growing up, experimenting with petting and making out in parked cars. Robin, KT and I just wanted to have fun, laugh, cut up, act crazy and dance to music. We were constantly talking about boys. We were free spirits. A girl cannot act maturely all the time. I was beginning to feel smothered by Matthew. My plan was to date different guys instead of just one. It was time I told him that I didn't want to date just him. I thought he was cute and fun, but I was just not ready to settle down with one guy. I waited to tell him at the end of the evening, before he walked me to the door. He was disappointed.

Momma and I, with Leeann and Charlie, had started attending a Methodist Church on the corner of Ann Street and Highland Avenue. Pastor Ken was a fiery little preacher. It was a small congregation. There was a boy home from college for the summer that was going to help Pastor Ken with the youth. He was good looking and was a great preacher. Not boring at all, on top of that, he could sing. That's when my opinion of Christian boys would change. He said he was called by God to be a minister. I thought how could you look that good and waste yourself being a preacher? I looked forward to church just to see him.

Mom was always singing and dancing while she cooked.
(Notice the kitchen cabinets that are open, we did not have much in them.)

9
THE VOICE OF GOD

I WAS DOING MY housework. I had to use a broom to sweep the carpet to get the dirt out of the house. The vacuum cleaner was broke. The radio was blasting on my favorite Big Bam rock station. I sang along as I swept doing a few dance moves to the beat of the music. All of a sudden there was an interruption in my thoughts.

I heard a voice in my head, "***You're going to be married to a preacher.***"

I heard the voice but I had no control over it. The loud rock music was playing and the voice came through my thoughts. It was like a speaker saying, "We want to interrupt this program to give this announcement: You're going to be married to a preacher."

I stopped sweeping and stood still to see if there was anything else the voice had to say. But the voice did not speak. I knew at that moment God just spoke. It was like an earthquake shook in my body that makes that moment stand still in time.

I put the broom down and went into the kitchen to call Momma. She was a bookkeeper for a women's boutique called Benson's. She answered the phone and I said, "Mom, God just spoke to me."

She asked, "Denice what did He say?"

"Momma He said, I'm going to be married to a preacher."

I could hear a soft, sniff on the other end of the phone and then she responded tenderly, "Denice, that's wonderful."

To this day I am still amazed at the fact Momma did not laugh at a fourteen year old telling her, she just heard the voice of God. We had never heard of anybody but maybe Moses, in the Bible, hearing the voice of God. She just believed what I said.

I began to think it might be that young boy at church who was in college and who had a call to ministry. He was good-looking, could sing and was a dynamic preacher.

That Friday night Robin, KT and I were on our way to hear a band and dance the night away. It was still early and we did not want to get there before the crowd. We drove around cruising. We passed the little red brick church Momma and I were attending. We noticed the youth group standing in the front yard of the church. Bart the handsome college boy was there, helping Pastor Ken with the youth group.

I told Robin and KT, "Let's stop and talk to them to see what they are up to." I parked the car and the three of us got out. As we were walking toward them, Bart spoke out, "Denice I'm glad you came to go street witnessing with us."

I said, "Oh, Bart, I'm sorry, but we already have plans to go dancing."

His face turned red as he pointed his finger at me, "Denice, if you go dancing tonight, you will dance in hell."

I swallowed as I blinked my eyes to take a second look at Bart. I couldn't understand what he said. Did he just say that I would go to hell tonight if I went dancing, instead of witnessing?

Then he said, "You must get your priorities in order."

"Bart," I said, "We wanted to stop to say hello before we went dancing, I'm sorry you feel that way." We split. I put the keys in the ignition and turned the radio up loud. I shook my head as we drove away and said, "I didn't know they danced in hell!"

Robin and KT laughed. I was disappointed in him. We headed toward the YMCA. We arrived late. We walked toward the cop, who standing by the door and paid the woman who was sitting behind a folding table at the entrance. She stamped the back of our hands with the word in red, "PAID". We walked through the double doors into a big open room with wood floors and basketball hoops hanging from the ceiling. A stage was brought in Friday nights for bands to play. The band was already playing, and the lead singer was singing a James Brown song, *"I Feel Good"*.

The room was packed with teenagers. Everyone had formed a circle in the room around a couple that was dancing.

"What is going on?" I said to Robin and KT. I pressed through the crowd to see whom everybody was watching. It was a boy and girl dancing.

We stood there moving to the music with the crowd as they all had their eyes on the couple. The boy was swift on his feet and exuded a confidence I had never seen. He was dressed in khaki pants, madras, and plaid, button up shirt with a burgundy belt and burgundy penny loafers. I could tell he was a wealthy, upper class college student by the way he dressed. He had brown hair with sideburns that looked stylish. My mind raced as I watched him dance with that girl. I could not take my eyes off him. He took my breath away. Where in the world did this guy come from? What is his name? What gives this guy the confidence I see expressed from head to toe? He was doing the James Brown dance. I had never seen a guy dance the way he did. He was loose and tight all at the same time.

Robin elbowed me, covering her mouth so no one else could hear. "You think you can get a date with any boy, let me see you get a date with that boy," she pointed at him.

Still not willing to take my eyes off of him, I responded with excitement, "Give me two weeks and I will have a date with him, better than that, he is the boy I am going to marry."

Robin laughed and said, "Yeah, right, let's see."

The bet was on. I now see and realize a young girl had no sense to be even thinking of marriage, but a college education and planning a future was not in the cards for me. I still believed in destiny. God's pull in my life was like a magnetic force pulling me toward Steve and my destiny. That is truly how it felt.

I knew for the first time in my life I felt something bigger than life itself when I looked at him. I was looking at a real challenge in this guy. He looked like a man compared to every other boy. The way he handled himself shouted masculine man. His body language shouted, going places in life. He didn't wear rags. I could also tell every girl in the room would give their eyeteeth to date him. I didn't know anything about him, so with my eyes still fixed on him I asked the girl next to me.

"Who's that boy?"

She looked at me as if to say, where have you been? "You don't know who that is? He is a college student at the University of Alabama and that girl he is dancing with, he's been going steady with her for the last two years."

I took my eyes off of him to look at her, to check out my competition. She was older than me, with real breast of her own, not like my padded bra. She was cute and in all appearance and by the way she moved her body, I was sure they had been intimate.

Not only was she stacked, she looked like a woman. She wore a tight skirt with a button up V-neck fitted sweater, wide belt and a pair of flat shoes. Her highlighted blonde hair was ratted and smoothed out with bangs, styled in a flip. She wore fake eyelashes with her dark brown eyes and big dimples on both cheeks. Her pink lipstick told me she kept up with the latest in style. I looked like a little girl up against her. I am only in the ninth grade. I reminded myself that my inner strength was more powerful than hers.

I felt I had the upper hand. I'm fresh and won't give myself away, it did not matter who he thinks he is. That will be his challenge.

The girl next to me continued talking, "He is the manager of the band that is playing and has his own band. He is the lead singer of a band and plays the keyboard. The band's name is, "*The Swinging Jades*." She added, "His girlfriend was Miss Georgia Peach."

I took my eyes off Miss Georgia Peach and put them back on the best looking thing I had ever seen in my life. I thought to myself—I couldn't look at what I don't have, like boobs. I have to have a whole lot of confidence to come up against this guy and that girl. I leaned in closer as I whispered, "What's his name?"

"Steve Vickers," she whispered back.

Right then it felt like a flash of lightning hit me in my gut. I realized that he was the big brother of Tommy Vickers who gave me my first kiss.

The band began playing "*Wooly Bully*" and everybody in the room began to dance. Robin, KT and I split up dancing with boys in the room, but my mind was on finding a way to meet that Steve Vickers. I danced to three other fast songs.

Steve was leaning against a table, his arms crossed, watching the band play. He was alone. When the song ended I turned to the boy I was dancing with and said, "I'm going to take a break."

I walked toward Steve, and the band began to play, "*The House of the Rising Sun*". I took a deep breath, pulled my shoulders back and told myself I had all that I needed to turn his head. I was five feet seven, slim, and I know I am easy on the eyes and I am not stuck up, just confident. I was wearing a short, fitted, dark purple sleeveless dress with a purple satin ribbon tied around my waist. I had penny loafers on. My dark hair was midway down my back, makeup was perfect: black mascara, eyeliner, pale pink lipstick and a pair of dangling silver loop earrings.

I walked up to him and stuck out my hand to shake his, "Hi, my name is Denice Perkins," I looked straight into his eyes and smiled. He laughed and smiled as he reached to take my hand and came back with a remark to make me laugh, "What do you want me to do, melt?" His eyes danced and never left mine. I have never looked into eyes that spoke to me the way his did. My heart was racing.

I thought, what a confident jerk. I was not prepared for that, think fast you have to have a confident come back, quick, speak, "Most boys do. Why shouldn't you?" I replied.

Leaning farther back against the table crossing his feet, staying in total control, he smiled back with those brown eyes flashing. "I'm Steve Vickers," he said.

I smiled and said, "I know who you are. Hi."

He looked at me from head to toe. He started at my feet and worked his way up, then looked me directly in the eyes, raised one eyebrow and smiled. His confidence was off the charts. I thought I could melt right there and then.

His girlfriend walked up, moved in front of me, and stood between us. I stepped to the side of her. She placed her hands on his shoulders, began to shake him, "Steve Vickers, I can't trust you for a moment. I can't even go to the bathroom." She looked at me as if to say, "And when are you leaving?"

He is now looking at her and smiling. I spoke up and he turned his face away from her toward me. "I guess I better go before I cause you more trouble." I smiled.

He winked, smiled and said, "I'll see you around."

I thought, yes you will big boy. I walked away. She was still fussing at him and giving him, her what for. I turned and looked back to see if he was watching me walk away or if he was listening to her. His eyes were on me as I strutted my stuff. She was still fussing at him.

The next week destiny would come into play. Momma let me take her car so we could go to Treasure Isle. I parked the car and told Robin and KT that I would go in and get us some drinks. I walked out with a tray of cokes in my hands. I could not find the car. Robin and KT had driven away to cruise up and down the Atlanta Highway. Looking everywhere for my car, suddenly someone tapped me on the shoulder. I turned around and it was "Mister Wonderful" himself.

He said, "Hey Denice, who are you with tonight?" He remembered my name.

"I'm with my girlfriends but they seem to have left me." I said.

He asked, "Why don't you come sit in my car, and we will talk while you wait for them?"

I wanted to! I had a bet with Robin that I would have a date with him within two weeks. This was my chance. I had not been able to get him off my mind. Every night I lay in bed thinking about him. He took my breath away. He opened his car door on the driver's side and I slid in.

"What are your plans tonight?" He asked.

"I don't have any. I am just hanging out with my girlfriends." I responded.

Robin and KT pulled in about two cars away from us. They saw me in the car with Steve.

I turned to Steve and said, "They're back. I guess I'd better go." He leaned back against the car door with his arms folded and smiled as he asked, "Why don't you tell them to come back in an hour and you and I can go for a ride? We can get to know each other."

I tilted my face to one side as I thought about my decision, "Ok, just a moment, let me go tell the girls."

Walking over to the car, I tried to keep my cool. They were ecstatic bouncing up and down in their seats.

Robin asked, "How did you do this?"

I told them how it happened, "I'm going for a ride with him, come back and pick me up in an hour.

He was driving a brand new white 1965 Cadillac convertible. It was apparent Steve was from a different background than mine. He was not the average run of the mill guy. It was also apparent that he was used to fine things by the way he dressed and the car he drove. The way he handled himself also told me a lot about him. We drove away with the radio playing a Rolling Stones song, *"I Can't Get No Satisfaction"*. Steve sang out loud as he moved to the beat of the music while tapping the steering wheel. His dark eyes flashed with such life in them. He turned, smiled at me and kept singing. It was not long until, sure enough, he turned down a back road and headed for the Lights.

I knew everyone would ask, "Where did you go with him?" I would have to say the Lights and everybody knows that is where you go to make out. Steve parked the car and turned the music down low. I felt the back of my seat going back slowly and tilting. My mind started racing. You better plan your next move. He might try to rape you. Girl, you're over your head on this one. I looked around for a light, maybe a house to run to.

Steve turned in his seat toward me. I stretched out my arms keeping him at a distance. I was not going to let him think this was going to be a making out date, so immediately I said, "Tell me about your girlfriend."

He kind of laughed and asked, "What do you want me to talk about her for?"

His arm was resting on the steering wheel and the other on the back of the seat. He leaned forward to kiss me. He missed and kissed me on the end of my nose because I was shaking.

I said, "I need to go. Take me back to Treasure Isle. I have to get back now."

The smile he gave me was a smile like, "you're cute, sweet girl". Steve raised the seat back up, cranked the car, turned the radio up loud and began to sing as he drove to take me back.

We arrived at Treasure Isle. I got out of the car, leaned my head in the window and said, "It was good to see you again." I was thinking, man he looks good. The attraction I had for him was like a magnetic pull.

He said, "Yeah, you too," and he drove away.

I jumped in the car with Robin and KT and said, "Oh, he is so tough. He is the coolest."

I had won the bet. What they didn't know was, I had just gotten the scare of my life. I also knew this boy had captured my heart that night. This boy seemed bigger than life—Steve Vickers. In the weeks ahead, I could not get Steve off my mind. I soon heard he broke up with his girlfriend. I would see him around town, always with a different girl in his car, blonde, brunette or red head and they were all beautiful and older than me.

One night the phone rang. "Denice, this is Steve Vickers. Do you remember who I am?"

Calmly I answered, "Of course I remember you Steve."

"Do you want to catch a movie with me tonight?" He asked.

"Sure, I would love to."

He then said, "I'll pick you up around seven."

I hung the phone up and I screamed and ran around the room dancing and cheering, *I got it. I got it. I can't help it! It's a good thing and I got it!* I jumped into the shower washed my hair, rolled it, got under the dryer, put on my make-up, dressed to kill, and the doorbell finally rang. I opened the door and there he was.

He was a total gentleman. He opened the car door for me. We went to a drive-in theater and we watched the movie. He didn't even try to kiss me. He drove me home and walked me to the door. I put my hand on the doorknob, turned and said, "I had a great time."

He gave me that gorgeous smile of his, "I did too; we will have to do it again.

I responded, "I would like that, good night." I opened the door and went into the house. I leaned against the door for a moment, just to catch my breath. I got in bed and the phone rang. It was Steve.

He said, "What are you doing?"

"I'm in bed." I was surprised he called.

He said, "Well, I'm in bed too. I just thought I would call you and just talk for a while."

We talked for hours. We talked about anything and everything. I could hear him breathing over the phone and I thought his breathing was sexy. I began to feel sleepy.

I said, "Steve, I've got to hang up I'm so sleepy."

He responded, "Me too, good night"

He continued to date other girls. I knew why, I didn't put out. He always called me at the spur of the moment. We went out and had fun, but there were still the other girls. The girls that gave him what he wanted. He never tried anything with me; he could tell I wasn't that kind of girl.

One Saturday afternoon Robin and I were out cruising. We pulled into Treasure Isle where I asked a girl if she knew where Steve Vickers lived.

She said, "Go down the Atlanta Highway until there are no more businesses, just keep driving, it's out in the country. You will see a dirt road to your left, turn there and you will see it."

We did just as she said and just as we turned down the dirt road, to my amazement, there sat a Southern plantation home. Pecan trees, apple, plum, pear, fig, magnolia trees, and azalea bushes with honeysuckle growing all along a fence mixed with pink baby roses were around the house. The large white columns across the front porch were impressive. The side entrance had huge white columns on each side as you walked up the steps. A wide staircase led up the side entrance, which led to the sitting room. In the back of the plantation home was a water well that was built of stone with a little door. It looked like the plantation home, Tara, from the movie, "Gone with the Wind". I screamed out loud, "Wow, look at that."

Steve was on the side of his house washing his car. We pulled up beside him and got out of our car. His radio was blasting.

I said, "Hey Steve, what are you up to?"

"Oh, just taking in this beautiful day and washing my car. What are you girls up to today?"

He dropped the hose and bent down to put the sponge into the soap bucket. I told him we were just cruising around town checking out friends. He asked if we would go up to his house and get some liquid soap for his bucket from his mom.

"Just ask my Mom for it."

I was taught a good girl does not call boys, and she definitely does not go to his house. I was not sure what Mrs. Vickers would think. We rang the doorbell and a black woman in a white uniform came to the door. We asked to speak with Mrs. Vickers. Mrs. Vickers invited us in to sit down and have a Coke with her. Robin and I sat on the Victorian chairs looking at each other while she went into the kitchen to get the drinks. We were trying to appear proper. Mrs. Vickers returned from the kitchen with a napkin around each cold Coca-Cola bottle before handing it to us. We sat for a few moments and talked to her, she was so sweet.

We gave Steve the soap and left. I swear, that boy Steve Vickers did take my breath away and if I were ever going to be a bad girl he would be the one whom I wanted to be bad with. I also knew that was just not who I was. I knew what separated me from the other girls. My innocence and knowing about my own self-worth made me different. I believed there was more to me than the pretty face and body to give away. I had self-respect that I did not want to lose.

One night Steve called, "Are you going to hear the band tonight?

"Robin, KT and I plan on going together," I said.

"I'll see you there," he said.

When I got there he acted as if I were not there. He was talking to other girls, so I went into the girl's restroom to freshen-up my lipstick. A girl named Jackie walked in, lit up a cigarette, and leaned up against the wall across from the vanity I was using.

"You're Denice Perkins, aren't you?" she asked.

She took a drag off her cigarette, blew the smoke out slowly and looked at me from behind. I glanced at her through the mirror as I rolled lipstick across my lips. She was one of the girls I had seen him with. She was all decked out. She wore false eyelashes, her dark hair cut into a short bob. Her long painted fingernails held a cigarette between her slender fingers.

I responded, acting nonchalant, "Yeah," and continued to look at her through the mirror as I combed through my long black hair.

She took another drag as she blew the smoke out slowly and asked, "Would you like to know what Steve Vickers said about you?" I just looked at her as she told me.

"He said you're a cute girl, but he knew he could get a date with you any time he wanted to. He said it makes you not attractive to him."

I turned to look at her as I was putting my brush back into my purse. "He did, did he? Well Steve Vickers doesn't know me very well." I walked out. I knew I was a threat. The girls I always saw him with were older than me and definitely not the innocent girls. It was obvious he liked spending his time with them. They were usually all over him. I walked into the dance room and found Steve standing in front of the band listening to them play. The room was already packed with couples dancing. I walked up behind him and stood to his right. He turned and looked at me as if to say hey! I was so ticked, not just at him, but also at myself. I was mad at myself for him being able to see thru me, he saw my excitement to see him or talk to him. I had let down my wall. Now, I was so ready to let him know the world didn't stop when he was born. He wasn't God's gift to all women. I went up to him, pulled him away from a girl he was talking to and said, "You go to hell Steve Vicker."

He did not know what had happen and I did not care to explain to him. I was mad at him and myself. I walked away not giving him a chance to respond. I left the dance and went straight home. I walked into my bedroom, my closet door was open and on the top shelf was a stack of my schoolbooks. I grabbed my science notebook and wrote across the front of it with black ink. *I, Denice Perkins will not date Steve Vickers again until I am ready.* I threw myself across through myself across the bed and cried. Steve was eighteen and I was fourteen yeards old.

～∾ 10 ∾～
THE CHALLENGE

1966

HOMEWORK WAS NOT MY cup of tea. I did my math because it was to be turned in. When it came to reading science or history books, well, I guess it would have been like trying to pull my own teeth. I just didn't want to do it. I came home from school and got my housework done. My routine was to lie across my twin bed, grab my pink princess phone, just in case a friend called, and do my homework. The radio was on. Sonny and Cher was singing, *"I Got You Babe."* The phone rang. I thought it was probably Robin wanting to know what our plans were for that night. I answered. "Hello"

"Denice this is Steve Vickers". My heart began to race.

He said, "I thought you and I might go out tonight."

I answered him, "Thanks, Steve, but I have other plans."

We made small talk for a few minutes and hung up. The next week he called spur of the moment at around five o'clock to ask me out for that night. I gave the same answer. This continued week after week. It was hard saying no and I could tell it was getting to him.

"No Steve. I have other plans." I always said the same thing.

He was patient with me but persistent. He was not used to the answer, "no" or "I have other plans," from any girl. I really thought he would give up, but he continued calling. One night he called and he was ready for me.

"Denice, do you want to go out tonight?" he asked.

"No Steve. I have plans." There was a moment of silence.

He spoke soft and direct, "Okay Denice, I get it! What about let's go out tomorrow night?"

He was not enjoying the chase. This was not the way he played the game. He called all the shots. I was going to prove him wrong. I wanted more from him and I was not going to be just another girl to him.

I answered him, "No, Steve I have other plans".

He then asked, "What about next Friday night"

I answered, "I have plans next Friday."

I took in a deep breath and let it out slowly, knowing he was getting the message and if I pushed him too far, he might give up. I could hear him breathing over the phone as if he had enough.

He then said, "Denice, two Friday nights from now, are you going to tell me you already have plans?"

Softly but firmly, I said, "Steve I told you, I have other plans."

He said, "It looks like you have plans with everybody but me." I could hear the hurt in his voice and his words.

I responded, "You've got it."

I knew I was acting like a jerk. I felt he needed it. He was finally getting the message. My mind was made up. This boy was going to earn me. He hung up. Then, I laid across my bed and cried. I was determined to stick to what I had written across my science notebook, I, Denice Perkins will not date Steve Vickers until I am ready.

That night I planned to stay home, watch TV with Momma, Leeann and Charlie when the doorbell rang. I answered the door in my pajamas. There he stood!

He said, "I thought you had plans."

"I do," I said, "I plan to stay home tonight."

I was shocked. I couldn't believe he was coming after me like this. He pressed against the doorframe with both hands leaning in toward me as if to say, I am in-charge.

He asked, "Are you going to invite me in? I'll watch TV with you."

I said, "Steve, I am going to spend the night with Momma."

He said, "OK."

He put his hands up, to let me know he was backing off. He dropped his head down as he turned to walk away, humiliated and crushed. I shut the door, walked over to the window and watched him drive away. It didn't feel right being rude. He stopped calling that summer. Summer came and went. I thought I had blown it.

PAM WAS STILL LIVING in Florida with her husband's parents. William was assigned to a ship. She enjoyed her job at the department store. Janice and Pam always knew they could come home if they needed to. Janice and her husband were still in Miami. She sent me a photo of her and her husband and boys all in white shorts and baby blue T-shirts getting onto a private airplane. I'm not sure where they were going, but they were all smiles.

Summer ended. School always started at the end of August. It was my first year in high school. I was now a tenth grader. Robert E. Lee High School had been the number one marching band in the nation for five years under Johnny Long. Football season was in the air. The University of Alabama and Auburn University are two Alabama colleges that divide the people of the state during football season. Everybody was into football. They were the two colleges that most of our high school graduates went to. If you could not afford season tickets, there was no need to miss the game. People just parked their cars in the stadium parking lot; pulled out their lawn chairs and charcoal grills, turned their transistor radios up loud and they were there. That would become a phenomenon—tailgating.

Robert E. Lee High School, known as the "Generals", and Sidney Lanier High, named the "Poets," had the same football rivalry every year. They were the only two white public high schools in the city.

Thursday, the night before the Lee and Lanier football game, students of both schools went out to cruise the main drags. Atlanta highway was the main street with the Treasure Isle hamburger joint for the Lee students. Fairview Avenue with Suzy's hamburger joint was the strip for Lanier students. This night, every year, they invaded each other's territory. Lanier students arrived in a procession lining their cars up and down the Atlanta highway on the side of the street opposite Treasure Isle.

Robert E. Lee students were ready for them as students parked their cars up and down the street. They were standing beside their cars, while some sat on the hoods. Convertible tops were down and packed with students as they chanted at each other. They threatened each other about the upcoming game. They debated over what the score would be for that year. Lee Generals, in turn, later that night invaded Lanier Poet's territory in the same manner.

The police were everywhere, not to stop us, just to control traffic and to protect the General Lee statue from vandalism. Lanier students always found a way to paint a yellow stripe down the General's back. Lee, in turn, would find away to distract the police during the night and graffiti was then painted on the front of the building. In bright red letters, they would paint the words Robert E. Lee and the previous year's winning score, to remind them of their loss.

Steve Vickers transferred from the University of Alabama to a small college in town. He had been partying too much at his fraternity, and his grades had dropped. His parents made him come home until he brought his GPA back up. That meant I would be seeing him around town more often during the week. I saw him when I went to Treasure Isle, Putt-Putt golf course or even to fill my car with gas. I saw him every time with a different girl.

Matthew and I were at the Lee Generals football game. The crowd stood up to clap and cheer the football team onto the field as the band began to play. The cheerleaders ran out in front of the players cheering them on. I scanned the bleachers behind me and there he was high up in the bleachers with a group of his friends.

Turning to my date, I said, "Matthew, I am going to the restroom. I will be right back."

He asked, "Do you want me to go with you?"

Of course I didn't, I hoped to run into Steve. I answered him, "No, you just watch the game. I'll be right back."

I walked up the bleachers to get to the landing that entered the concession stand, Steve saw me. I was sure he would. Just as I hoped, he was waiting for me as I walked out of the restroom.

"Hey Steve"! I smiled as I stopped and I was thinking, *boy I am good at this.*

"Who are you with?" he asked. I was glad to answer him.

"Matthew Folsom," I said with a smile.

We talked, but the conversation was mostly centered around asking me questions like, how long had I been dating Matthew? Why won't you go out with me? I just answered saying, "I am not ready. I do not want to date you Steve Vickers until I am ready."

He looked at me with those dark brown eyes questioning, "Ready for what?"

I answered, "You, Steve Vickers, ready for you."

I knew he just didn't get it. I wanted more than he could ever give, I wanted it all.

He asked, "Are y'all going anywhere after the game?"

"I'm not sure." I answered, waiting to see what he was going to say.

"Why don't you get him to take you home early and I will call you?"

My heart told me why not and I responded, "Okay."

He called that night; we talked about life and what we both wanted out of life. I realized that night on the phone with Steve that he had never had a conversation with a girl like this.

Steve knew Matthew. They had a few classes together at school. He began to speak to Matthew as if to counsel him, giving him advice on how to get me to go steady with him. It was his way of staying in my business.

I was walking home from school. I noticed Steve's car parked out front of my house. He was leaning against his car with his feet crossed, smoking a cigarette.

"What are you doing in front of my house, Steve Vickers?" I asked smiling at him, thinking how cool is this that he just dropped by.

He said, "I came to talk to you about something."

Holding my books, I relaxed my posture as I leaned against his car.

He said, "Matthew is going to be asking you to go steady with him."

I gave him a look as if to say, and what business is this of yours.

He asked, "What is your response going to be?"

"My answer will be no." I wanted him to see I was in charge.

"If I ask you to go steady with me, would you?" He asked.

"Steve, I'm not going steady with anybody. I don't want to be committed to any one guy. I want to be free to date whom I want and when I want."

Steve had this expression—his left eyebrow would rise when he was uncomfortable about something. His left eyebrow went up as he looked at me with those dark brown eyes. I told him I had to go on into the house to get the dishes washed before Momma got home. He left. My home life was so different from his. He went home to housekeepers.

EVERY YEAR IN OCTOBER the state fair came to Montgomery. Schools let out early for Fair Day. Robin, KT and I went. We heard Steve's band was playing at the fair that year. I was sure I would see him.

I wore black and white herringbone plaid hip hugger pants with a white belt running through the loops of my pants showing a little flesh between my waistband and the top. The top was a sleeveless, black fitted V-neck shirt laced with a white shoestring to close the front instead of buttons.

Walking through the crowd on the Fair Ground, I saw Steve and his band from a distance walking toward me. I pretended I did not see him when he passed by. I was laughing and busy talking to Robin as we passed.

Steve turned, came up behind me and grabbed me by the arm, swinging me around to face him saying, "Do you know what you look like?"

I just stared at him. His eyes were flashing with anger. He continued, "You look like a French whore and the girl that I'm going to marry is not going to look like this."

Jerking my arm away from him, "What makes you think I'm going to marry you?"

He did not like that I looked so cute for other guys looking at me and was not with him. He talked back as if he were my boss. "You're going to go out with me tomorrow night and you are not going to give me any excuses."

He waited for my reply expecting me to say no. I was stunned at his boldness to order me around. I responded, "Okay." I felt I was ready and that this time he was ready for me.

The next night he picked me up. As I was getting into the car, he said, "Here, hold this," while handing me two glasses and a bottle of champagne.

We had not gone a block when I said, "Take me home."

He pulled the car over. "What's wrong?"

I said, "I am not going out with you if you are going to drink."

I think he did that to show me who was boss. He threw the glasses out the window.

I said, "Steve, if you are going to date me, there will be no cussing, no drinking, and you will be in church with me Sunday morning."

Looking at me, he moaned, "Oh, no, you are kidding me aren't you!" The determined look on my face told him I was not kidding.

From that night on, we went out together and Steve was in church with me on Sunday.

Only one time, he called and said, "I'm not going to make it to church today."

I answered him with "Well, that's something. I'm not going to be available for our next date."

Steve made it to church that day and sat on the last pew. I was walking out and there he sat.

One Sunday night at church, a boy was singing solo, *"Fill My Cup Lord."* I cried as he sang. After church, Steve and I went outside to our backyard swing

He asked, "Denice, why were you crying tonight when that boy was singing?

I did not tell him. I was thinking about the day I was sweeping the carpet and God spoke to me and said, "You're going to be married to a preacher". I knew Steve was far from being a preacher. I knew I was falling in love with him.

After a few minutes of silence, looking up at all the stars, I said, "I just want all God has for me. I don't want to miss my destiny in Him."

It shook him when I said that. He had never met a girl that took life this serious.

He said, "Denice, you need to go get you one of those church boys. I hurt people. I want to be a good person. I guess some people are born bad. You are pure and innocent. I don't want to spoil you. I ruin what I touch. You need to run from me. Don't get me wrong; I want you so bad that it hurts. Your different than anyone I have ever met. I can't help but admire you, but I want you too."

Steve would tell me he was in love with me, but I could not say it back to him.

He would say, "It hurts to say, 'I love you.' Denice, why can't you say you love me?" He asked me that all the time and I would answer him, by asking him. "Steve, how many girls have you said that to, to get what you want from them?

He looked at me and said "I mean it when I say it to you. I have never been in love until now. Denice, I am in love with you."

I smiled as I threw my arms around him and said, "Steve Vickers, someday I am going to marry you and I am going to have a little boy named Stephen Vickers." He smiled at me as he said, "You are, huh?"

I shook my head as I said, "Yeah, I am."

I said that with a knowing that God had his hands on my life. My heart and soul was crying out for God to be involved in my life and yet this force was so strong between Steve and I, but he was far from being a preacher.

STEVE'S BAND WAS getting recognized and was booked through the Christmas holidays. Momma, Leeann, Charlie and I planned to spend Christmas in Miami with Janice, her husband, and their three boys. Steve and I talked about not wanting to spend Christmas apart. He decided to tell the band he was going with me to Miami, which split up the band. They could not believe he would give up music for a girl.

He wanted to be with me every opportunity. He would go to my house before I got home from school. He cleaned the kitchen so that after school he could spend time with me. We never locked the doors. It was easy to get in. He learned how to plug the hole in the sink with rags, and he remembered to check the pot under it and empty the water. Momma would come home from work, cook us breakfast for dinner and put on a pot of coffee for the evening. He stayed every night, staying up late, talking with Momma.

I looked at him and I said to Momma, "Tell Steve to go home. I've got to go to sleep. I have school in the morning."

Steve just laughed and said, "Go to sleep; I'm talking to your momma."

I would go to bed. He and Momma talked about life, love, and God. Steve loved her. He loved that he could speak so easily to her. She told Steve to trust God, that He was Steve's answer to life. Every morning he showed up to drive me to school.

Our friends were still being drafted to war. Local draft boards determined who would serve; resulting in uncertainty for the potential draftees during the time they were within the eligible age group. One day I was standing at the sink washing dishes, Steve's car pulled up in front of the house. I walked out to greet him. He stepped out of the car. He was wearing a sailor's uniform and his head was shaved.

He said, "Denice, my number was coming up. I was going to be drafted off to Nam. If I were going to war, I would rather be on a ship. I joined the Navy. I will have to serve six years and three of them full time duty. I am going away for those three years. Will you wait for me?"

I looked at him and said, "No. I won't wait. I can't just throw my youth away waiting for a boy gone for three years and hope he doesn't forget me."

He responded, "Then, let's get married."

A few nights later, we were on a date. Steve parked the car, opened the glove compartment and pulled out a small white box. He turned in his seat, toward me, and asked, "Denice, do you love me?"

"Yes Steve, I am in love with you."

"Will you marry me?"

Knowing he was all I wanted in life, I said, "Yes, I will marry you".

The box held a diamond ring. I was sixteen and Steve was twenty. Momma accepted that we were getting married. The date was set for August 4, 1967. All my girlfriends would be bridesmaids. June rolled around. I had already seen a doctor and started birth control. Steve and I were into heavy kissing. Our passion was building, but we always stopped before we went further. One night we were parking, lying down in the seat making out in each other's arms. We both were aroused and wanted to make love. I did not want to wait any longer. I wanted Steve to touch me and make love to me.

I said, "If you want me, Steve, you can have me."

He sat up, cranked the car and took me home. Before I got out of the car, he said, "I want you so badly, believe me when I say I want you. I always thought if given the chance I would take you, but I can't hurt you like that. I will wait for you."

I went into the house, washed my makeup off and got into the bed. I lay there in my thoughts. I had offered myself to Steve and he had turned me down. He really loved me. He cared about my true feelings and not those made in an emotional moment. I could not wait until the day we'd be intimate.

We had ourselves in the same place of making out, lying down, our bodies up against each other, we found ourselves in the same state of passion, but this time we made love. When it was over, Steve started the car, not saying a word. It was late at night. He drove to the Methodist Church his mother attended. It was a stone church with heavy old world Gothic doors on the front with iron door hinges and door handles. The lights were turned off in the building. He got out of the car, walked over to the passenger side and opened the car door, grabbed me by the hand and walked me up the front stairs of the stone church. Steve put his hand on the big heavy door handle and pulled; to our surprise it was not locked. We walked in. Holding my hand in the darkness, we walked up the isle between the pews to the front. The stained glass windows were lit up as the streetlights shone through them. The church had high ceilings and heavy wooden beams. He sat me down on the front pew. He then knelt down in front of me, grabbed my hands.

He wept and said, "Denice, I am sorry."

I could not stop crying. I looked at him and said, "Steve, it was my choice too."

He moved to the wooden altar, knelt down crying out loud, "God forgive me," he felt bad because I was a virgin. He took me home.

The next few weeks were filled with planning the wedding. I had eight bridesmaids and Steve had eight groomsmen. Robin was my maid of honor, Leeann my flower girl and Charlie my ring bearer. Pam and Janice were two of the brides- maids, along with my girlfriends. They all wore fuchsia satin empire waist, bell shaped full-length gowns. We were married in the same church Steve took me to the night we made love. The church was filled to capac- ity. Six hundred guests were at our wedding.

After saying our vows the min- ister turned us toward the congre- gation as he spoke, "Ladies and gentleman I would like to introduce to you, Mr. and Mrs. Steve Vickers."

The organ began to play as we walked down the aisle and exited the auditorium into the foyer of the church. Steve grabbed me and spun me around in a circle saying, "We did it. You are mine."

A reception followed at a Hotel. After greeting everyone, we changed into our going away clothes. We ran through the crowd as the rice was tossed and we jumped into Steve's red car that had been painted with "Just married" on the sides, with strings and cans drag- ging behind. We drove about an hour drive away and stopped at a

Hotel along the interstate. The exit was to a small country town with only a dinner. We decided to get a bite to eat before we checked in. I was really worried about Steve seeing me with no clothes on.

Our car was parked out front. You could see it all painted with "Just Married".

The waitress came over to our table with her pencil and pad in hand. She was middle aged, but her face had signs of a hard life. She had on tight fitting blue jeans and a T-shirt with a motorcycle on it that said, Harley. She also had a small pink apron on that had

a ruffle. Her hair was blonde, a little messy and was pinned up in a twist. Her white chain earrings hung down with a ball that looked like orange bubble gum out of a gumball machine.

Chewing her gum she said, "Are y'all the ones that just got married?"

I smiled, "Yes we are."

Her voice had that familiar twang heard in small country towns in Alabama.

"Well, honey, you've got to get it annulled immediately." She continued snapping her gum as she chewed it.

Steve and I looked at each other and I spoke up. "Why do say that?"

"Well, honey, I was just reading my horoscope, and someone was coming in and I was to give them help. You know—a warning. When I saw that paint on the side of the car, I knew what the message was to be."

I responded, "Well, I don't believe in horoscopes, thank you anyway."

She said, "Well, I had a boyfriend living with me and see this cut on my forehead", she pointed to a scare. "He beat me and broke a bear bottle on my head. Then he took off with the Harley I paid for. I haven't seen that damn fool since.

She popped her gum with a smack sound and then said, "Okay honey, what do you want to order? We have a steak special tonight. Honey, you got something in your hair let me get that out for you." She, pulled a grain of rice still in my hair, then she smiled and said, "I'll be right back."

Steve took me by the hand as she walked away. "She's crazy Denice; don't pay any attention to her."

"I'm not," but the truth was, I was shaken. I had seen through Momma that men would only hurt you. I entered the marriage knowing he would one day break my heart, but at that moment I just didn't care. All I could think was I'm love with Steve Vickers. Steve opened the door to the honeymoon suite and swept me up in his arms. We both began to laugh as he swung me around in his arms.

We kissed and he told me, "Denice Vickers, I love you."

We kissed again and I said, "Steve Vickers, you're my man. I love you."

Steve said, "Go into the bathroom, change, and I will open this bottle of champagne."

I changed into my sheer white, baby-doll pajamas with tiny pink roses across the top and wondered if I should leave my bra on. I was nervous. I had always worn a padded bra and now Steve would see I barely had any breasts. Will he still think I am beautiful? Will he be disappointed? I knew I was going to have to let him see me eventually, so I took the bra off. I cracked the door to see Steve putting the champagne bottle on ice. He was wearing pajama bottoms. How do I make my entrance? Without further hesitation, I threw open the door, jumped to the center of the bed, grabbed the pillow and covered myself. Everything worked out the way honeymoons always do.

Our honeymoon lasted for five days in Gatlinburg, Tennessee. We came home to a little redbrick house we had rented on Atlanta Highway. It was a cute one-bedroom, one-bath home with living room, kitchen, and a small dining room. Mrs. Vickers bought us all new furniture for the house, even a washer and dryer. For our wedding, we had received every gift we could possibly hope for. It looked like our marriage was off to a good start. Nevertheless, my own insecurities about men and Steve's ways were soon to be roadblocks in my quest for happiness.

~ II ~
MARRIAGE AND SUSPICIONS

STEVE ATTENDED HIS RESERVE meetings and it was a year before he had to leave for active duty. We had settled down to married life. He took a job in the camera department of a department store. He was making a hundred dollars a week. That was considered good since our rent was only forty-seven dollars a month, which included utilities. The average family of four lived off four hundred dollars a month.

Summer ended and a new school year began. I was in the eleventh grade. Steve was at work around beautiful women all day. It bothered me. Every time I went to see him at work there always seemed to be a girl, who worked in another department, standing there talking to him in his department. She was older than I was and very attractive.

One day I stopped by to see Steve and there she was standing at the counter. Steve was waiting on a customer. I walked up. She did not know who I was. She was looking at some photos that had been taken of her in the outdoors. I spoke up as if I were waiting to be waited on.

"Those are beautiful," I said.

She smiled as she was looking at them and said, "I am so happy with them."

I asked, "Who was your photographer?"

She said, "Oh, the guy that works here in the camera department took them for me on his day off." She flipped her hair off her shoulder. I felt my insides boiling, yet not wanting to show it.

I asked, "Do you mean Steve?" I smiled, "Well, he is my husband."

I reached out my hand to shake hands to greet her. "My name is Denice."

She went on to say, "He did such a good job for me. Didn't he tell you about it?"

I could tell she felt a little uncomfortable by the way she shifted her body. I tried to act as if it were fine with me.

"He probably did, I just forgot about it. They are really good photos. You look beautiful," but really I was dying inside.

Steve gave me all kinds of reasons why he had forgotten to tell me that he took his day off to do that for a friend who wanted her engagement photos taken and so on and so on. His quick excuses became a song and dance routine that he was very good at. I became increasingly suspicious of him, believing I could not trust him. Steve was always flirting with other women. I noticed when he didn't think I was looking. He was checking the ladies out from head to toe. Women didn't care he was married. They hit on him anyway. I felt he ate it up and fed it too.

JANICE HAD DIVORCED again. She called to say she met a truck driver and that he invited her to go on the road for a few days with him. I asked, "Where are you going with him?"

"I'm going to a music concert that's going to last three days," she exclaimed with excitement. "I got the cutest outfit to wear, it's a brown suede fringed jacket with knee-high boots. I have painted a piece symbol on the side of my cheek and I am ready to party. Tell

Momma not to worry about me. I'll be fine. Tell her to keep the boys for me until I get back." The boys had already been at Momma's for a few days playing with Charlie and Leeann and now Janice was going out of town.

I asked, "Janice, where did you hear about this and who are you going with?"

She said, "Just tell Momma I have gone to Woodstock, New York."

The event was held at a 600-acre dairy farm 43 miles outside of the town of Woodstock. There was Janice and 500,000 concertgoers. There was a sense of social harmony, plenty of music, and free love. They were called flower children. It became known as a moment that changed the history of Rock and Roll. Janice always seemed to have that wild hair Pam and I didn't have. Nothing was thought out; she just dove in. If somewhere, something was happening, she was the

STEVE WAS CALLED to active duty and received orders to go to the Great Lakes Naval Training Station in Illinois. I was going with him. We packed our U-Haul truck, decided to stay the night at the Vickers house and then leave the next morning after we finished the last minute packing.

There was an office party at a girl's house that night. Everyone was drinking and dancing with everybody else's spouse. I did not want us to go, but Steve said the going away party was for him. He thought we should go. He was dancing with all the women. He reminded me of Daddy.

There was one particular woman, named Brenda, who looked and acted loose. Her breasts pushed up and out, overflowing in her bra. Her fried, bleached blonde hair rested against her brown tan, but failed to cover the sun damage on her face. She looked like a dried up prune with fake eyelashes and shiny pink lipstick. She was thin, wearing a tank top and hot pants. Her tan wrinkled legs weren't as sexy as she thought. I do know that trashy doesn't have to have a pretty face to turn heads.

Brenda walked over to me. "Denice you are so cute", she said in a cutie patootie way.

I responded "Thank you." Thinking, nature had played a cruel trick on her.

Two other girls joined in the conversa-tion and were in their appearance just as trashy. The three of them stood in front of me. I was backed up against the wall. One asked as she took a sip of beer from her Budweiser can, "So baby, how long have you and Steve been married?" The three of them giggled.

"One year," I answered them, knowing I was their entertainment. I was thinking they had fallen out of the ugly tree and must have hit every branch on the way down. I was looking for a way to get away from the fort they built around me.

They looked me up and down.

Brenda then asked, "Have you gotten the itch to flirt with other men yet Denice?"

They laughed elbowing each other.

I'm thinking the sun had fried her brain and wondered if I throw a stick will these dogs go away?

I answered her, "No, I don't plan on getting an itch."

Brenda looked at me and said, "Well honey, you will, trust me. Life can get a little boring if you don't dabble a little on the side."

One of the girls tapped her on the shoulder laughing and said, "Brenda, you leave her alone and don't put your ways into her; she's sweet."

I thought, sweet, did she say sweet? I may look sweet, but in my mind, I was talking to three chipmunks.

Walking between them to release myself, I looked back their way again. Brenda was checking Steve out as if she had a secret with him.

I walked over to Steve and asked him. "Why is she looking at you that way"?

He looked at her and she smiled. He looked at me sheepishly, "Oh, she's a store tramp. Don't pay her any mind."

I told him I was ready to leave, so we left the party.

We were finishing up the last bit of packing the next morning. I was still bothered from the night before, so I decided to look in Steve's wallet. There it was—a slip of paper with a phone number penciled on it. I wondered whose it was. I kept telling myself, no big deal. But, I had to know.

I dialed the number and asked, "Who's speaking, please?"

"Brenda"

It was her, the tramp, Chipmunk Brenda. She was making a play for my husband. I slammed the phone down and went to Steve to show him a piece of paper. That was, my green thread.

"What is this, Steve? What are you doing? Why would you take her phone number?" I felt my blood boiling, feverish, faint.

He answered, "Well, she was just trying to let me know, if I have time, come see her before I leave town—as a friend."

I looked at Steve as I turned to leave the room, "Yeah, right are you that stupid?"

I went straight into the other room to call the chipmunk. "Hello Brenda, this is Denice Vickers, you know, Steve Vickers' wife.

151

She said, "Oh, hey Sunshine." I wanted to say, hey Chipmunk.

I continued, "Steve gave me the lowdown on you, he gave me your phone number. He was laughing about how you tried to make a play for him. Do you want to know what my husband said about you? He told me you're the store tramp and you try to go with younger men. He was saying the men at work say you've been beaten with an ugly stick. Is that true Brenda? He said it's the only way you can make yourself feel young again. Are you still trying to step into the past? Has life chewed you up and spit you out, honey?" She started huffing and puffing. I kept talking.

"Brenda, I have one last important question to ask you. What are you going to do for a face, when the monkey wants his butt back?"

She responded in anger, "What did you just say to me?"

"Sorry, Brenda, it's too late for you, baby. It's my time now; you need to be young and fresh like me. You're all used up." I slammed the phone down, got in the car and went to speak with Pastor Ken.

I was going to tell him about the phone number and ask him if I should go with Steve to Illinois. I was driving too fast; I noticed in my rear view mirror a blue, flashing light, it was a cop pulling me over. I was crying hard and driving too fast. I watched in my rear-view mirror as a police officer walked toward my car. I was mad at all men. I rolled down my window.

"Lady, where's the fire?" He asked.

I retorted, "What's your problem?"

He backed up and looked at me. "Listen to me young lady."

I replied, "No, you listen to me. I don't like my husband, I don't like my father, and I don't like you. So don't bother me." I rolled my car window up and was about to drive off.

He tapped on the window with his ink pen. I rolled the window back down.

He said, "Lady, what's your problem?"

I said, "I'll tell you what my problem is. I just found a phone number in my husband's wallet. Therefore, do not bother me, let me drive." I began to cry.

Then he asked, "Where are you going?"

I said, "I'm going to talk with my pastor."

Thank goodness he was compassionate. "Okay, just don't get yourself killed.

Drive slowly," he said. I drove away crying. He was just another man in my space.

The pastor was not home. I sat in the car and thought: You do not know anything for sure. He just took her number and he did not go to see her. You love him. You can start over. I realized we were moving out of town. It would be a new start. I drove back to the Vickers' house.

Steve's Dad met me at the side door of the Vickers' house. Mrs. Vickers overheard our fussing. She was always the peacemaker, but Mr. Vickers did not like me. He stopped me as I was walking in. "Why don't you leave my son alone? Let him get on with his life."

I said, "I want to see my husband." I walked on in past him. I told Steve I was moving with him. We loaded the truck and left the next morning.

While we were at Great Lakes, we got an apartment. Mrs. Vickers had given me of the green stamps that she collected so that I could decorate our apartment with curtains and wall art. S&H Green Stamps were given to customers at checkout counters of supermarkets, department stores, and gasoline stations. They could be redeemed for products in the S&H catalog.

We discovered a friend of ours from our hometown, Sully Johnston. Sully was in the same naval training school as Steve and was going home to Alabama to marry and bring his bride back with him. The four of us became great friends. Her name was Stacy. She had blonde streaks in her hair and wore it with bangs and her hair ratted and smooth out into a bubble flip. She wore false eyelashes and had long fingernails that she kept manicured, which made the way she held her cigarette look sexy. She was different from me, but I really liked her. I made her laugh and she made me laugh. We were opposites, but we became great friends. We got to know each other. She couldn't believe Steve was the only guy I had ever had sex with before marriage. The four of us went bowling and shot pool on base every weekend.

You haven't lived, Denice." Stacy said.

I would just laugh at her and say, "Steve is enough for me."

IT WAS MY SENIOR year, so the first day of school I went to enroll, a guidance counselor said, "In this state, you cannot be married and attend school. I suggest you go to night school. It appears all you are really lacking to graduate is history and math. Your other alternative would be for you to take your GED test to get your degree."

We couldn't afford to pay for me to go to night school. I left and went to the mall where Stacy worked and got a job at the same department store, working in the cosmetics department.

Steve and I loved each other, but we were two people going in two different directions. He had something wild and sneaky about him. Lies rolled off his tongue with ease. Stacy and I surprised Sully and Steve at the military base. Steve was already drinking in the middle of the day.

Momma always said to me, "God is the answer," I began my search in a local Christian bookstore that was in the mall. I began reading books on how to find happiness, success, how to be a total woman, and whatever self-help book was out there. I would buy six books at a time, reading them on my lunch break. Stacy found it amusing that I was always on this journey. She and I took our lunch breaks together.

Now that I was married, sex was great. I wanted it all the time. I think I scared Steve. Lord, here I was such an innocent girl and now I was hot to trot. I couldn't get enough sex. I wanted it more than Steve did.

I decided it was time I speak to someone about this. I went to the military base doctor to have my yearly Pap smear. It was the first time I had ever had an appointment with this doctor.

He said, "Put your clothes on and come into my office and we will talk."

I did as he instructed. I noticed my urine specimen was sitting on his desk.

He said, "Denice, it is good to have you as a new patient. Do you have any questions?"

I thought well here goes, he asked for it.

I said, "Well doctor, I seem to want sex a lot more than my husband. What should I do?"

He laughed and asked, "What was it like before you married?"

"Well, he wanted me and I was a virgin. I had given myself to him a few weeks before we married. Doctor I must say I really love sex. As soon as he gets home from work, I want him in bed."

He laughed and said, "I think you have scared him. You've turned into this little tiger."

I smiled and nodded, yes.

He said, "You turned the tables on him. You see, one chases and one is caught. You're doing the chasing."

I said, "Well, I want to be caught by him. I don't want to be the chaser."

He went on to advise me on how to turn the tables. I told him if I do that, we would never have sex.

He said, "Yes, you will. You're just turning the tables on him. He is going to be the chaser and you are going to be the one he catches." He laughed as he talked to me. I think he found me to be refreshing. I laughed with him and told him I just loved sex. I felt I could tell it as it was, since he was my doctor.

He said, "Your husband's a lucky man."

I got up from my seat to leave his office. I was so nervous and wanted to thank him for his excellent advice. I reached over his desk to shake his hand and knocked the urine specimen over. It spilled all over the papers on his desk. I just looked and him and said, "Thanks Doc."

He shook his head laughing, lifting up the papers soaked in my urine.

He smiled and said, "Good luck Denice."

I don't think he ever met anyone like me, and I must say, over the years I believe that he gave me the greatest advice I have ever been given. It still works to this day. Steve's doing the chasing, and I'm letting him catch me and he doesn't even know it.

One night in the club, Sully, Stacy and Steve drank while I sipped on my Coke. Stacy told me "Denice if you don't join 'em, you'll lose 'em."

The following Sunday, I went to church by myself. Steve just wouldn't get out of bed. After the service, the pastor stood in the doorway shaking everyone's hands. I walked by and he grabbed my hand and said to me, "We're glad you visited with us this morning."

I looked at the Pastor and began to cry, *"Please help me! Pastor, please help me!"* I was searching for just one person who would stand up and say, "I have the answer. This is what you've got to do. This is what you need." I cried out, but the pastor didn't know what to do. He patted me on the back and pushed me through the crowd.

As he said, "Now you come back and visit us again, you hear?" He pushed me out the door. He was too busy being popular with the church people in the foyer rather than helping the hurting and broken of life.

I got into the car, sitting in the parking lot, beating the steering wheel, screaming and crying. I yelled out, *"God, where are you? God what about me? What about me? Do you even care? Do you have an answer for my life? I don't care what you have done in everybody else's life. God, you have got to do something in my life! God, I'm so tired of searching for you and never finding you. If you're really here, you better get busy and show yourself because I am so tired and I need your help. Are you so small you can't prove yourself to me?"*

I dried my eyes, cranked the car and drove home to Steve. He was watching football. Steve had no clue about what was going on inside me, my soul was screaming out for more. I wanted to live life big with a big God. I got busy cooking lunch in the kitchen.

Stacy once asked me "Denice, what's the big question? What is your search all about?" My response was, "I have this great pull inside of me. I can't explain it. All I know is it's away from everything you have told me like 'that I need to loosen up and that I haven't lived until I experience other men and things.' I have this drive to find out who God is. Did he put us down here to survive all the hurt and pain life dishes out? We live for self, hurting each other and then we get to go to heaven? Is that how small God is? Is that the all-powerful God? On the other hand, can God possibly be so significant in this thing we call life that He could step into our life and truly make a difference. Can He turn things around? Is it possible God can move on my behalf? Stacy, I have this hunger and thirst in my soul that only God is going to fill. I don't know why, you don't need Him like I do, but I do."

Stacy looked at me with a look of confusion as she questioned, "What is it you need from Him so badly?" She just did not understand. She did not need God at that time in her life but I have learned, sooner or later, we all need Him.

I told her, "I don't know, but what I do know is, it is going to be found in Him."

I was eighteen. Stacy was twenty-one and she had been a college student, living the college life. I married at sixteen. She was not on a search or journey like I was. I think now it was the call of God calling me to come. Come find more, come find my destiny.

Time passed at Great Lakes Naval base. Our spouses were assigned to a ship. Stacy and I turned in our resignations at the department store. We both would be moving back home to Montgomery, Alabama. Steve and Sully were going to remain at the naval school for a few weeks before they caught up with the ship they were assigned to.

The manager of the store called me into his office. He was a well dressed man but in a self-conscious way. I had never had a conversation with him. I did not know he had noticed me. He said, "Denice, take a seat. You have been a great employee. We really hate to loose you. I looked forward everyday to seeing you in your department. You know, you are a beautiful woman." I was wondering where he was going with this. I just looked at him kind of dumb-founded.

He said, "Our Company has a penthouse that is fully furnished. What would you think about staying here while your husband is out to sea? Everything you need would be taken care of. You name it and you will have it. Shopping money for clothing and anything else you will need. I will take care of you. You would not have to work and all you have to do is keep me happy!"

My mind was trying to take this all in as he described it to me. He finished talking; it clicked. I looked him and said, "You are an extremely, unbelievably, stupid person." I pushed my chair back, *"Mr. Kilpatrick, you have just made an offer to the wrong girl. There is nothing and I mean nothing, that I find the slightest bit interesting or attractive about you that would turn my head away from my husband to look at a man like you! All I can think of right now is, asking myself how many times will I have to flush my mind, to get the gross offer you just made out of my head?"*

He leaned back in his desk chair at my boldness to speak up, as he stood to his feet. I wanted to vomit. Gross! I put my hand on the doorknob to exit and turned toward him to make one last statement. "Why don't you make that offer to your wife? She just might take you up on it!"

I returned to my department. I passed Stacy and she stopped me to ask what he had wanted. I told her of his offer and my reply to him. She laughed as she pounded on the counter and said. "Denice, he had no idea whom he was dealing with." I walked away from her and pointed my finger down my throat to let her know he made me want to gag.

Stacy and I packed our things to move back to Montgomery and the guys left to hook up with the ship they were assigned to. Stacy was complaining about her right arm hurting. She went to see a doctor and he told her she had arthritis. None of us thought much about the report. I moved in with Momma, my little brother and sister. Stacy rented a small two-bedroom home.

Steve found out that his ship would be in port in Norfolk, Virginia for two months, which was great because Pam and her husband were stationed there. His ship was out to sea and she and her baby girl Melissa, a toddler, were alone. Pam told me to come to stay with her those two months so Steve could come home to me every night.

Pam was so excited when I arrived. She looked good as always. Pam had a cute figure. Her hair was in the same short blonde hairstyle with bangs. She showed me her little apartment and asked me how Janice, Momma, Charlie and Leeann were doing. I caught her up on all the latest news.

Steve went to the ship every day and Pam and I spent the day together. Pam was always trying to advise me. She and I were outside hanging the damp clothes on the clothesline.

She began, "Let me tell you what I am doing. I keep a Webster's Dictionary beside my toilet. Every day I learn a new word and its definition." She snapped a clothespin to the damp clothes on the line.

She continued, "While you are here, I want you to start doing this."

I replied, "Why would I want to do that?" I had no desire to use words that I couldn't understand.

I asked her, "Why would I want to put people through that when I speak?"

She said, "So you will become polished."

I interrupted "But I don't want to be polished."

She stopped pinning clothes on the line, put her hands on her waist and said in a firm correcting way, "Denice it will make you a great speaker."

"Pam, I don't want to be a great speaker. I like who I am."

She continued hanging the damp clothes on the line and ignoring my answer, she continued instructing me on how to become polished.

She said, "Denice, you will take your new word for the day and use it in a sentence."

I said, "Pam, you go ahead and get polished, this is as smooth as I want to be." I teased her about being "polished". I said, "Pam, here is my new word, Cracked." She looked at me knowing I was goofing off and instructed me to use it in a sentence.

I answered, "Blessed are the cracked in the head, for it is she who lets the light in."

She laughed and said, "Ok, get on with yourself, be who you are Denice."

We laughed and enjoyed every minute of our time together even though it was short. Steve's ship was then sent to ports in Boston, Mass, and Jacksonville, Florida. I loaded our green Volkswagen with a few pots and pans, and drove to Boston. I sang as I drove:

"I know the Lord will make a way for me
If I live a holy life, shone the wrong and do the right
I know the Lord will make a way for me" . . .

I was eighteen years old, driving all the way to Boston alone. I spent the first night on the road. I promised Momma if I got the least bit drowsy, I would pull over. I pulled into Buddy's Diner in South Carolina.

I walked in, both men looked at me. There was a white man back behind the counter who was around fifty years old wearing a red baseball cap with the letters S.C. on it. His white tee shirt and apron had grease spots on them from frying food all day. He stood at the grill flipping a hamburger for a customer that was sitting on a bar stool at the counter drinking a cup of coffee. The jukebox was playing a Marvin Gaye song, *"Heard it through the Grapevine."*

I'm sure they thought it was odd for a young girl to be pulling into a diner this late. I said, "Excuse me. I'm going to park right in front of your window here and take a little nap. Could you please keep a check on my car while I rest?"

He said, "You go ahead young lady. You'll be just fine. I can see from here everything that goes on."

I slept for a while then went in the diner and let him cook me some eggs and grits. He had a fresh pot of coffee waiting for me. I thanked him and got on the road driving to Boston. I arrived just in time for Steve's ship. It was pulling in to port.

We rented a place and I got a job, even though it was just for a few months. I wanted to be near my man. I was always able to get jobs as a store clerk or bank teller. We rented an apartment in a rough neighborhood. On the front door of an apartment building, someone had scrawled, "Beware of rats." I thought it was a joke, but to my horror it was true. There was a long dark hallway with all the doors that led to the various apartments. Everyone stood his or her trash out in the hallway. The girl next door to our apartment played a cello all hours of the night and was a prostitute in between her cello practice. Our apartment was one room, lit by a hanging bulb in the center of the room. It had a small kitchen with sink and an apartment-sized refrigerator. The oven did not work. The apartment had a bed and the drapes fell apart when I washed them at the Laundromat.

At the Laundromat, a freaky guy exposed himself to me. I threatened to beat him with my purse, which seemed to work. He pulled up his pants and high-tailed it out. I guess I said it in a manner that he understood. I told him, *"I will kill you with my purse."* Weird huh?

I hung sheets to replace the drapes. Outside my little kitchen window was a fire escape. The fire escape had a street person that slept right by my kitchen window every night. Thank goodness we weren't there long. Steve's ship was going to Jacksonville, Florida for a few months and then on to the Mediterranean for nine months. I loaded my green Volkswagen up and moved to Jacksonville for those few months so that Steve could live off ship at night. I got a job as a bank teller.

THE USS ALBANY, Steve's ship, went to St Thomas in the Virgin Islands for a couple months. I was busy at work, which helped pass the time until he was back. We had already met some other sailors and their wives who lived in an apartment building near ours. The ship returned to port and one of the sailors and his wife had a welcome home party. Two single sailors that were on Steve's ship had a bunch of photos they had taken on the beach in St. Thomas.

Steve would not let them show me the photos. One of the guys spoke up and said to another guy about Steve, "He just doesn't want Denice to see what he and Janice Joplin were doing on the beach." The other sailor cut his eyes at him as if to say, shut-your mouth.

Janice Joplin was an American singer-songwriter known for her blues and rock music. She was an icon for her counter culture movement in the USA and had performed the night before in St. Thomas and now I hear he spent the day on the beach with her.

"Steve, what was on those photos?" I asked.

"Nothing, Janice Joplin was there on the beach that day, that's all it was."

I said, "No, those guys said you were sunbathing with her. How did you end up with her and what did you do with her?" I felt sick at my stomach. I knew that girls sunbathed naked on those beaches.

I asked, "What were y'all doing?"

He said, "Nothing just hanging out on the beach."

I asked, "Then why did you grab the photos from them as they were about to show me?"

I said, "One guy said you were putting lotion on her." I felt myself literally shaking inside. I never saw the photos and Steve would not give me any straight answers. He said he did not want to talk to me anymore about it and to stop asking questions.

Taking on my mother's pattern of playing detective, I tried to find a clue to prove Steve was being unfaithful. I looked in his pant pockets for the telltale thread, the green thread. I examined his collars for signs of makeup, constantly imagining that Steve was out with another girl when he was supposed to be on the ship. I just didn't trust him. I knew I was going to be hurt by him. That is what men do. They hurt you. Don't they?

The ship was leaving for its nine-month tour as I dropped him off to board. I looked at him and said, "I missed my period, but it's too early to do a pregnancy test."

He smiled and said, "You mean a baby?"

"Yes, maybe" I tilted my head to the side.

I moved home to live with Momma. A month later I had a test, the doctor said, "If the rabbit dies, you're pregnant."

A few days later the doctor's office called, "Denice, the rabbit died, you're pregnant!"

I sat down and wrote Steve that he was going to be a Daddy. He wrote me back and said, "I am so happy about you and me having a baby together. You are the love of my life!" I was nineteen years old and would turn twenty just after the birth of my first child. Steve was twenty-four.

Immediately I got a job at JC Penny's in the girls' junior department. I didn't tell them I was pregnant. I was determined that by the time the manager found out, I would be her best employee so she couldn't do without me.

It was a new store in town and I was working for their grand opening. Every department was amazing. In the kitchen area, a man was giving a demonstration of a new invention. It was a small box with a door on it. He told the crowd of people that he could take this cake mix that was mixed in a bowl, put it in the paper cupcake holder, stick it in that electric box, and in one minute it would cook the cupcake. To everyone's amazement, in sixty seconds out came the cupcake, fully cooked. The crowd cheered. It seemed like a magic trick. He said the electric box was called a microwave and that one day every home would have one. That seemed unrealistic.

Every day I spent my lunch break writing Steve love letters and telling him when the baby moved inside of me and how it felt. I referred to the baby as Stephen.

I stayed in touch with Stacy about the pain in her arm, which was getting worse.

Pam's husband was also gone on a Mediterranean cruise. Pam, her daughter, and her baby boy, got an apartment around the corner from Momma.

One evening Momma and I were sitting at the kitchen table talking over a cup of coffee. "Denice, why don't we spend these nine months you are going to be with me searching for God together? Let's not limit our search to Baptist or Methodist just because we were born and raised Baptist, and let's not limit God to a denomination. We'll begin our search this Sunday and visit a different church in the city every week." One Sunday we decided to visit a church called Evangel Temple.

Momma said, "I keep hearing something is happening there."

I asked, "What could be happening in a church?"

That was enough to make us want to go visit. The church was a small one-story building with brownish brick and a small foyer. We entered the auditorium that had the same brown brick walls with Gothic arched rafters made with tie beams of timber. There were dark stained wood pews with hunter green carpet running down the aisles toward the kneeling altar. In the choir loft, there was a Baptismal in front of a stained glass window. The wood organ was to the left of the room. On a small platform was a wood pulpit and to the right was a piano.

We sat on the last pew. The people started singing, clapping and raising their hands in the air as they rejoiced in song. I got tickled and began to laugh. Tears ran down my face as I tried not to laugh. Momma kept elbowing me, trying to get me to stop.

I jokingly said, "They can't possibly all have to go to the bathroom at the same time!"

Again she elbowed me as she laughed, "Hush."

165

The pastor began to speak as he paced the platform back and forth with his fist in the air, red faced, and every vein in his neck bulging. Boy, he was preaching! I had never heard anyone preach with such passion. As he paced back and forth, everybody's head turned following him. A woman stood up and gave a "message in tongues". I thought she was from a foreign country. The pastor told us what she said. I was impressed he understood her language. The service came to a close. Mom and I headed toward the door.

A woman walked up, hugged me and said "We are so glad to have you here today Sister."

Momma and I headed home. We talked. I said, "Momma that just isn't for me. That woman thought I was her sister."

Every night at the kitchen table, the service became one of the things we talked about.

Stacy and I had not talked in a while. One day she called and told me her pain in her arm was cancer. The doctors told her it was terminal. She was already in chemotherapy. Sully's ship was still out to sea, so the Navy was going to send him home right away. I drove over to see her. She told me to come on in and go straight to her bedroom when I get there. I couldn't believe my eyes. She was so thin with her eyes sunk in and no hair. She was always such a perfect picture of beauty. She looked so weak.

I walked into her room, "Hey". I was holding back the tears. Her teeth were yellow.

She smiled and said, "Hey. Come in, Denice."

She propped her bed pillows up so that I could sit on the side of the bed and talk with her. She was twenty-two. I did not know what to say. I told her about everything I had been doing and asked her about herself.

I said, "Steve called me and asked me to fly to Europe and be with him for two weeks."

She said, "You're going to Europe!"

I stood up and did my happy dance, throwing my arms in the air and yelled, "I'm going to be a world traveler." When I get back, I will come over and see you and tell you all about it."

I made preparations to visit Steve in Europe. I scraped up enough money and flew to Germany. From there I took an airplane to Switzerland to meet Steve. In Switzerland, I was to go to the train station in Geneva where Steve was to meet me. All around the station were little flower shops, gift shops and restaurants. While I was waiting for Steve's train to arrive, I decided to buy a postcard to mail to Momma. I noticed a man watching me. He was well dressed in a business suit. No one seemed to speak English. I was trying to determine if the box on the wall was a mailbox or trashcan. The man was following me and watching every move I made. When I stopped walking, he stopped walking.

I saw two young men behind the counter that sold hotdogs. I thought if I stayed by them I would be safe. Suddenly he walked up to me and began speaking in French. I thought to myself as he was talking, this man is trying to pick me up. I must let him know with my expression, if I said, "No", that I meant it. He was talking very softly to me. I thought, he isn't going to understand what I am about to say, but he will get it by my response.

I looked at him, threw my head back and said very firmly, "*Shut up!*" He took off running. The two young boys that were selling hotdogs understood what he said to me and I guess they understood me because they began laughing and were hitting each other on the back, as I walked away. I now realize the man was probably trying to compliment me as a beautiful pregnant woman.

Steve didn't arrive on the train that day. It was getting dark, so I decided to rent a room for the night. I took a taxi to the nearest hotel. I entered the room, locked the door and pushed the chest of drawers up against the door to make me feel extra safe while I slept. I rose early the next morning, returned to the train station to look for Steve. He arrived late that night and stayed a block away from my hotel. When he saw me we ran toward each other and instead of grabbing me he grabbed my belly, "Denice, you're so beautiful!" Steve never saw me pregnant. I was seven months along and was really showing.

We stayed in Geneva for a few days and then flew to Nice, France on the Riviera. It was lovely. We were walking one day. Steve kept looking at me.

"Denice", he said "I can't take it any longer. I miss you. I don't want to be away from you." Biting his lower lip he paused then said, "Denice, you are what's right in my life, I just don't want to be away from you anymore." I could tell he felt peace when he was around me. All I knew was I loved him and was just glad to be with him. He treated me like a China doll. We spent several days on the Riviera, enjoying each other and the sights. One day, we sat in the park discussing names for the baby.

I said, "Steve, if it's a girl, I would like to name her Stacy.

He agreed, but both of us felt it was going to be Stephen. All too soon our time together ended. I returned to the States knowing the next time I saw Steve would be at the Montgomery airport with our new baby in my arms.

After getting back to Montgomery, I went to check on Stacy and let myself in. I called out her name as I walked toward her bedroom.

"Stacy, the world traveler is back."

She looked thinner and weaker, but she gave me a sweet smile and said, "Come sit", as she patted the side of the bed. I began to speak trying to make her laugh. I told her all the crazy things that happened to me in Europe. She laughed as I told her the stories. She suddenly lifted the sheet off herself, stood up and walked over to a full-length mirror. She stood there looking at her reflection. All she was wearing was a pair of white panties. Her body was thin and weak. Her eyes were sunk deep in their sockets and not a hair on her head. Stacy was beautiful and full of life, now she looked different.

"Summer's coming, "I said.

She turned sideways to look at herself in the mirror, "You know I'm dying!" She said as she looked at me to see my response.

I looked at her as I said, "Stacy don't say that." She walked back over to the bed, lying down slowly. I took the sheet and pulled it over her.

She said, "Denice, I need to talk to you about something." Reaching over to her nightstand she handed me a book titled, "I Believe in Miracles", by Kathryn Kuhlman.

"This woman believes in miracles that God can give me a miracle. Do you believe that?"

I said, "I believe God can do anything."

Stacy looked down as she paused for breath and then said, "Denice, I want to apologize to you about the things I told you in the past. How you were too serious about God and that you need to live it up more. Last Sunday my Mother and Sully took me to church. The balcony was empty, so they laid me on pillows and let me hear the preacher. When he gave an altar call, I couldn't go down but I did ask God to forgive me of my sins. I gave Him my life."

I smiled and said, "Stacy that is wonderful!

She said, "Denice I am sorry if I ever hurt you about you and God."

I said, "Stacy, no you didn't hurt me. I was on my own journey, and I knew you didn't understand. I've always felt I walked to a different drumbeat than other girls."

With out skipping a beat she changed the subject as she looked at me, "Now I want you to do something for me. I am never going to get pregnant and have a big belly like yours. I have always wanted to see a pregnant belly. I heard your navel gets turned inside out." I knew where this conversation was headed, so I stood up and lifted up my maternity top as we both began to laugh.

I told her, "Steve and I talked and if it's a girl, we are going to name her Stacy"

"After me?" she asked and her smile lit up the room for me.

I said, "Yes you, you beauty queen."

We talked and laughed together until I could tell she needed to sleep, so I left. The next week I returned to her house. A hearse was in the yard. I walked into the living room where some of her kinfolk were gathered.

Her aunt said, "Stacy has not passed away but it is close and the doctors told us to go ahead and call a hearse. Sully and Stacy's Momma is in the bedroom with her. She has been in a coma for three days."

I walked back to the bedroom and tapped on the door. Sully opened it, "Come on in."

We had small talk for a few moments and then Stacy's Momma said, "Sully, let Denice sit with Stacy for a few minutes while we go in the kitchen and have a cup of coffee".

They had hardly left the room. Stacy opened her eyes and looked at me and said, "Hey,"

I stood up and said, "Stacy, stay awake, let me go get Sully!" I ran into the, kitchen. I said, "Sully, she's awake."

The three of us hurried back into the room. Sully leaned over her, she again opened her eyes as she lifted her head forward trying to speak, but words could not come out. One more breath and she left us that simple, that fast. Sully walked into the kitchen as I followed him. He faced the corner of the room and pressed his body and face into the wall as he wept. His body shook as he pressed himself against the wall as if trying to disappear.

Sully would go on to marry two more times and have three children. He never got over the loss of Stacy. He was known to have spent many nights lying on her grave, weeping and wishing he'd died with her. One day, he walked into Steve's office, gave his heart to the

Lord and then a few months later was killed in a car wreck at the age of thirty-two. It was ten years after Stacy had passed that Sully died.

IT WAS getting close to the time of the birth of my baby and I moved in with Pam and her two children, so that she and I could split the rent. We were around the corner from Momma, so we went there a lot for supper. It was eggs, biscuits' with gravy and a large pot of coffee. Pam and her daughter, slept in one bedroom, and I slept in the other bedroom in a twin bed, sharing the room with her son, he was in his baby bed.

One night, in the middle of the night, Pam came into my bedroom and touched me on my shoulder to wake me. She was crying. "Denice, wake up."

I woke up, "What? What is it? What's wrong Pam?" I asked, just as when we were young kids.

She said, "Can I get in bed with you? I'm scared."

I scooted over. She slipped in beside me. Here we were two young married girls, her with two children and me as pregnant as pregnant could get in one twin bed. We spooned together, melting into one. Just like when we were children.

We cuddled while I asked her, "What are you scared of?"

She whispered in my ear, "I'm scared of dying. I'm scared of being placed in a coffin. I'm scared of being placed under the ground.

I jumped up out of the bed and turned on the light. I said, "Pam, I am tired of this, I am tired of you dealing with this fear, and we are going to get rid it. I want this fear to be, gone out of your life."

She shook her head weeping and said, "I don't want this torment anymore, Denice."

I walked over to the telephone and called the little fiery preacher from the Methodist church we attended before Momma and I started looking around. It was the middle of the night and I woke him up. I told him Pam and I needed help.

"My sister needs prayer."

I asked if he could come over. Within thirty minutes, Pam and I stood in our pajamas talking to him. I was actually doing all the talking; trying to explain to Pastor Ken how long Pam had battled fear. Looking back on this, I think it's funny we didn't even think about getting dressed. Bless that Pastor's heart.

I said, "Pam is full of fears and I am ready for her to be free."

Pam wept with her face buried in her hands as I talked. He then walked over to Pam, put his hands on top of her head and commanded the spirit of fear to leave her.

Pam, weeping, repeated over and over "Yes, yes, leave me.

We thanked the pastor for coming and he left. Pam was free. She was free at last and never dealt with fear again. It was a miracle. She slept like a baby that night in her own bed. We would learn one day in the future that the Bible says, "Whom the Son of God sets free, is free indeed." John 8:36 God knows I am telling you the truth!

The next morning I woke up thinking I had wet the bed. Pam walked into my room as I said to her, "I wet the bed."

She said, "You're in labor. Your water has broken."

Pam put her two small children in the car and called Momma, for her to meet us at the hospital. She also called Janice and Steve's parents. Everyone was at the hospital except Steve. His ship was at port in Athens Greece. I gave birth to Stacy Elaine Vickers. He received a telegraph of the birth of his baby girl.

ONE NIGHT, PAM, Janice, Momma and I were sitting at the kitchen table. Pam told us that when she was in the third grade, our cousin made her do things. He was a married man with children of his own. He and his family came to visit us. He would take Pam to the swing in the back yard, expose himself and make her do things. He always wore a white belt. At night, she kept seeing that white belt in her sleep. That's why Pam always wanted to sleep between Janice and me with her legs and arms, intertwined. It made her feel safe from the white belt. Pastor Ken prayed for her and she did not have nightmares after that night. The fear was gone and Pam could talk about it.

Janice got so mad she called our cousin out on it. It was at least thirteen years since we had seen him. Let me tell you, it's not smart to fall into the hands of an outraged Janice. The phone call she made that night scared the fool out of him. I think she said something about nailing his penis to a tree. All he could do was stutter on the phone. He never came around again. A real Daddy would have protected his daughter. But we learned we had to stand up for ourselves.

Pam and I realized that the night the pastor came over, laid his hands on her head, and told the spirit of fear to leave her, it worked. We decided one day to try it out ourselves. Pam's daughter Melissa had seizures since birth. She would start choking on her tongue as her eyes rolled back into her head. The doctor told Pam to hold her tongue down with a spoon until the seizure was over. It scared us; it was getting worse, and happening daily.

One day, Pam and I were pushing our strollers down the street. Melissa, who was around three, began to convulse. Her eyes rolled back and she started choking on her tongue. Pam began to panic. I picked Melissa up out of the stroller. I laid my hands on top of her head and asked God to heal her. I commanded the seizures to stop. It worked.

Steve came home on leave to see our new baby girl, Stacy Elaine Vickers and the left for nine months to return. When he returned this time I knew we were on to different roads in life. I knew I was going with God with or without him.

~~∿~~ 12 ~~∿~~
THE COMFORTER

1970

STEVE WAS GIVEN A three-week leave from his ship, the USS Albany. It was going to be his first time to meet his daughter Stacy Elaine Vickers. I dressed her in a beautiful pink gown and wrapped her in a soft pink blanket. I watched people coming off the airplane. My eyes went to the sailor in a white uniform. There was my man. He always took my breath away. Our eyes met as he ran toward me. We kissed and he looked down at her and smiled.

He said, "*She's beautiful,*" kissing my face as he looked at her.

Even though it was going to be a short leave home, we decided to take advantage of the opportunity and buy a home with a VA Loan. We found one in a new subdivision. It was a three-bedroom, two-bath home, with around 1200 square feet.

It would be a month or so before Stacy and I could move in, waiting for all the paper work to go through with the mortgage company. In the meantime, Steve went back to the ship and we stayed with Momma. She was attending Evangel Temple. I was looking forward to attending a service. We arrived late, so we sat in the back of the church in the last pew. Buell Pitts, an Evangelist, walked up to the microphone.

"*Tonight my sermon is on the gift of the Holy Spirit. God has a gift for you to receive.*"

Then with strong exhortation he declared, "*He is called, The Comforter.*"

I had never heard of anything like that. I couldn't understand what he meant by the gift of the Holy Spirit. My mind began to race with thoughts of the mess my life was in, knowing that one day Steve and I would probably get a divorce and wondering what Steve was up to as the ship pulled into all those ports in the Mediterranean. I had a hard time focusing on the sermon.

He sang out his sermon as the congregation backed him.

"*This gift will give you Joy.*

"Amen brother."

"*This gift will give you Peace.*"

"That's right, Sir."

"*This gift will give you Assurance.*"

"Yes it will."

He threw his hand up in the air, held his Bible up and declared, "*The Holy Spirit brings comfort to your life. He is the comforter and teacher of your very soul. The Bible asks you the question, have you received since you believed?*"

"Amen! Hallelujah!"

"Preach it, Brother!" were shouted from the audience.

Like a sponge, I soaked up every word. Joy, I thought, I need joy. I need peace and I need assurance. I stayed in constant turmoil. I knew God was there. I had heard His voice. Was I just another drop in a sea of people or was He really aware of me? Many nights I lay in bed wondering, did He ever think about me? Does He listen as I cry out to him? Was He hearing my prayers?

Brother Pitts paced back and forth across the platform; waving the handkerchief he uses to wipe the sweat from his brow.

He said, *"The Holy Spirit will endow you with Power."* He stopped pacing, looked straight at the congregation, his eyes piercing my soul.

"If you want this gift, it's yours. All you have to do is come and get it."

I had never heard of coming and getting a gift from God. It all sounded like a little gift, wrapped up with a beautiful bow, waiting for me to come and get. He made it sound so easy that I decided I would go and get this gift. How was God going to get it to me? Who would hand it to me from God? I didn't care. I was going to go get it.

I stood up and made my way down the aisle toward the altar. I wept all the way because God had a gift for me. The Evangelist was there to receive those who responded to the call.

"Yes, come and make your way to the alter of God. He is here to receive you."

As he said again, *"Come,"* tears were running down my face. I made my way to the altar. I felt like someone drowning, wanting to be rescued. I thought this is it, the turning point. It was an appointed time in my life, it was! Finally, someone with an answer to my search had found me and I had found him. This man knows something I don't know about life, about God. He is throwing me a lifeline and I am being rescued. I walked straight to the Evangelist.

He reached out his hand to receive me. *"Young lady, what do you want from the Lord?"*

How strange, I thought. I wiped the tears from my face. I thought to myself, he said come and get it and now he wants to know what I want.

My thinking was, tell him you want joy, peace, assurance and power. All I could do was look up at him with an over powering emotion of tears. I tried to speak. I meant to say, I want joy, peace, and assurance, but instead a language I had never learned began to flow out of my mouth. I cleared my throat and I tried again to say what I wanted, but again a language I knew nothing about flowed like a river from deep inside me.

The evangelist started laughing. I thought, he thinks I'm retarded. He thinks something is wrong with me and I can't speak. Why can't I talk? I couldn't utter one word in English.

He looked at me and said, *"Young lady, you have received the Baptism of the Holy Spirit and now lift your hands and surrender to you heavenly father and just let it flow."* He turned to the rest of the people who had responded.

"Those of you who are thirsty drink from the river that will never run dry."

Leeann, who was nine years of age and Charlie, seven years old were also talking in this unknown tongue. Tears flowed down their faces. Mother and Pam were crying. We were all having the same experience. Our whole family received the Baptism of the Holy Spirit that same day.

Janice was living in Jackson, Mississippi. A black lady who was a neighbor every Sunday morning would knock on Janice's door and invite her to church. This Sunday Janice was dressed and ready for her. Janice planned to go with the lady to her church and after service she would tell her she did not like it, so the lady would just leave her alone. Unbeknownst to Janice, God had made His own plans. Janice went and the very same day we were in that service in Montgomery she received the same experience in Jackson Mississippi. Janice called to tell us what happened to her and we were telling her, it happen to us. How strange is that. How could this happen to mom and all five of her children, even when one was States apart?

Everyone in our family had received this gift from God at the same time. It was a miracle! All the years of Momma's tears in the dark crying out for God to help her and her children, God answered in a moment. This was an appointed time for us. The statement that life can change on a dime is true. I do not care if you believe this. It's a fact; God knows I am telling the truth. Lee Ann kept speaking in tongues all the way home. We undressed her and put her to bed while she cried and spoke in tongues. Mother and I tucked her in bed.

I turned to Mom and asked, "Momma, do you think she will ever speak English again?"

Momma whispered, "I don't know."

We didn't care. All we knew was that something had happened to all of us, something we had never heard of or understood. We knew it was from God. Momma and I went into the kitchen. We could not stop smiling and laughing as we sipped our coffee. I reminisced how I had felt, almost as though I had died and gone to heaven at that altar.

I kept saying, "Momma He touched us." We realized that God was indeed a God of miracles.

That night I lay in bed crying talking to God, "You touched me. You touched me. For the first time in my life you touched me!"

It was such a shock to me that I experienced the person of Jesus. No longer did I only have to know Him by faith. He touched me! I discovered that only Jesus could satisfy my soul. For the first time in my life, I was so touched and impressed with a person to the point that it was life changing. It was the person Jesus. It was the person of the Holy Spirit. I could hardly hold my pen when I wrote Steve to tell him what had happened. I wondered what he would think of this new knowledge. I had been writing love letters to Steve, but now I found another love in my life. It wasn't to replace Steve. This love filled an emptiness I had inside me and for the first time, I felt complete. My letters to Steve were about Jesus.

I would read my Bible and write Steve about it, "This is for me! This is for me! This is Jesus talking to me. I don't know where the

Pentecostals have been. Why haven't any of them told me of the glory of being filled with the Holy Spirit? All those years of searching and none of them had come to me and told me. It introduced me to a dimension in God where His power and might is."

He wrote back, "Denice, what happened to you is really great, but please don't write me about religion anymore. Tell me how much you love me, how much you miss me. Tell me, what you're doing during the day. Tell me about Stacy. Is she crawling? Is she walking?" It hurt me, but I was glad he wanted to know about Stacy.

The Vietnam War was still raging and the hippie movement was everywhere. It was taking the country by storm. On Sunday afternoons, I began to go to Oak Park. It was a beautiful park, full of hippies. They called themselves flower children, with their peace, love and anti-war slogans written on their clothes and painted on their face. Speed, cocaine, angel dust, music and free sex were everywhere. Some sat under trees playing their guitars and singing while others danced. Music played on their transistor radios. The sound of confusion was in the air. No boundaries, no answers, and The Beatles singing, "Imagine there's no heaven..." John Lennon said they were more popular than Jesus Christ.

With Bible in hand, I stepped up on top of a picnic table. I lifted my voice as loud as I could.

I said, *"I have found the answer!"* Immediately my loud voice drew a crowd.

"Listen to me! Let me tell you." As I pointed to them looking them straight in the eyes, I said, *"I've searched for twenty years and now I have found the answer. God himself has touched me. You do not just have to believe; there is a God. You can experience his touch. His touch goes dipper than any surgeon's hand. You look for peace and love in this world. You're not finding it because it fades. This book I have in my hand has the answer you're looking for. I met Jesus for myself. He touched me."*

One hippie in the crowd spoke out at me, "Hey, this babe's high, man. She is really tripping."

Another in the crowd yelled out, "She's high on something!" The crowd laughed.

Then they were getting bolder as the crowd grew "Baby, come down off that table and I will touch you and change your life. I'll touch you in places you've never been touched. My touch will go deep." The crowd laughed.

I said, *"Man, you're right! I am high! I'm high on something, and I never am going to come off."*

I turned to the guy who was bold at talking sexually to me. *"You take your drugs, tripping, but you have to come down. Then you have to search for another high, a stronger high. You steal. You sell your-self and your very soul for another high that doesn't last. You always hit bottom. It doesn't last. In your lonely moments of hopelessness and despair, you wonder if anybody cares. You feel hopeless because you know the next fix won't fix it."*

He spoke out again, "How do you know my thoughts?"

Looking at, him, I answered, *"I don't know your thoughts, but God knows who you are. He hears every thought you have, every word, even the ones you don't speak."*

I said to him, *"You wanted to kill yourself last night."*

His face became almost twisted as his anger rose, his face turning red with rage.

"Stop dipping in my Kool-Aid, you bitch," he yelled as he ran away.

I began to spend all my Sunday afternoons at the Park, spreading the Word and then taking them with me to the evening service. I was radical and proud of it. I spoke with a knowing, and the hippies and flower children listened. These were the times we were living. When the world goes through dark times, God causes light to shine.

They were just like I had been—searching for answers. I had found the answer they were looking for and I knew it. The church people weren't excited about the way some of them came dressed, but the Pastor was excited about the new faces coming in.

I was always praying to God, *"Let me be a woman of knowing. I will be the voice that points them to you."* These were radical times for the world. Everyone was radical one-way or the other and I went my way. There are the silent people, in the middle, gray people who stand for nothing, but that is not enjoying the journey. I had a fire in me; I was not going to keep quiet.

God had gotten under us, in us, and a hold of us. We'd sit around Momma's table, read the Bible and pray together. We'd laugh sometimes for hours about how free we were in Jesus and how everything had turned around. We were excited about our future. We now had a sense of destiny. Momma had just had a hysterectomy and began taking hormone pills and her nerves were calming. I believe with that and the work God was doing started to release her from depression and hopelessness. She no longer needed a psychiatrist. She was happy, no more bad days. She shared with people how she had tried to take her life. They couldn't believe it.

Momma had compassion for the unlovable and the hurting. I saw the love of God in her life and so did others. God had been listening to her as she cried alone in the dark. He was listening all along the way and He had a plan. His eyes were on us and we didn't even know it. I was thankful that at last I had found the dimension of the Holy Spirit. He was now my teacher and guide in life. He would help me as I faced the difficulties and plains of life. I knew I was not alone and I never would be again.

~~ 13 ~~
GOD, HELP ME, IT HURTS

STEVE'S SHIP WAS ON another ten-month cruise. His active duty time ended during this time. He was to be processed out of the Navy. He had served his country and now he could come home for good. Steve missed Stacy's baby stage. She was already walking.

Steve's parents drove Stacy and me to the airport to pick him up. He stepped off the plane and there I stood holding Stacy. She had changed so much and didn't know her Daddy. We took a few pictures and then he put his sea bag into the trunk of the car. We sat in the back seat as we headed toward the Vickers' house. They wanted Steve to spend some time with them before we went to our house. He couldn't get over how big his baby girl had gotten and he just kept kissing me.

He said," I'm finally home for good."

He gripped my hand the entire way, but sometimes he stared off into the distance at nothing in particular, just quiet. The radio was playing a song by Captain and Tennille, "Love Will Keep Us Together." Tennille was from Montgomery. It just seemed to be the right song for that moment. I couldn't wait for Steve to hold me and make love to me. He was home. That's all that mattered.

I put Stacy down for a nap. I then began to undress. I felt shy as I slipped out of my dress knowing Steve was sitting on the edge of the bed looking at me.

He spoke softly as he hung his head down, "Denice, I can't touch you."

I looked at him and asked, "Steve, what's wrong? Why?"

"Denice, there's something different about you," he said.

I responded, "Steve, I love you, that's all that matters at this moment."

He stopped me, "Wait. Let me speak. When I received your letters, at first, you wrote how you couldn't wait until I held you in my arms and made love to you. You told me all the things that I needed to hear. They were building me up. I read your letters until I nearly wore the ink off the pages. Then, all of a sudden, your letters changed drastically. They weren't love letters to me. They were love letters about God. I've become jealous of Him. Denice, how can I fight God? He is my competition. Last night another sailor from my ship and I got drunk. I seemed to be two different people. The reason I wanted to get drunk was that I knew I wanted to see you, yet part of me wanted to move as far away from you as possible. Baby, when I got off the plane and saw you and Stacy, I wanted to run to you. You are so beautiful, but when I got close to you I felt unworthy, unholy. I felt something around you, something good, and I am not."

I said, "Steve, I am madly in love with you. You are the love of my life. You are the most handsome man in the world. You are my man. Touch my body Steve. Make love to me. I've been waiting for this." I took his hand and placed it on my breast. "Make love to me, Steve." I kissed him and nature took its course.

That night as we were talking, I asked, "Tomorrow is Sunday. Will you go to church with me?" He responded he would. Partially, I suppose, because he knew I had him over a barrel. He had just gotten home and wanted to keep me happy.

We walked into the church. We could hear the people saying amen, clapping, and people worshipping. The music was loud, and the choir was singing, *"I've Got A Mansion Just Over The Hill Top"*. People were swaying in the isles as they sang. "Steve's eyes widened. He hesitated and almost turned back toward the door. I could see the absolute terror that came upon Steve's face as he heard what he thought was racket."

Reverend Vaudie Lambert was the Pastor. He was on fire with a message of truth for the people. The congregation was backing him up with, "Amen" and "Preach it, Brother!" What he was saying was so heavy with truth. Steve could hardly stand it. One thing I must say about Brother Lambert, his messages never condemned. His messages built up and exalted the Lord Jesus Christ. He declared what God had done for us and how He could change our lives. I will forever be grateful to Vaudie Lambert for answering the call of God.

He never stood still when he preached. He paced the platform, face red, veins popping out from his neck with an expression of force and passion in his voice.

Steve was breathing heavily, as though he could barely catch his breath.

I asked, "Steve, what is wrong?"

He said, "I can't breathe in this place."

Grabbing my hand, he said very sternly, "Denice, let's get out of here." He hurried us out of the church and we headed home.

I was discouraged. I had been hoping that Steve would like the church. We walked into the house. I was silent. I could tell he was angry. I knew the speech was coming. He paced back and forth across the living room, his face red and sweating. He stopped to speak forcefully and direct.

"Denice, don't you ever ask me to go back to that church again. I can't breath in that place. I don't like that place. I don't like that preacher. I am never going back. I'll go to any other church in town, but never ask me to go back to that church."

I suppose the reason Steve was so uncomfortable was that he was able to sit in other churches and not feel anything. There was no conviction. That Sunday the presence of the Holy Spirit, which convicts us of our sins, was there. The Holy Spirit was invited into that Service. He always shows up where He is invited.

After much silence and prayer on my part, I finally got up enough courage to speak. I certainly did not want an argument on his first day home.

"I'll make a deal with you. If you'll go back one more time, like tonight, you'll never have to enter that church door or any other church door again."

I thought, Oh, God, what have I just said? I've given him a reason never to go to church again. I've just fixed him for the rest of his life.

He responded, "Now let's get this straight. If I go back tonight, you're saying you will never speak to me about church, God, the Bible, prayer or any of that for the rest of our marriage?"

"Yes," I said.

He looked at me, "I'll do it but know this. I'm going to hold you to it. I'll go tonight but never again."

While Steve was gone, I realized there were good, decent men that lived for God and their family. Steve's remark didn't seem to freak me out. My mind was made up. I was going to live for God. I am going to have the life God has for me. If it meant getting rid of Steve, I was ready, if that was the path Steve wanted.

We arrived at the church. The people had already begun to worship. Brother Lambert gave a powerful message on the changing power of God. Two ladies in the church played the piano and organ and the choir began to sing,

Softly and tenderly Jesus is calling

Calling for you and for me

See, on the portals he's waiting and watching

Watching for you and for me
Come home, come home
Ye who are weary come home
He gave an altar call and Steve jumped up from his seat. I thought he was going to run out of the building, but instead he ran toward the altar. He literally ran and threw himself upon the altar. The rafters of the church made a sound as he threw himself on the rails of that altar.

I got up from my seat, walked down the aisle and knelt beside him. He was slumped over the altar on his knees. I had a flashback of our four years of marriage. Can he really go a week without lying? Can he go a month without my finding out something he has done behind my back? Will I find phone numbers in his wallet? I guess in my flesh I didn't really believe he could. How long will this last? There is no way he can change. He is just who he is.

I couldn't believe my ears. He was sobbing as he cried out loud, "Lord, if you still want me, I want you, but you are going to have to change me. I am not a good person. I can't do it myself." He was weeping for the sins and errors of his life. He shed tears of deep sorrow.

Steve was so moved by what happened to him at the altar. He wouldn't stop talking about it, as we were getting ready for bed.

"Denice, as the preacher was preaching, all I could hear in my head was you're no good. There is nothing good in me. Yet, within myself, I felt something drawing me to respond to the altar call. I knew it was now or never. I told God all of my life I've really wanted to be a good person. Denice when I fell in love with you, I was attracted at first to your looks, but then I saw something deeper in you. You had a hunger for more in life for everything that was pure and right in life. I have had no right to your love. I was ruining your life and our love. I knew I was doing what people said I would do to you. All these years I've tried to hold on to you, on the one hand,

and yet I've lived in filth on the other. Baby, you have been my only contact with goodness in this world. I have been like a starving man who has a diamond ring to sell, but I'd rather starve to death. I told the Lord, if you still want me, I want you, but you're going to have to change me. I told Him I would give him my life."

I looked at Steve and said, "Steve, God is transforming you into the man you were meant to be. What happened at the altar is real."

The next few weeks Steve experienced regeneration in his life. He wanted all of God he could have. He got a job selling life insurance, going door to door, but right away it seemed that all he could see was their need for Jesus. He spent all of his time telling them about Jesus and praying for them.

His paycheck was only twenty-two dollars his first week at work. He was supposed to be making good money. It became obvious that if he was going to sell insurance, he was going to have to sell it to make a decent pay check, not spend his time praying with his potential clients.

A week's revival meetings had started at our church. We were sitting there with a twenty-dollar bill and two one-dollar bills in Steve's wallet. This was all the money we had in the world. Our refrigerator was empty except for a jug of water. There was no food in the house. Those twenty-two dollars had to pay bills and buy a few groceries.

Steve said, "Denice, I think the Lord wants me to put this twenty dollar bill in the offering plate. I'm going to do it."

The twenty dollars was dropped into the plate. It was gone. Fear gripped me as I thought, well, here we are with two dollars. When we got home that night, the couple that lived behind us called and said, "Denice, this is Diane. Have you looked in your refrigerator yet?" I said, "Diane, I know what's in there—nothing."

She said, "Just go look in the freezer."

Steve was standing near me, "Steve, look in the freezer."

He opened the freezer door, and it was jammed full of roasts and steaks. They didn't even know our needs, but God saw Steve put that twenty-dollar bill in the offering. God began teaching Steve and I about giving and from that point on Steve gave. Remember, in the South we didn't need to lock our doors. That's how they filled our freezer. It was a different time we lived in.

Weeks passed and I noticed I wasn't seeing any cigarette ashes in the ashtrays. Steve had been a chain smoker, going through one to two packs a day. There was always a cigarette in his mouth.

"Steve, where are you putting all your cigarette ashes?" I asked.

He looked up from the Bible, smiled, "You know; I just quit desiring cigarettes."

He forgot to take a cigarette out of the pack and light it up. He had tried to quit many times before and hadn't succeeded, but now the habit was gone. That addiction was taken from him with ease and no struggle. Smoking isn't a sin, it won't send you to hell, but you will just smell like you have been there. It's not healthy.

I began to see other changes in Steve. God was moving swiftly in his life. He accepted the Lord as his Savior and he was baptized in the Holy Spirit. I woke up at night and would hear him praying in "unknown tongues," seeking the face of God. He would even go into the closet at times so that he could be alone to pray. Our lives were changing. We were hanging out with Christian couples. Things were going along too well for anything to be bad again, or so I thought. I had one more dreadful lesson to learn and it would tear right at the core of my being.

Several months of joy swept over us after Steve's commitment of his life to Christ. For the first time in our marriage, it seemed as though I was free. I had peace and a feeling of contentment. Together we pursued our relationship with God.

One night Steve was distressed and came into the bedroom to talk to me as I prepared to get dressed for the midweek service. I could always tell when Steve had something on his mind—he starts to bite the corner of his mouth.

"Denice, sit down, I want to tell you something." The aggressive undertone in his voice sounded as if he were going to tell me something he did not want to tell, but something God was forcing him to get it out.

My mind began to say, "*Oh no. He's going to admit things to you. I don't want him to tell me anything. I don't want this bubble around me to burst. I don't want him to say a word. I like things the way they are. God, please don't let him confess anything to me. Let me live in this realm of total happiness, peace and joy. God, just tell Steve that we've begun a new life, to forget the past. I don't want to hear it.*" I felt sick to my stomach.

I then heard this still small voice say, "Denice, listen to him. Hear him out. You can take it. Let Steve be free once and for all. I will see you through this." I stood to listen to what Steve wanted to tell me.

"Denice I'm going to tell you something. When I tell you, I know you're going to take Stacy and you're going to leave me. I know you Denice. I've got to get this off my chest. I can't go on like this. I want to walk in total freedom with nothing to hide. I am not going to live any longer with the threat of my past. I am going forward. As long as this is within me, I know I cannot be free from my past. I've got to tell you."

Steve had reason to be worried because I had told him that if I ever caught him with another woman there would never be a second chance. One strike and you're out!

Steve continued, "Denice, I've weighed the cost. I've thought this through. I know that no matter what happens I've got to go all the way with God. You might as well know. This sounds hard, but I've got to walk with God first, even above you and Stacy. Even if it means I lose both of you. It's not what I want to happen, but I know how I can mess my life up. From now on I am doing it God's way."

I knew this moment was a turning point in our marriage. It was going to determine our destiny together or not.

He continued, "The entire four years that I have lived with you, I have been lying to you. I have lied to cover up lies to cover up lies. I was going out to drinking parties and getting drunk while you thought I was on night duty. His lips quivered, tears in his eyes, "Denice, I have committed adultery." He told me of the times and places. I watched the expression on his face. I watched his lips trembling as he spoke. He bit the side of his lip. I could see the suffering as he tried to relieve himself of his pain. I knew all along that there were times Steve had lied to me. When the word adultery came out of his lips, it was as though he had just plunged a knife deep into my gut and turned it. I felt dead inside.

Steve looked at me, waiting for me to scream, yell, cry, throw a fit, or show some emotion. There was nothing there. I could not even feel anger. My marriage with Steve Vickers died. It was over. He waited for my reply. I was silent and I only looked at him, lifted my hand for him to keep his distance.

I said, "I've heard every word you just said. I don't know what I'm going to do about what you've just told me. Don't you come near me; the thought of your touching me makes me want to vomit. You will never touch me ever again. I can't live with you anymore."

If God had opened a hole in the earth that led to the fiery furnace, I would have kicked him in it without one thought. I felt nothing for him. Steve slept in the other bedroom. In the middle of the night, he came into the bedroom and softly shook me to wake me.

He said, "Denice, Denice," his voice was just above a whisper and it trembled as he said, "pray for me. God can't forgive such great sin."

He was on the floor, on his knees crying with his head buried into the side of the mattress. He was asking me to pray for him. I didn't love him anymore. I didn't care. I wanted to say, Jesus just phoned. He said He hates you after all. I knew my heart was wrong and that I had to care about the torment he was in and should pray over him, so I did.

I placed my hand on his head and said, "God, show Steve that he is saved and that you have forgiven him." At the same time, I heard a voice say, *"But you can't forgive him."* I knew He was right.

I knew he needed a touch from God. I wanted him to have God, but I didn't want him to have any part of me. However, I continued laying my hands on his head and praying for him. "God, show Steve you can forgive such great sin."

Steve returned to the other room to sleep. I'd wake up in the middle of the night and hear him praying. His prayers could be heard throughout the house. I would see Steve reading his Bible. My feeling of nothingness for him turned to anger, and the anger turned to torment. I was mad because men were always hitting on me but never was I tempted. I didn't deserve this from a man. For three nights in a row this scene repeated itself: Steve came into my bedroom, shook me and cried, "Denice, pray for me. God can't forgive such great sin."

All my mind could see was Steve with the other women. I pictured him in bed with them. I cleaned the house and would become sick at my stomach and throw up in the toilet. I soon discovered three things that would save me from being tormented. I read the Bible, played Christian music in the house, or spent time praying.

One night I was in agony. I could not stop thinking about his adultery. I called Pam.

I was crying out of control, "Pam, I'm dying! Is there such a thing as dying of a broken heart?"

She answered me, "I don't know." She too was crying.

I told her, "If there is, I'm telling you, I am dying Pam. I'm dying!" Tear drops of pain poured from my eyes from my innermost being. My scream was loud. My pain was deep. Pam cried with me.

I said, "Pam, Daddy did this to us and now my husband is doing this to me. I'm tired of this. I am so tired of this pain, I think I'm dying." I sobbed.

She said, "Denice, I know. I know," as she moaned in pain for my pain. That's all she could say. We cried together on the phone. We were like to little girls crying together.

The next morning as I was vacuuming my mind raced with pictures of Steve with other women. I turned the vacuum cleaner off, threw myself on the living room carpet and buried my face in my hands.

I screamed and it echoed throughout the house, "God, help me! Help me God. It hurts, it hurts, I'm hurting." I screamed out like a mad woman, "God please let me out of this marriage, I don't love him any more."

When I said that, I felt the Holy Spirit all over me. It was as if He stood at attention when I called on Him. From an inward voice I heard, *"Denice, if you'll see this man through this, I will give you the man you never dreamed you could have."*

I talked back, "God, you give me a man I never dreamed I could have, but don't let his name be Steve Vickers. I don't love him anymore."

The Holy Spirit spoke back to me, *"This man."* I had heard His voice. I got up and continued to clean the house.

Later that day I realized that I was no longer hurting. The house seemed peaceful. I realized I wasn't being tormented about Steve. I laid across my bed, flat on my back. I lay there trying to imagine Steve in bed with another woman. It didn't hurt. I had the idea I'll make it worse, make it kinky, dirty and in color. I could see it in my mind, but it didn't hurt.

I said, "Lord, what's going on? It's supposed to hurt. Why doesn't it hurt?"

I heard God within me, *"You said it hurts. So I took the pain away."*

I questioned him back. "You can take pain away?" All my life I have had this pain inside of me, first Daddy and now Steve. Now, at the age of twenty, I'm finding out that He can take hurt away. I was changed in a moment. I learned happiness is within you. It is in your way of thinking. It is in what you allow God to do inside of you.

Steve came home from work. He sat in the living room to read. I walked past him as I went to cook dinner. He is so handsome. Steve's dark eyes, his brown hair and mustache had always taken my breath away. I told myself not to look at him. I wanted to look at him again, so I walked toward the bedroom and glanced at him again. Look how handsome he looks, sitting in that chair, reading his Bible. I don't want to look. What's wrong with you? You're getting attracted to him again. Don't look at him. He doesn't deserve your love. Three voices were speaking. The enemy of my soul was speaking, God's voice and my voice. I had to choose which voice to listen to.

I felt like a schoolgirl again, seeing him for the first time. I felt myself being drawn to him. I became afraid that he would notice that I was looking at him. So I tried not to look at him because I did not want to start loving him again. I couldn't help it. It all happened so fast. It was a whirlwind.

Steve had been a gentleman during those weeks when I had nothing to say or do with him. I was in pain. He had not forced himself upon me; instead, he had continued to seek God. Passion started to build within me. I knew God had said to me that He took my pain away.

I walked over to the chair and knelt down beside him. "Steve, I love you and I want you to move back into the bedroom." I looked at him to see his response. He choked back the tears.

"Denice, are you sure? If I move back into the bedroom, I'm never going to leave it ever again. Are you sure Denice?"

I replied, "Yes."

Our eyes met as if for the first time, I knew we were in love with each other. I looked into Steve's eyes and all I could see was truth. I was no longer looking for a green thread. He was not going to be the man like my Daddy with plastic, nothing real. There would be no plastic tulips to fool people. I saw what I was going to have as a husband. I didn't have to wonder anymore. I knew for the first time in my life that God had given me a man I never dreamed I could have. I had been married to Steve for four years; it was as if I was looking at him for the first time. We were free for the first time. We were both free from our past!

Action does not always bring happiness, but there is no happiness without action. I read once that a foolish man seeks happiness in the future. The wise man grows it under his feet. It is said, you can take an image of your earthly father, how he makes you feel and how he treats you. If you turn the picture over, you see God, and you transfer those feelings to Him. Until you can connect why you feel the things you feel you will not understand and you will quickly blame Him the way I did when Steve confessed to me.

My earthly father only showed up in my life every few years to hurt me, tell me what a rotten kid I was and to show off his latest conquest. I am seeing my heavenly Father in a different light. I cried out to Him and He answered me. He showed up.

~ 14 ~
DEATH AND LIFE

I HAD JUST STARTED a job as an orthodontic assistant. At the interview, I told the doctor that I did not have a high school diploma and I was not trained in orthodontics, but that I loved to be around teenagers. I assured him I was a quick study and that I would bring fun to his office.

"I'm a party waiting to happen and teens need someone like me around when they come to your office to get their braces checked." I smiled and added, "You won't regret training me. I will make coming to your office something they look forward to."

The whole time I was talking he was smiling at me. He stopped me in the middle of a sentence and said, "You're hired."

After a few weeks of working, I explained to my boss I had a family problem that needed to be taken care of. He asked me was there anything he could do to help me. I explained that I had just found out my Daddy was running a black prostitution house downtown and that I was going to go shut him down. He didn't judge me for who my Daddy was and told me it was fine for me to leave to take care of it. He said he was sorry I had such a disappointing father.

I said, "Yeah, I know."

I drove down the street that I knew to be a rough neighborhood. One knew not to drive into that area because of all the shootings and drug problems. I was in my early twenties, a white girl at that, who had no business around that part of town. There were blocks of slum houses in a state of disrepair. The old wooden shack homes had porches falling apart with broken down sofas and recliner chairs sitting on the porches. Cars were jacked up in the yard, no tires on them and grass growing all around. The yards were filled with junk.

I pulled up in front of the address that was given to me by an informer. I walked up to the porch and noticed two black girls in sheer lingerie sitting on the porch swing.

"Hi, Sugar, what do you want?"

"Is Charles Perkins here?"

"Just a minute Shug, "she walked over to the screen door, "Charlie, there's a young girl here to see you." She then walked over to an old rotting white column, leaned her back against it and propped one foot up against the column. She was checking me out while the other girl filed her fingernails, never looking up at me.

"He be here in a minute." She said.

He was forty-five, dressed in black dress pants with his white starched shirtsleeves rolled up and no tie. He was still a tall slim man with jet-black hair. Daddy had a smile that charmed everyone. His smile normally seemed to say, "I have the world by the tail". This time, as he looked at me through the screen door and pushed it open, there was no smile. He did not like that I had found him there.

He stepped out onto the porch and asked, "What do you want?"

"Daddy, I heard you have this house you're running and I know you still work for JSH Company. Leeann and Charlie are still in elementary school. I don't want them to know about you and what you are doing. I'm giving you twenty-four hours to clear out of town. If you don't, I am going to your job and then to the police to tell them about these prostitutes and you."

He did not say a word, just a blank look on his face as he turned to go into the house. I went back to work and found out the next day that Daddy had taken me seriously. He moved to Jasper, Alabama, near Birmingham. I didn't want to see or hear from him again.

THERE WAS A TRANSFORMATION in Steve's life. I wanted to believe that I could believe in this man—that he could be trusted. The Holy Spirit began to teach me how to treat a man. He would tell me things to say to Steve and I would obey.

One morning after I had invited Steve back into my bedroom, he was in the bathroom shaving. I turned him around to face me with his face all lathered up.

I looked him straight in the eyes and said, "Steve, I really do love you."

He looked at me as if he questioned it and asked, "Do you, Denice?"

I looked him straight in the eyes and said, "Yes I do."

God began to teach Steve and me tender words and tender touches toward each other. Steve was caught up in the freedom he was experiencing in God. The change in him had an effect on Momma and my sisters.

Momma told Steve, "Steve, you've renewed my faith in men. Watching your life and seeing what God has done has made all the difference in me."

Life was good. Steve and I both ran after God and each other. I loved the man he was becoming and I let God teach me how to love and treat a man. Peace prevailed in our home.

Wednesday night, while I was in choir practice, Steve sat in the back of the church talking with Pastor Lambert. Steve was weeping, telling him, "If I could do anything for the rest of his life it would be preach the gospel. I want to help the hurting, broken and bruised of life and tell them of the greatness of God."

Pastor Lambert prayed with Steve and then said, "Son, that's the call of God on your life. Just say 'Yes' to God."

After choir practice Brother Lambert said, "Denice, it looks like you and Steve will be leaving us to go to Bible College." I remembered when I was fourteen years old sweeping the carpet, I had heard God speak to me and say, *"You're going to be married to a preacher."* It was God's plan and my destiny all along, as he watched over me.

We knew we had to tell Steve's parents. We dreaded the reaction we would get from his Daddy. He had great plans for Steve to be a lawyer and then go into politics. Steve knew he never measured up to his Daddy's plans.

His Daddy would say, "One of the most valuable things in life is when you walk down the street and hear people say, 'There goes Steve Vickers.'"

Steve and his family always had everything first class. Vick, Steve's father had the precise appearance of a Southern gentleman. He wore a white suit and he walked with a black cane that had a brass handle. His hair and mustache were white and he had deep blue eyes. I pictured that's how Steve would look because he was built just like his Daddy. His Daddy always reminded me of Clark Gable, who played Rhett Butler in Gone with the Wind.

Vick and Nettie always retired to their master suite to watch TV after dinner. In the South no one locked their doors and since we were family, there was no need to ring the doorbell. Their bedroom door was open, so we walked in. His Daddy, as usual, was sitting in his easy chair smoking his pipe. He looked so distinguished in his black silk smoking jacket. Nettie was sitting up in bed while they both watched the Lawrence Welk Show.

Steve said, "Momma and Daddy, I want to share with you my plans. I'm going to be a minister. "Steve looked at his dad to see his response.

His father's head dropped down as he shook his head, biting his bottom lip in disappointment. Steve and I knew the speech was coming. I also knew he would blame me for his son missing the mark.

He looked at Steve as he spoke. "Son, you know there's no money in that. How will you provide for your family? Son, you must focus on success and how you are going to get there, not this religious stuff."

Steve replied, "Dad, I don't care about money, this is what I want. I want to spend my life helping people. Dad, God has called me."

The air was filled with tension. His dad was frustrated, shaking his head in disappointment.

Nettie, Steve's mom, was a complete picture of order; neat in her appearance and the way she presented herself, giving a feeling of class. She reminded me of a person who had just stepped out of a Vogue Magazine, who was not trying to be in style but rather had style. Mrs. Vickers had Indian in her. She had short black hair with some gray running through it. The Indian in her meant she never had to shave her legs or arm pits. Her grand mother was a full-blooded Cherokee Indian. She moved over to the edge of the bed so sweetly, trying, as always, to keep peace in the family. She had on a long pink nightgown with a matching silk scarf to hold her fresh fixed hair as she slept at night. Slipping into her pink satin slippers, she walked over to Steve and placed her hands on his chest. Her nails were perfectly manicured with pale pink polish.

"That's wonderful son. I hear Sanford in Birmingham is a great Bible College. "I could tell Steve's parents were ashamed we were Pentecostals."

Steve said, "Mother that might be so, but I think that the Lord wants me to go to Southeastern Bible College."

We knew he could get his BA in theology there and it was where he would be able to get the Bible teaching we knew and believed in.

"Okay, son" she said in her gentle way.

His Daddy spoke up, "Your mother and I love you and we want you to be happy." Then he grit his teeth, "But if you're going to be a damn preacher, you better be the best damn preacher there is."

Steve responded, "Yes sure."

That was typical of Steve's dad, "You better damn do it right and be the best d*** one at it." He was a man of quality and drive. When he set his mind to do something, he did it and he did it perfectly. Deep down, I did respect him. We were alike in many ways. I was firmly established in my drive for spiritual things and him in natural things. I think we both lacked balance.

WE MOVED TO LAKELAND, Florida in January 1972 so Steve could get his degree. We spent the next four years working hard getting Steve through college. I was able to get a job with an orthodontist. Soon after, I was managing his office. For me, lacking a college degree has never been a problem. I was making a lot more money than all the other wives of other Bible college students and all of them had college degrees and some had Masters. It just reinforced my belief that I had not missed out.

Confidence in one's self goes a lot further than knowledge. Knowledge I can get, confidence you must put on from within. We both had full time jobs and Steve attended school. We stayed very busy. Stacy was in a good day care at our church.

Once settled into work and school, we began to meet other couples in College. Friday nights we had married couples over for a bag of Taco Bell and a movie. Every couple lived on a tight budget so that was a treat for all of us. I made Momma's fudge and it was a hit!

Momma was invited to go to the Dominican Republic to be a housemother with a mission team. I think she was so tired of working and providing that it sounded like heaven to her. She took Charlie and Leeann, but Leeann only stayed a week. I guess she had some culture shock. As a teenager, she did not want to live there. Momma asked if she could live with us. Here we were, in our early twenties, raising a toddler and a teenager. Leeann was easy to have in our home and we were able to put her in a Christian School on a scholarship program. Leeann was the typical teen. She had thick brown hair and a cute little figure. She liked makeup, just like me. She also loved her loud music so she could dance around the room with her girlfriends.

Steve came home from class before leaving for work each day. He would open the door to the apartment and Leeann and her girlfriend would run and change the radio to a gospel music station. They did not want him to know they were listening to rock music. He knew what they were doing and we did not care. The city had two Bible Colleges and a great Christian radio station that we listened to a lot.

Steve and I laid in bed at night laughing about Leeann and praying for God to give us wisdom on parenting a teenager. We were young ourselves. We prayed for God to bring the best young boy into her life for her first kiss. She loved cooking and was good at it. Many nights I came home to a cooked meal. She was very respectful to us, which made it easy.

Momma and Charlie spent two years in the Dominican Republic. Charlie was a natural at learning Spanish and with his green eyes and light blonde hair, he stood out. They returned to the states and moved to Lakeland to live near us. Momma got a bookkeeping job at a car dealership. Leeann moved back in with Momma and Charlie. We were all attended the same church together.

Daddy paid a visit. He called Momma and said he wanted to see them. She told him he could come. She felt it might be good for them to see him. He had left when Leeann and Charlie were babies. He was going to stay at mom's house in Leeann's room and Leeann would sleep with mom. It was going to be a short visit.

All of us thought maybe God was going to do something in Daddy. Maybe he would put the family back together and we all could live for God. We believed God was able to change a life and we were hoping this would be it for Daddy. He arrived Friday. Saturday, mom had to go to the Laundromat to wash clothes. The apartment she lived in did not have a washer and dryer hookup. Charlie stayed home with Daddy. Dad had never given us any reason not to trust him around Charlie. Dad's problems had always been with women.

Charlie ran to the Laundromat sobbing. He told Mom Daddy molested him. He was twelve years old. He told Momma what happened. She shook to her very core. She called Steve and he told Daddy to get his things and get out. Steve wanted to beat the living hell out of him. I kept him from being the one to do it. Charlie was just a boy, an innocent child. He longed for his Daddy and this is what his father did. It is not a child's fault when an adult takes advantage of them.

A lot came out after this happened. We all talked about everything dad did in front of us. Janice had also been a victim. She hated Daddy. She said he showed up when she was seventeen. She had just gotten a divorce from her teenage marriage and Daddy asked if she would have sex with his brother. She didn't, but she hated him for asking her. It made her feel cheap. She told me she hated him and if he died she would not go to his funeral. She said that when she was young, she remembered she had slept in bed with him one night and he wrapped his legs around her legs and some wet stuff came running down her leg. Now that she had been married she knew what it was. I told her that I had a memory of seeing him have an erection, but at the time I was so young I wasn't sure what was coming out of the leg of his shorts.

Life was better when Daddy was not around. He always brought pain when he showed up in our life. We preferred to move on without him.

JANICE AND HER NEW SPOUSE, her third, with whom she had another son, moved to Lakeland to be near all of us. Janice was convinced she could own her own furniture store. She had no money to open one, but she was convinced she could do it, so she did. It was not long before Janice owned two stores. We were all together again. The only one missing was Pam, who had moved to Camden, Alabama with her husband and three children. He left the Navy, went back to college and became a pharmacist. Pam and her kids came to visit during the summer to go to Disney World.

Steve graduated from college and was named the salutatorian. The week after graduation, I gave birth to our second daughter, Misty Shae Vickers. Stacy was five years old and wanted us to name her new baby sister, Ronald McDonald. I assured her Misty Shae was a better name than Ronald McDonald.

We went on staff as Youth Pastors of our home church in Montgomery, Alabama, under Pastor Frank Martin of Evangel Temple. It was a great year working with a man we respected.

One morning Pam called, "Turn on the radio. The DJ just said Elvis is in the hospital and they are playing his music." Pam loved Elvis. She had gone to see him in concert in Birmingham and even got to meet him afterward. I turned the radio on just as the disk jockey came over the air, "Elvis is dead."

Pam began to cry over the phone with me as they played one of his songs. The DJ said, "Rest in peace Elvis, we love you." The next few days they played his music on the radio all day and the television kept reporting his passing. People were outside Elvis's home standing at the gates of Graceland and bringing flowers and candles as they wept over Elvis's passing. It was hard to believe he was gone, but not forgotten.

Steve felt the direction of God. We were to start traveling as an evangelist, holding revivals in churches across the country. We bought a used twenty-eight foot travel trailer and pulled it behind our van as we traveled from state to state preaching the gospel.

Steve was driving the vehicle, a trailer in tow, and I was reading out loud the life story of Smith Wigglesworth. He was a man who believed God and saw miracles. He had stepped out in faith and God did miracles in his services.

Steve began to weep. He pulled off the side of the road, got out of the car and walked over onto the grass. At first I didn't know where he was going. He stood beside the car on the interstate with his hands lifted up toward heaven crying as he said, "God, I believe in you. God, let me see miracles. Use me God. Use me for your glory."

I was sitting in the car crying, too. I knew that God wanted us to be children of faith. I also realized how significant our God was. I began to see that God was as big as we let Him be in our lives. God wanted to use us in a mighty way. He wanted us to be a voice for Him.

Steve opened the car door and sat down and looked at me. He said, "I believe God. I am not going to settle for less. I am going to see God move in me and use me. I am going to see blind eyes opened and the deaf will hear. I will see the lame walking and the captives set free. I am going to tell them of God's love and mercy. That God will change their lives and bless them if they will only cry out to Him. I'm going to tell them God is faithful and that God cares about their every need. If they will cry out to Him, things will happen that will turn their lives around. Denice, are you with me?"

I shouted out, "I'm with you, Steve!"

I knew that he was going to see these things in his ministry.

I thought back to the day while we were youth pastors. I was walking down the stairs and noticed Steve sitting in his chair reading the Bible. God stopped me at the foot of the stairs and spoke to my heart, "Do you see that man over there?"

I replied, "Lord, you know I see that man over there."

God spoke back, "He is not yours. He is mine. I'm just lending him to you."

In our revivals, we saw God do many great things. One of the first to come forward at the alter call was a little elderly woman. She was small in her frame and frail in her posture, but her hair was what caught my eye. It was salt and pepper colored hair, more salt than pepper. It was pinned up loosely in a bun. There was a glow about her face. Her skin was as smooth as a baby's rear-end and she had beautiful blue eyes.

I moved over to her and asked, "What can I pray with you about?" She looked at me with tears flowing down her cheeks.

She said, "I cannot hear at all out of my left ear and I can just hear a little out of my right ear. Tonight, I know God wants to heal me." Her words were said with such confidence, I felt sure God would honor her faith and heal her.

I went over to Steve, "Steve come over here. This woman knows the Lord. She believes that God is going to give her back her hearing tonight." Steve asked her a few questions. He then turned to the congregation. He asked the piano player to stop playing.

Steve said, "You all know this woman. She can't hear out of one ear and her other ear is infected. She is under constant doctor's care. She believes tonight God wants to heal her."

He placed his fingers over both of her ears and prayed a simple prayer. He removed his fingers and her head jerked back.

She sobbed as she cried out, "I can hear. I can hear."

Steve and I looked at each other. We were as shocked as she was. We knew that it wasn't Steve. It was God. All we did was step out in faith—faith in a big God who will do big things, if we'll just let Him. That night we let Him and He did.

That night as we lay in bed holding each other, we knew God wasn't looking for flamboyant preachers. He was looking for someone to believe in Him and let Him be God.

Steve held me and said, "Baby, God is faithful. What He says, He will do. I want us to be all He desires. Together, let's keep our eyes on Him and follow wherever He leads."

One time, Steve was preaching in front of a large audience about how Peter and the disciples were in a boat that was being tossed about in the storm. Peter called out to Jesus who was walking on the sea. He said, "Lord, if it is really you, tell me to come to you walking on the water."

Jesus said, "Come." Peter stood up and walked on water. Steve was preaching with passion, Bible in hand, throwing his hand up in the air as he said, "What we need are more Peters to stand up."

I have always been a visual person, and when I heard him say that, I smiled and strained to hold back the laughter, because that's what I saw. Upon realizing what he had just said, he attempted to correct himself, but it got even worse. I choked and wiggled in my seat and held my breath so that I would not scream out in laughter. The third time he attempted to correct himself, the audience was in hysterics. He had said, "Peters" walking on water.

Steve and I did follow God. I watched him in services as God used him a powerful way. I knew it was all God and that Steve was the empty vessel filled with God, desiring to be used by Him. We were a voice for God. We let people know that He would step into their life in a minute, turn things around, if they cried out to Him for help. Our lives were proof. We could say look on us. Many times I was reminded of the Scripture, "To whom much is given, much is required." Luke 12:48

We were sold out to God. Many times, Steve's daddy shook his head at us, as though we were such a disappointment. The ministry was not his idea of success. He took Steve out of his will because he was unhappy with the direction Steve had taken in his life. I would tell Steve, "If he gets saved, I will be able to believe for anybody."

Steve's dad came down with terminal cancer. He told us he was listening to a TV preacher named Charles Stanley. We began to see a difference in him. He softened and was open to talking about God. This was the man who cussed TV preachers out as he changed the channel.

He yelled at the television, "That damn preacher, all they want is my money."

He had hated preachers and he didn't like me for changing his son. I knew it wasn't me who had changed Steve. He did not understand. We asked God to let us know without a doubt that he would spend eternity in heaven. A few nights before Vick died, the hospital called and said for us to come. They said that Vick had been asking for me.

He kept asking, "When is she coming?" I walked over to his bedside. He looked at me, smiled, and put his hand out toward me as I placed my hand in his.

He said, "You made it," and folded his hand with mine. "Denice, I want you to forgive me. You were right and I was wrong." He said this in front of all his loved ones. This is a man that has never admitted he was wrong about anything.

He continued, "Now I understand everything you ever told me about God. I want you and Steve to know I'm proud of you. Keep up the good work that you are doing." His heart had changed toward his son but he did not have time to put Steve back in the will. He never left the hospital.

On the day of the funeral, we drove behind the hearse. Steve's Momma reached over and put his Dad's diamond ring on Steve's finger.

She spoke softly, "Your Daddy wanted you to have this."

What a powerful ability we have in our freedom to choose. I thank God repeatedly that I chose to seek Him first and hunger after Him. God is who He says He is and He will do what He says He will do, if we will let Him. I thank Him that He keeps His Word. I do have a man I never dreamed I could have. Steve and I became one and I willingly staked my life on him and his stability because now I knew who he was. I knew who he was in Christ. I saw that God was bigger than my circumstances. He took our hurts and turned them into our victories. When Steve drew me close to him and held me in his arms and whispered, "Baby, I love you," I could look into his eyes and respond, "I know. I love you too." Steve's walk with God was amazing to me, and under God, Steve was my breath.

Our time traveling was coming to an end and we both knew there was change coming. We just did not know what it would be. I was homeschooling Stacy, who was in the second grade, while we traveled. I was ready for us to get settled. I told Steve I wanted us to buy a home and let Stacy go to public school for the third grade. Steve was still traveling, preaching from church to church. We made the decision and bought a beautiful new home.

It was around that time that I took a good look at myself. I was tired of wearing a padded bra and hearing about breast implants. I decided it was for me, so I did it.

Steve was home for a while, relaxing in our bedroom reading. I had just stepped out of the shower. I stood naked in front of the mirror brushing my long dark hair. I looked at myself in the mirror. I saw my slim figure and now beautiful breasts. I had married Steve when I was sixteen. I stood in front of the mirror, I was twenty-seven, naked and I realized I was a woman, a beautiful woman. My body was curvaceous and I had full breasts. I walked over to him.

He looked up from his book. He asked, "What?"

I said, "Steve, looking in the mirror, I just realized when you married me I was a little girl. I am not a little girl anymore. I am a woman, a beautiful woman."

Steve smiled and said, "I knew this day would come. I have always thought you are the most beautiful woman I have ever seen. I knew you did not really know how beautiful you are. Denice I thought if you ever saw yourself the way others see you, you might not stay with me. You would think you could do better."

I said, "Better, Steve Vickers, get in that bed and let me show you what this woman wants."

We had a craving for each other. It was sexual, emotional, spiritual, and it was beautiful. It was a love affair between two people, body, mind and soul, completely given to each other—living for each other and both living for God. You can't get any stronger or better in this life than that.

PAM HAD RECENTLY gotten a divorce. She moved back to Montgomery with her three children.

She asked me, "Who is going to want me with three little children?" Even as beautiful as she was, I too, wasn't sure what man would want her with three little children. I knew sharing my concern would not bring her comfort. I told her she could trust God and I shared Romans 8:38 with her: "And we know that God causes all things to work together for the good for those who are called according to His purpose."

I said, "Pam you can trust God."

She shook her head as she said to me, "I will."

Pam was always burying her face in her Kleenex. Pam was an umbrella and Kleenex person. She was funny like that. I'm neither. I would rather get rained on and look for Kleenex when I need one. Isn't that funny how different we were?

Janice, now with four sons and single again, ended back in Montgomery. I laughed and told Momma, "Isn't it something, all these single women in churches go to the altar praying and believing God for a husband and Janice can marry as many times as she wants. Men just like Janice and Janice sure liked men. The key for her, I guess, was how she made men feel about themselves."

Janice had gone through the hippie movement, smoking weed, going to Woodstock, the whole nine yards, trying it all. She would go to the Copa Club, wear her white Patten knee high boots and short fitted Minnie dress. They always let Janice be one of the girls dancing in a cage. So she did get her cage after all. Remember, she wanted to grow up and be a heart surgeon or a go-go girl in a cage. Well, there you go.

Now, here we all were back in Montgomery together with Momma. All of Momma's adult kids, Leeann and Charlie, who were now teenagers, were back in the same town. We were all going to the same church and trusting God to teach us and show us our way through life. You can see we were not perfect people and life wasn't perfect, but we ran after a perfect God.

ONE MORNING WHILE I was getting Stacy ready for the school bus, I noticed Misty was not out of bed. She was a rambunctious five years old.

"Misty, don't you want to get up and have some breakfast with Stacy?" She did not move. I walked over and felt her forehead. She was burning with fever. I said, "Misty, getup baby, I'm going to take you to see a doctor." She could not walk. I laid her in the back seat of the car with Stacy and drove her to the doctor's office. The doctor immediately realizing she was unable to walk was running a fever and had extreme fatigue, requested blood-work.

"Mrs. Vickers, we are going to need to hospitalize Misty to see what we are dealing with." Within hours of being in the hospital, I was told Misty had Osteomyelitis, an inflammation of the bone in her right leg. The doctors began to talk to me about possible amputation. They said that the disease had already eaten through the growth plate of her leg. The diseased bone has to be removed along with tissue around it to stop it from spreading. It could mean death, if they did not move fast.

I called Steve, who was out of town. He cancelled his meetings and rushed home. Misty was in the hospital for ten days with IV treatments of antibiotics given around the clock before considering removing her leg. Sitting up all night in the hospital not being able to sleep, I was suffocating with fear. I was overwrought with the knowledge of possible amputation or death for my five year old. I sat beside her bed with my hand on her leg, crying all night.

All I could say out loud was "Now God, now God." I felt like someone was holding a pillow over my mouth. I could hardly breathe. I knew only God could turn this around. Daily the doctors discussed with us amputation. My mind was made up, not my daughter.

In prayer, God told Steve not one bone would be broken. Steve and I switched out the next morning. While he sat with her, I went home to freshen up.

Sitting in the bathtub, I cried asking God, "Why? Why God? We have dedicated our lives to you. We are spending our lives serving you. Why, God?"

I heard that inner voice speak, *"When the enemy comes in like a flood, the Spirit of the Lord will raise up a standard against him."* Isaiah 59:19

I jumped out of the tub like a mad woman. That's all I needed, a Word from God. I drove as fast as I could to the hospital to tell Steve. I threw open the door of her hospital room. I pointed at Steve and declared, "When the enemy comes in like a flood, the Spirit of the Lord will raise up a standard against him."

Steve jumped up and began to dance around saying, "Yes!"

We got our miracle. One word from God mixed with our faith turned things around. They did not amputate.

We did not have medical insurance and the hospital bill was going to be over a hundred thousand dollars. I was sitting in the hospital room when the door was opened slightly and a blonde woman with the most beautiful smile poked her head around the door without stepping into the room.

All she said was, "I am a representative. Go to the Cripple Children's Clinic. They are waiting for you to sign the papers. They will pay your bill." Then she left.

I told Steve what happened and he said, "Let's go.

I told them that their representative came by and told me to come to sign some papers. They said they had no one who does that. I looked around at all the desks and I could not find her. The lady was so amazed at my story that she came back into her office with the forms for us to sign. Our medical debt was cleared.

We checked Misty out of the hospital, the double doors opened for us to exit. I turned to Steve and asked, "Do we have the victory?"

He responded, "Yes, we have the victory."

We looked down at our Misty walking between us, healed and no medical bills to pay. We had a taste of victory in our mouths. There is nothing like that taste, sweet, sweet, sweet victory. Her leg was not supposed to grow. It had eaten through the growth plate, but it grew just as her other leg grew. She would one day become a physical trainer with the most perfect body you have every laid eyes on. The Doctor wrote across his medical records, "Unexplainable phenomenon."

ONE AFTERNOON I MET Pam for lunch and just as we were leaving the office where she worked, a young man with dark hair and a dark mustache walked by us and said, "Pam, I will see you after lunch."

"Who is that?" I asked.

She said, "My boss"

I said, "You have worked for him now for two years. Is he the boss who is single?"

Pam laughed, "Yes." She knew what I was about to say.

I told her, "He is gorgeous. I would throw that man down on the ground and lay my lips on top of his mustache."

Pam laughed and said, "He is dating someone."

Pam laughed as I began to instruct her on flirting.

She said, "Denice, I haven't flirted in years. I have forgotten how."

As we sat at lunch, I went over flirting instructions. We both laughed at my way of catching a man. Every day I called her to ask, "Have you flirted with him today?"

She laughed as she whispered over the office phone, "I don't think he got that I was flirting."

Eventually he took the bait and they married and had two more daughters to add to her two sons and daughter. That made five. I call that, "Woman Power".

I HAVE ALWAYS BEEN one of those people that if something crazy is going to happen, it's going to happen to me. That summer on our vacation Steve and I took our kids to Disney World in Orlando. There is a building you can enter to see a short film about how Walt Disney came up with Disney World. We thought that would be exciting.

The crowd pushed their way into the dark room to stand in front of the screen and somehow we got separated from each other without me realizing it. I love cuddling; it was dark and I placed my arm around Steve. We were hip-to-hip and cheek-to-cheek. The lights turned on and I turned my face toward Steve, whom I had snuggled up during the show. I was shocked. It wasn't Steve. Instead, it was a short little Japanese man.

Gasping for breath, I stuttered, "I . . . I thought you were my husband."

He smiled and in his half broken English said, "It's okay."

I left the building and found Steve and the kids. I asked Steve, "Do you know what I was doing in the dark just now?" I excitedly tried to express my discomfort, "I was in the dark hugging on another man."

Steve laughed at me, "Why didn't you check to make sure it was me?"

I said, "Steve, you walked in with me. How could you leave me like that?" He just laughed and shook his head.

Misty said, "I saw you, Momma"

I asked, "Misty why didn't you tell me I was hugging on that man?"

She said, "I thought you knew."

Somewhere in this world, there is a short Japanese man who tells all his friends, "Go to America. The women there will surprise you in the dark and you will love it."

We decided to go to a water park. I have a little daredevil left in me and I decided to try out the waterslides. I slid down the slide head first right after Steve. I did not realize the water pressure was pushing the top of my bathing suit down. The slide spat me into the pool. I jumped up, stood waist deep in water waving at Steve, not realizing my breasts were exposed. Cameras began to flash as people spotted me. I did not know why everyone wanted to take my picture. I waved at Steve to wait for me so I could catch up with him. I dipped down in the water to make sure everything was in place.

A man came up to me and said. "Ma'am, please don't do that again. I don't think my heart can stand it."

Not knowing what he was talking about I smiled and said, "I know. It was wild, wasn't it? That slide just spits you out."

I caught up with Steve on the climb and he asked me why I wasn't embarrassed. I then found out what the cameras were all about. We left the water park.

~ 15 ~
THE BIRTH OF CHRISTIAN LIFE CHURCH

1980 Montgomery, Alabama

W E FELT GOD WAS changing the direction of our lives. We noticed every church we went to, we were falling in love with the people and did not want to leave them. One night while Steve was preaching out of town, I prayed, crying out to God, "Tell us what you want us to do and we will do it." Tears were running down my face. "Just tell us what it is you want. God, what do you want us to do?"

I fell asleep as I kept asking over and over "What do you want us to do?" I awoke at sound of the ringing phone. The voice on the other end of the telephone was a woman's voice.

She said, "You do not know me and I do not know you. I was praying this morning. God gave me your phone number. God has a question for you."

My thought was I've got some flake on the phone, an airhead, and a real space cadet.

I said, "Ok what is the question God has?"

She answered, "He said to ask you, '*What do you want?*'" She instantly had my attention.

She continued, "I am to hang up and let you tell Him."

I had fallen asleep with tears running down my face asking God to tell me what He wanted us to do. He is asking me what I want. I knew this was God.

"Woman, you have heard from God." I hung up.

I never thought about what I might need. We lived life by prayer and obedience. The vital question was what do I want?

I lay there, took a step of faith and said, "I, Denice Vickers, want Steve Vickers to pastor in Montgomery, Alabama."

I was amazed at what came out of my mouth. I responded to that out loud, "*dadgum.*"

The Bible says it's within you. Just ask Me for it. I was learning God's plan. I called Steve and told him what had happened. It wasn't long before we had our first church service in our living room. Momma, Leeann, Kenny, Charlie, Janice, Pam, a dentist and his wife, two young single brothers, Norris and Wayne Braswell, my Avon lady, and of course, all our children. That was the birth of Christian Life Church August 1980.

One month later, we moved into a tiny rented church building. Our first Sunday in that building, I told Steve I knew how we would know that the hand of God was on us to pastor. The sign would be, if He sends a Black family to our church and they choose us as their pastors. You would never see that in the South, Blacks and Whites attending church together. Our first Sunday service Sam and Willa Carpenter, a handsome Black couple walked in.

I turned to Steve, smiled and said, "Now, let's have church."

The first year of the church, the neighbor who had taken my father from us, Maria, came to a Sunday morning service. I wondered how she could come knowing Momma and all her kids would be at the service. There was no way she did not know I was married to the pastor. I knew she came with a purpose. She answered the altar call at the end of the service.

I walked over to her and asked her "What do you want me to pray with you about?"

She put her hand on her chest and said, "My heart."

I knew she wasn't talking about heart trouble, but rather that her heart hurt for what she had done. A scripture came to mind, Luke 20:43: "Until I make your enemies a footstool for your feet." I knew right then I could wipe my feet on her or I could give her mercy. I chose to give her mercy. I pointed at Momma and all her children and said, "Because of God we survived and we are blessed by God. You go now and suffer no more. We are all right." I prayed for her, and she left. I never saw her again.

I was amazed how God brought her to me. He wanted to give me the opportunity to wipe my feet on her, but He knew I would give her mercy. I kid you not. I thought if given the chance, I would have knocked the fire out of her. Isn't God something?

One night in my sleep God spoke to me, He said, "Seek the Father as hard as the Father is seeking you." I woke up, sat up in bed and pointed to Steve, who was sitting in the bedroom chair reading his Bible, and quoted to him what I had been told in my sleep.

Then I put my hand on my chest and said, "All my life I saw myself as running hard after God. I never knew He was running hard after me."

Our fourth year of Christian Life Church, we were pastoring six to seven hundred people. A young black attorney walked into one of our services. His name was Jock Smith. Jock became one of our most faithful attendees. He always sat behind Steve and me. As Steve preached, Jock would get so excited about the message he would begin to rock in his seat. I would often look back at him and see tears running down his face.

He would say, "Pastor delivered it today."

One Sunday God spoke to me and told me to tell Jock something. I turned to Jock, "God says to tell you, He is going to raise you up in high places, and you are going to stand and walk with people of authority. Just keep your face toward God and He will take you there." Jock wept as I told him.

Steve and I watched as God worked in Jock's life. Jock ended up having the biggest, documented, privately owned collection of game-worn sports memorabilia and the largest African American sports collection in the United States. He talked to youth and adult groups across the country. Jock started a ministry for athletes, Scoring for Life. He made a special appearance at Super Bowl XXXI as a guest of the NFL Players' Association. He obtained record setting verdicts on behalf of his clients, including an $80 million dollar verdict for an elderly black female whose house was destroyed by termites, and a $700 million settlement in the nation's largest environmental case.

There was a landmark $1.6 billion verdict for a mother of three who was a victim of fraud. This verdict was reported as the single largest verdict in civil law in the country and the verdict remains the largest civil verdict obtained by an African American attorney. In 1996, Jock met nationally acclaimed lawyer Johnny L. Cochran, Jr. He was well known for the OJ Simpson trial, famous for the line, "If it doesn't fit, you must acquit," talking about the bloody glove. They were called, "The Dream Team." Together they formed Cochran Sports Management, a sports firm that represented athletes in contract negotiations.

In 1998, Jock Smith facilitated the meetings with Cochran to form the national law firm of Cochran, Cherry, Givens and Smith. This partnership became well known as The Cochran Firm, one of the country's most recognized civil and criminal defense law firms. In the first few months after forming Cochran, Cherry, Givens and

Smith, Jock called Steve and said he and Johnny wanted to fly all their partners and spouses in for a Sunday morning Service to have Steve pray over them for God's blessing on the firm. We had a fabulous service. Johnny Cochran told Jock if there was a church like ours in L.A., he would never miss church.

Jock was opening his beautiful new Law firm in Tuskegee, Alabama and had a dedication ceremony and banquet with people of every background flying in to attend. Steve and I sat at the head table with Jock and Johnny Cochran. I sat next to Johnny. Cameras were flashing with reporters and fans wanting autographs from him. The fans were so enamored with Johnny. He laughed, leaned over to me and apologized for all the distractions.

I said, "Johnny, I admire greatly your accomplishments in life, but it is so hard for me to think about you what I see in their faces. I already have met the greatest of them all, the King of Kings and Lord of Lords. After you have met Him, all others are just people with achievements."

He laughed and said, "You're right Denice. I see what Jock loves about you."

We flew to Atlanta. A Limo picked us up to go to the grand opening of the new office of the Cochran firm. We celebrated at the home of "Home Run King", Hank Aaron. Stevie Wonder was performing in the back yard.

One Sunday morning Jock leaned over my shoulder and whispered, "This week I have been asked to meet with President Obama." I laughed and said, "God has truly done for you what He said He would do."

Jock never missed church on Wednesdays and Sundays all those years, until one Sunday morning, January 8, 2012, he passed away at the age of sixty-three, in his home in Montgomery. We loved him.

For twenty-five years Steve and I preached to thousands. It was not uncommon for a politician to want to meet Steve and ask for his backing. Steve always welcomed them to the services, but it was unusual for Steve to say anything from the pulpit about their presence. Only twice do I remember Steve giving pulpit time to say that a politician was in the service and that was only if he knew they were Christian and he believed in what they stood for. One was Bobby Bright, who became Mayor and then later a Senator.

Steve was a man of prayer. It was normal for our children to fall asleep while hearing their Daddy pray out loud to God for guidance. His hunger to feed the people the full word of God was real and passionate. We took every service with absolute seriousness. We knew you never have the same people in each service, and we knew people walk in with thoughts of taking their life, divorce, pain, torment, addictions and just plain unhappy. We were the voice God had sent them to hear.

We made a great team. We walked, lived, and breathed telling people how big God was. We were told by Pastor John Osteen, whom we considered our mentor, that if we would build a fire, people would come to warm themselves. We knew what he meant. All we had to do was be on fire with the word of God and people would come, and come they did. We had a fire in our belly, knowing in us that we had found the answer to the empty space in people's lives, and we were going to shout it to those whom had ears to hear heard and received. Only God could fill that space. I prayed for God to make me a woman of knowing.

I would hear God ask me, "Denice, what do you know?"

I would say back to Him. "I know you!"

The Bible says, "My sheep hear my voice". I felt His pleasure.

Steve, being a man's man and a strong leader, spoke with passion and conviction. He was a polished orator. He made straight A's in college and came from an upper class home. They say opposites attract. Steve liked me just the way I was. I worked at looking good. Every morning, Monday through Friday, I put the kids on the school bus, went to the gym, worked out with a group of girls. We did speed walking. That all stopped when I was diagnosed with rheumatoid arthritis. The discomfort of the disease slowed me down.

When going in front of the congregation, I always liked dressing in stylish clothes, high heels, makeup and the latest in fashion. The tomboy in me loved to dress down in my blue jeans and T-shirt. During the week, it was common to see me out shopping in my jeans, which in the South was almost taboo. There is an unspoken rule that the pastor's wife should always be at her best in public. It was always a shock to new people in the church to see me out in my casual attire.

I noticed the socialites would turn to Steve and me in their time of need, when they were drowning in this life. We pointed them to the one who could help them. Many Pastors guide by a scripture verse and then prayer. I always went a step further and gave the same counsel that I would give if it were my child asking for help.

One morning at the gym, a woman well known in the city, was working out. She approached me as I was sitting on the gym floor wiping the sweat from my face.

"Denice, can we talk?" she asked.

"Sure, sit down," I said.

She whispered, "My husband is in an affair. He never touches me anymore. I am losing him, Denice."

I knew she had not shared this with anyone.

"Do you still love him?" I asked.

She answered, "Yes, and I do. I do not want him to leave me for her."

I told her, "I am going to tell you some things to do and I want you to do them. I also want you and me to pray together and ask God to help you turn things around." I am a believer in having to do our part and God will do His.

I told her, "Whatever you did to catch him the first time will catch him again."

She responded, "What do you mean?"

"Find the young girl inside you, the girl you used to be. How did you act when you first met him? What did you act like toward him? How did you make him feel about himself? He is still your husband. Tonight I want you to put on the sexiest outfit you can find, darken your eyes, put on red lipstick and seduce your husband." She asked what I meant by "darken her eyes".

I said, "Take your eyeliner and darken them to seduce him, like Cleopatra."

We both laughed. She didn't even wear make-up.

I told her seduction would say a lot to him. He will think about himself, "I'm the man". It will take confidence in yourself as a woman, but you can do this. Her eyes were wide with a look of shock as I gave her this advice. She was unsure of herself. I guess, coming from a preacher's wife it sounded a little strange.

Weeks later she walked up to me and told me he had stopped the affair and returned to her. She said they were both so excited about their new love together and she thanked me for not just praying with her and for helping her see where the love had been lost.

MOMMA, JANICE, Pam and their spouses were always sitting in the audience listening to Steve or I speak.

Pam would call me the afternoon after I preached and would say, "Denice, that was powerful today. You speak with such authority and passion. You really helped me today."

It always meant a lot to me because when we were young she tried to "polish" me. I was now one of her favorite speakers and I would hear her laughing in the audience at the things I said. Steve and I had a daily TV show called, *Heart to Heart*.

The church drew men who needed to be taught to be godly men. We attracted doctors, lawyers, teachers and ditch diggers—all backgrounds. It was beautiful, our church, with black and white sitting together, side by side, not caring who they were or what they did in life. It was beautiful seeing an elegant woman sitting next to an ex prostitute, and doctors and lawyers, next to an ex drug addict. Nobody cared. They were there as brothers and sisters in the Lord wanting to be fed the Word of God. All were treated equal. We had very strong marriages in our congregation and marriages were the foundation of the church. Most churches are held together by women, but not at Christian Life Church. Steve led the men.

We went after marriages and taught what the Word says about a woman and a man. We were young and this helped draw in young couples and college students. We had our own TV show, Monday through Friday. The men in the church were always asking when I was going to speak, which I found to be a high compliment. I told jokes and made people laugh as I hit them hard with the truth and they never saw it was coming. Steve had a powerful ability to teach with authority; the authority God had given him in his calling. He talked with excellence and you could feel his heartbeat as the words came forth with passion.

I gave birth to our son, Stephen, just like I told Steve when we were dating: "One day, Steve Vickers, I'm going to marry you and we will have a son name Stephen." The first thing I said to my son was, "There you are. I've been looking for you for a long time."

Steve went out into the waiting room to announce the birth of his son to everyone, and what did Steve do? He flexed his muscles for everyone. He's the man. I recovered from childbirth and a few weeks later I went into the hospital to have a hysterectomy. We were sure we were through having children and I had a history of female problems. We felt it was the best decision. I checked into the hospital the night before surgery to be prepped for early morning surgery.

Just as I was falling asleep, my nurse came into the room and said, "Denice, your doctor wants you to call him at home." I called.

He said, "Denice, you have to go home. You're pregnant."

"Doctor, I can't be, there is no way."

He laughed "There is a way and you are."

I remembered Steve and I had gone to be on a television show out of town. Our son Stephen was three weeks old. I convinced Steve it was safe to have sex because I had not yet had a regular cycle. While we were there doing the show we had dinner with Dale Evans, one of my childhood heroes. Roy Rogers had already gone to be with the Lord. I was able to tell her that she and Roy, along with Roy's horse Trigger, were in my life every day when I was a child, and I had wanted to be a cowgirl, just like her. I remember whispering to Steve, at the table, sitting across from Dale Evans, "Can you believe this?" Under my breath, I whispered, "*Destiny!*"

Anyway, back to trying to explain how I got pregnant. I told my doctor I would not go home until he proved it to me. The nurse took me downstairs to do an ultrasound.

I asked her, "Do you see a baby on that screen?"

She answered, "I'm not allowed to say."

"Listen, I just gave birth to a baby, so keep your mouth shut and shake your head yes or no. Now I'm going to ask you again. Do you see a baby on that screen?"

She nodded her head in affirmation, yes.

I called Steve at the church office. When he heard me say his name, "Steve" in a stretched out desperate way, he started laughing.

He said, "You're pregnant."

I went home that day, holding Stephen in my arms. I explained to Stacy, our fourteen year old, and Misty, ten years old, that Momma didn't have surgery because we had a surprise for them, a baby.

Stacy was embarrassed and told us to "Stop it" We laughed.

The night I went in labor, unaware my labor was starting, I heard the voice of God prompting me, *"When the enemy makes a threat, it is not a threat, if you do not listen, but if you listen, it will turn into reality."*

I wrote it down on a piece of paper thinking I was to preach on that sometime in the future. I did not know that I would be the one needing these words in the very next hours. My labor began. On the way to the hospital, I told Steve what God had said to me.

He said, "Let's go have a baby and we will talk about that later."

I said, "I just want you to remember, we are to preach about what God told me."

Then I leaned forward in pain.

During the delivery, I noticed my doctor's look of concern. My baby was stuck inside, and the heart had stopped. The baby was not breathing. The doctor began to make the adjustments to pull her out, as it was too late to do a C-section. The baby was too far down the birth canal. I saw the look on his face. I knew I was in trouble.

I asked, "Steve is everything all right?"

Steve responded very firm, "Everything is all right."

The doctor listened to Steve and me as we talked back and forth. There was no way the baby, without a heartbeat and oxygen, was going to be born alive. It seemed to take forever, getting the lifeless baby out of my body. One of the nurses climbed on top of me and began pushing my stomach, until the baby finally appeared. The doctor held up the body of my lifeless little girl. She was on her back, arms and legs dangling over his hand. She was dark purple gray. She looked like a perfect little baby doll.

I looked at Steve behind my head and asked again. "Steve, is everything all right?"

He answered, "Everything is all right."

We stayed in agreement that everything was all right. I looked at the doctor; he shook his head hopelessly.

I looked at Steve and asked again, "Steve is everything all right."

Steve responded, "Everything is all right."

We continued to say that to each other. The doctor was holding our lifeless baby girl. Steve and I stayed in agreement. I remembered what God had said to me right before my labor started. "When the enemy makes a threat, it is not a threat if you do not listen, but if you listen, it will turn into reality."

Suddenly our baby girl gave out a cry. Steve took her in his hands, held her up toward heaven, and declared, "Her name is Denice."

Denice Lynne Vickers was born May 23, 1984. The word God had spoken to me now made sense. This had been a "threat". She breathed! She looked like a little china doll, with a head full of black hair. She and Stephen were ten months apart. It was like having twins, two in diapers and with bottles. The joy I had was so enormous, I wasn't sure I could fit it into my heart.

We had bought a new home at 3137 Fitzgerald Road, in the Hillwood neighborhood, one of the most desirable developments in Montgomery. It was a brand new home, with street named after famous writers who had once lived in Montgomery, like F. Scott Fitzgerald and Zelda Sayre from the 1930s.

The home across the street was bought after we moved in. It was gated with a guard gate at the entrance of the driveway. We found out Governor George Wallace lived there. We knew he was confined to a wheelchair and needed his privacy, but that did not deter my Misty. She was nine years old and had my personality. She got to know the guard at the gate and he got a kick out of her. It was Halloween. Stacy and Misty wanted to trick or treat at Governor Wallace's house, so the guard escorted them in after receiving permission from the Governor, who was glad to meet them. He welcomed them as he laughed at their costumes. Misty inquired about why he was in a wheelchair and she said to him, "trick or treat."

Wallace said, "I'm sorry, but I have no candy to give you." He told the guard, "Go get me two pictures and I will sign them for these two young ladies."

Misty came home disappointed that he gave her an autographed photo of himself.

She said, "All he gave me was this dumb picture with his name on it. I wanted candy."

We laughed at her. She did not understand who he was. He lived his final years in that house. The Alabama state troopers guarded his house around the clock until his last breath. In his latter years, Wallace had announced he was a born again Christian and apologized to the civil rights leaders for his initial segregationist position. He said that he once sought power and glory, but he realized he needed to seek love and forgiveness. About his stand in the school-house door, he said, "I was wrong. Those days are over, and they ought to be." He said he did not wish to meet his maker with unfor-given sins. He wrote a letter to a man in jail, the one who had shot him and told him that he forgave him. He did not get a response.

George Wallace achieved four gubernatorial terms across three decades, totaling sixteen years in office. Wallace's final term as gover-nor (1983-1987) saw a record number of black appointments to State positions. Governor Wallace was a very significant part of Alabama's history. He lived in a time that the South needed change, and he was wrong in his segregationist position. I greatly admired Governor Wallace; the man, not his politics at that time we lived in. If he were in politics today, I know he would run for President and he would have been a great President and made Alabama proud. Wallace was a man with conviction, passion, and a man that was a driving force. He led people and they followed. His politics on those subjects would be different today. I am proud to say, I met Governor George Wallace, from Alabama.

It was a wonderful neighborhood to live in. Our neighbors were successful, fun loving, cheerful, and colorful. One character, on Christmas Day, cruised the neighborhood on a motorized toilet with his trumpet in hand, announcing to all that Christmas was here.

I wrote my first book, "God, Let Me Out Of This Marriage", and began to speak on all the Christian television shows around the country. I struggled, wanting to stay home with my children and let the book do the talking for me. We raised our children: homework, school projects, braces, football games, cheerleading and barbecues around our pool. In the winter, we took the children on snow ski-ing trips with aunts, uncles and cousins to Steamboat, Colorado. Steve bought a ski boat so that we could spend Saturdays on the lake near our home. Our children loved to water ski and Stacy and Misty brought their dates along. Life was good, our two youngest children, Stephen and Denice loved doing everything the older sisters did.

I was diagnosed with rheumatoid arthritis, and dealt with a lot of pain, but I knew God would make a way of escape for me. We hired a full time maid to help me with the house and my two youngest children. They loved her and always greeted her with a big kiss on the lips.

Our church had as many blacks as whites. Our children never saw color. One night I sat Denice and Stephen on the kitchen counter. They were about five years old.

"Now, kids, this weekend Daddy and I are going to take y'all to meet Daddy's aunt that you have never met."

Denice looked at me and asked, "Is she black or white?"

Steve and I had a good laugh realizing that here we were in the Deep South and my daughter wasn't sure what color our kinfolk were.

My daughters were cheerleaders and Misty was voted homecoming queen. Their brother, Stephen, was a singer in a band and a stage actor. I know that this sounds like a mother bragging, but I believed my children were so beautiful that they could stop traffic. I made drapes and bedspreads for their bedrooms, making sure their rooms were their own space with their own private bathroom. I always had a project going on, ceramics, oil painting, or even painting the outside of our house. I loved digging in the dirt, planting flowers and vegetables. Somewhere in a hanging basket or the yard I had a plastic tulip reminding me from whence God had taken me.

We raised our children in a beautiful home with swimming pool, trampoline and a playhouse in the back yard. It was a lot different from my childhood. Over the years, we started buying rental property. Momma moved into one of them.

Steve earned his doctorate and became a pilot, two of his goals. He bought a jet as he continued to pastor, using the jet to get to churches all over the country. It was part of our mission. When pastors needed a pastor for themselves, they called Steve. He could get to them in their time of need. No pastor was unimportant to Steve. It didn't matter how small or how large the congregation, they knew he cared about them. Pastors go through the same trials and tribulations that their flocks go through, but it is hard for them to turn to someone for help.

I was seeing the world with Steve. We ministered in Bangkok, Koh Samui, Chiang Mai, Thailand, Switzerland, Germany, France; Monaco, the Philippines, Rangoon, Burma, Katmandu, Nepal, Mexico, St Thomas, Puerto Rico, the Dominican Republic, Kenya and in Uganda, where we put in a well for over five hundred families. We helped feed starving children in these countries. We preached to the pastors so that they could give good spiritual food to the people. We built churches in Rangoon and Africa. We began a ministry for African Pastors. They were crying out for help and instruction.

We were in Katmandu, Nepal and Steve got a driver to take us around to see the city. The driver stopped at the top of a mountain for us to take a look. I was excited and I open my door and stepped out. I did not realize he had stopped on the edge of a cliff. I took my first step out of the car and began to fall down the cliff in mid air. I could hear myself scream out, "Jesus." As my body crashed into an uncertain environment, breaking limbs that bounced me around for what seemed like forever. I finally landed face down in a huge mud hole, which turned out to be

a pig's pen. I jumped up, threw my hands up in the air, covered with blood, pigs poop, and mud, from head to toe.

I yelled out, "I'm alive."

Steve and the driver looking down from the top of that mountain had a look of horror on their faces. I was glad to be alive, not one broken bone. It provided us many laughs over the years. Steve always said, "Denice, living with you is an adventure in itself."

While I was in Jinja, Uganda, I was sitting on the porch of a small cottage by the Nile River drinking a cup of coffee, watching monkeys swinging from trees. I was thinking how amazing my life was. That a little girl, who could whoop any boy's tail, stuck frogs in her pocket from Alabama could end up in Africa. Then I heard the voice of God. "Go get a paper and pen."

I wrote the first page of this book. I stopped at the place where I asked, "Momma are we there yet?" and she answered, "Yes Denice, now stop you're wiggling. We will soon be there and we are all going to have fun. Yea!" It flowed out of me without even thinking of what I was writing down. I knew I had just started a book. I sat there thinking how amazing God is in our life. To think about when He spoke to that fourteen-year-old girl, sweeping the carpet. My, gosh! Just think if I had not believed that He could speak to his children. What a wonderful life I would have missed. I'm not saying there haven't been times of sadness, test and trials. But what I am saying is, He's been there all the way. We knew we were blessed as we ran after God and obeyed Him. Obeying God and *doing His Will energized our life*

My sisters and Momma continued to be my closest friends. We attended church, went to movies and dinners together and shared our Easters, Thanksgivings and Christmases. Thanksgivings were at Janice's house and Christmas Eve was at Pam's. Christmas day we stayed home. I always cooked a big meal ahead of time to serve mid-afternoon. On Christmas Eve, Momma was always showered with gifts from all her children and grandchildren. She went on everybody's family vacation. We put ski boots on her in the snow in Steamboat, Colorado and pulled her around on a flat surface. Momma was spoiled by all of us. She was our queen and the grandkids called her granny and duchess. She could do no wrong. She got lots of love.

Janice married her dream man, Colonel Tom Willard and had a formal military wedding. He worked at the Pentagon in Washington, DC. We always stayed in touch with each other. It was funny, the once hippie was now a Colonel's wife. They lived in Boston and Tom was commander over the building of Military Satellites. They came home to Alabama and bought an old Southern antebellum home for mom to live in. They decided to retire in Montgomery. Mom loved the house. Janice and Tom filled it with antique furniture they had collected. They also opened a store for mom to manage, "The Holiday House."

Mom rented out some of the bedrooms to single young men in the church. She loved mothering them and speaking into their lives. It wasn't long before Janice and Tom retired to be with all the family. Together they had six sons, Mike, Raymond, Chris, Ben, Mike and John. Tom and Janice took Momma on overseas trips to Korea, Germany, and Hawaii. Momma was becoming a world traveler.

Tom and Janice had been listening to our church services on tape. They would listen to a lot of other ministers like Kenneth Hagen, Kenneth Copland, and John Osteen. Wherever they were stationed, they always found a church to attend. There are many people that have told me, over the years, that Janice had been the one that led them to the Lord. One was a man that was installing hardwood floors in her house. He was the owner of the company. Janice told him about the Lord and how God could turn his life around and

236

right then and there on his knees, he prayed with her to accept the Lord as his savior. Janice has many stories like that. She is a soul winner. She has always been bold.

Pam and her husband had two sons and three daughters. Their children kept them busy with sports, cheerleading, and all that goes with raising children. Pam loved being a mother and was always reading books on parenting.

One day, Pam came to me and said, "I believe I have found my calling." I looked at her and listened with much interest because I never knew Pam was looking for her calling. She said, "I am an Intercessor. I will spend time praying for people. That's what I can do." I smiled and said "Well, that's great Pam."

I really did not know at the time where all this would take her. Pam was so neat in every way. The slightest odor in the room, Pam was the one to notice it. Blood and vomit were two words you would not use in the same sentence when in her presence. This would change. Pam drove her expensive car back and forth to Birmingham, Alabama, which was over an hours drive, taking women for their cancer treatment. They laid in the back seat, sick from the treatment. Pam provided them a bucket to throw up in. Pam prayed for them all the way there and back.

Mark was Pam's friend. Mark visited our church and answered the alter call for prayer. Pam was an alter worker. She met him for the first time at the altar. Mark was a drag queen. When I say Mark was a drag queen, I mean with hands going, hip moving, body swaging, head swaying, girl talking and hair flipping. Well, it was just plum confusing. Mark had some real disadvantages as a drag queen—he was white, tall, about six-four, too skinny, and ugly, dog ugly. It just did not work for him at all.

Mark's family had disowned him years ago and even gay people did not like him. He got on their nerves. Mark had nobody. Pam had compassion for him and as his friend he called her often for prayer with him. One day he came to her and told her he was dying of Aids. She led him to the Lord. Mark truly got born again. During Mark's last days in the hospital, there was no one but his only friend Pam, the intercessor. She stayed with him until he took his last breath.

Pam stopped by my house the day Mark passed away. With her perfectly folded Kleenex in her hand, she wiped away her tears, "Denice, Mark and I held hands and sang, "Jesus Loves Me", and tears ran down his face as he sang. He took his last breath still singing, "for the Bible tells me so." Pam stood in my kitchen and cried over Mark.

LEEANN AND KENNY had a daughter name Logan. Leeann had a dream of owning her own business. She began to decorate all the wealthy homes in town for Christmas. It became a hot ticket in town to have Leeann decorate your home for the holidays. The money earned decorating she used to open her first designer home store and then she began to build her first building. It was a beautiful Tuscan structure with a hair salon, spa, boutique and furniture store. Leeann became successful decorating houses, vacation homes and redesigning office and apartment buildings. It was a God given gift.

MY BROTHER CHARLIE AND JIMMY lived in Atlanta. Charlie met Jimmy when they were young and they moved in together in Atlanta, Georgia. We learned to love Jimmy. Charlie started his own business selling outdoor fountains and statues. The business did so well that he bought Momma a new car.

MOMMA RECEIVED A supernatural miracle. The doctors had diagnosed her with cancer of the liver and gave her a few weeks to live. We transferred her to a cancer hospital at Keesler A.F.B. Biloxi, Mississippi, to have a new test done. It came back with the same report. She only had a few weeks to live.

The doctors decided they would open her up to take a look. The night before surgery, around midnight, Janice, Pam, Charlie and I were at a restaurant. We were sharing with each other. We agreed that God is a big God and He has the last say in this matter. I told them we needed to go up to the hospital where Momma was and request the film of the cancer that was on her liver. I said," We need to look at our enemy and command it to leave."

The night nurse said it was illegal for her to show them to us. I looked at her and said, "Now you listen to me, our Mother has been told she is dying, and we believe in the power of laying on of hands and getting into the power of agreement. You are not going to deny Momma's kids from doing that, are you?"

She pushed away from her desk and said, "Follow me."

The nurse took us to a room where the files were kept. She held the film for us to look at. It looked like a huge cluster of grapes on her liver. We stared in silence. We looked at the enemy that dared take Mommas life. We laid our hands on the film and commanded the cancer to get out of our mother's body, in the name of Jesus.

The next morning, before they took Momma to surgery, we began to dance around her bed singing, *"Satan, the blood of Jesus is against you."*

Momma laughed as we were doing all the dances of our youth to that song. We stopped dancing and singing when the doctor walked in. I asked, "Doctor, Momma has always had a weak bladder. While you have her open, will you put a few tacks in her bladder so when she laughs, she won't pee on herself?"

His moved his head back with his chin down with amazement that I could ask such a foolish thing. He paused to gather his words. "We do not do corrective surgery at a time like this."

I responded, "Oh, I get it, but can you just promise me that if you open Momma up and the cancer is not there, you will tack up her bladder?"

He looked at me and said, "Sure, I can promise you that."

After five hours of surgery, the doctor walked out scratching his head. He stood talking to another doctor. I grabbed him by the hand, pulled him in front of Janice, Pam and Charlie as we all began to jump up and down screaming with joy.

I yelled, "Tell us you found nothing."

He looked up at the ceiling, paused and then looked at us and said in a profound manner, "I found nothing."

I asked, "Did you tack her bladder?"

He responded, "I tacked her bladder." We were shouting, jumping up and down like children in a candy store, laughing with joy.

The waiting room was packed with people waiting on their loved ones in surgery. They heard what was being said and began to line up for their own miracle. No one said to form a line if you want prayer, everyone just got in line. God took it out of her body during the night before surgery. It was a miracle.

Momma was being rolled out of the recovery room to return to her hospital room.

I said, "Momma, you got a miracle—the cancer is gone." She said, "God is a good God." We began to sing to her:

God is a good God,
God don't ever change
God is a Good God, that's why I will forever
Praise His name
I'm a telling you, God is a good God"

The doctor asked us, "What did you do to make it disappear?" We answered him, "*We prayed*".

The night nurse had left for her vacation, but next morning she called up the hospital to find out the results of the surgery. When she was told it wasn't there when they opened Momma, she said she called her grandmother to tell her about it. Her grandmother had always told her about these things happening, but she had never witnessed it for herself. She said it was life changing for her. Years passed and no cancer—a miracle.

MOMMA ALWAYS TOLD us how smart and beautiful we were and that we could be anything or go anywhere we dreamed in life. These were the blessings of a mother's words. We believed her. All of us were natural dreamers and believed if we could dream it, we could have it.

Every five to ten years, Daddy showed up at my house. He never came in the house, just stopped out front with a different woman in his car. I always knew it was to show off how successful his children were. He whipped in and whipped out, just being him, living for self and the moment.

One particular time he came by. Steve and I went out to greet him and the woman he had brought with him. He stepped away from his car to talk to Steve. I was always kind to Daddy's women. I couldn't blame them for being with Daddy. He was still a charmer, and his lies could really impress you. Why wouldn't you hookup with a single man that owns hundreds of rental homes and is a medical doctor or a politician? Hey, he might be an inventor. Who knows what he was telling her. I walked over to her side of the car to greet her.

I smiled and said, "Hello."

She spoke softly, "I have been wanting to meet all Charlie's kids. He told me how successful y'all are. I'm so impressed how your Daddy put you all through college. You have a lovely home."

I laughed and said. "That's a joke."

I realized there was no need in setting her straight on his stories. I knew she would eventually find him out. I decided I would just thank her for the compliment.

"Yes, thank you, I love my house."

We had small talk and they left.

I heard she and her brothers beat Daddy and kicked him out of his own house. There's no telling what he had done. I heard it had something to do with him inappropriately touching one of her children. Those men kicked Daddy's butt all over his front yard. I heard he had broken ribs and had to be put in the hospital, where he ended up having back surgery due to the injuries. His back gave him trouble from then on.

He continued to pop in and out of my life. He would stay a few minutes to brag on his latest woman and tell us how he's helping some politician run for office. There was always something crooked up his sleeve. I received him with grace and listened to his flashy lies, but I was never impressed. The strange thing was I called him Daddy. I always longed to feel a Daddy's touch, maybe a hug, or to see a look of favor in his eyes towards me. They were always empty when I looked at him.

~~ 16 ~~
LIFE HAPPENS

1990s

O UR TWO OLDEST DAUGHTERS, Stacy and Misty married. Steve and I became grandparents. My babies had babies. Stacy gave birth to her daughter, Stacy. At the age of twenty, Stacy has become a famous pop singer. She travels the world with rock rapper, Flo Rida. He saw her talent and opened the door for her future. She goes by the stage name "Stayc Reign".

My daughters, Stacy and Misty, went into labor at the same time and at the same hospital. They gave birth to my granddaughter Misty, and grandson Dylan. Steve and I were going in and out of two hospital rooms making sure both daughters felt their deliveries were equally important to us. Both daughters wanted us in the room when their babies were born.

Pam called every morning while she drank her cup of hot tea and I had my coffee. We talked about our children and grandchildren, and we tried to keep up with all the teenagers. We prayed together about whatever was going on in their lives. Sometimes we just wanted to take a broom to them. We laughed about how much easier it would be to lock them up in the basement while they were teens. Love keeps us all together and believing that God works all things out.

Life was like we were on a fast train, looking out the window, seeing it speed by. A lot of living was going on. I always reminded my children that the family is the strongest army on earth and don't forget it. People come and go through your life, but there is nothing stronger than blood. You accept each other's imperfections and you do it for life, no matter what, always believing the best will happen for them. I realize I have become my mother, always making declarations to my children. There is power in our words, for good or bad. I understand that, in a family, there are some family members that no matter how hard you try, they bite you in the butt. Love them forever, be there if they ever need you, and keep your distance, if that works best. That is, if it's the last resort.

Pam had her fortieth birthday party at the roller skating rink. We entered the rink and saw photos that had been blown up of her as a teenager. The place was packed with people in their late thirties and older. We were doing something from our youth that we had not done in years. Five people were sent to the emergency room that night. One with a broken arm, another with a broken wrist and Momma, yes Momma, in her sixties with a broken tailbone. We weren't skating drunk and yet we had the time of our lives. Everybody had flashbacks of their youth at the skating rink.

The emergency room wanted to know whose party it was.

⟨⟨ 17 ⟩⟩
SEPTEMBER 11, 2001

I HAD JUST POURED a cup of coffee, sat down in my chair and turned on the television.

The phone rang. It was Pam, and she asked, "Do you have the television on? An airplane has just hit the Twin Towers in New York City."

Just as she was speaking I saw it on the television screen. I called Steve to come and look. My two teenagers, Stephen and Denice, ran down the stairs to see what all the screaming was about. At first we thought it was an airplane flying low, but within minutes a second one hit the other Twin Tower. Every television station was taken over at this time with live coverage of the Towers' collapsing as people jumped from windows. Every airport was shut down, and the world was watching and asking, "Are we at war? What do we need to do to protect ourselves and our families?"

We listened as the anchorman tried to help make some sense of what was happening. Our world was changing. The United States of America would stay under the constant threat of a terrorist attack.

MOMMA WAS NOW on pills due to high blood pressure. The doctor told her to drink a glass of red wine every evening and said it would help keep her blood pressure down. Leeann got her a gallon jug of cheap wine. Momma put it on top of her refrigerator. I told her I thought she should drink it. Every time I walked into her house I looked at that bottle and checked the wine level. It never changed. Momma was not drinking it. I ask her, why she said she didn't know.

One afternoon, I was hurrying to meet Pam and Momma at a baby shower for a young girl in our church. The phone rang and Steve answered it, he talked for a few seconds.

He hung up and said, "The drug store just called, your Mom is there and has fallen."

We jumped into the car, drove as fast as we could. It was only two blocks from our home. We drove up and saw a fire truck and an ambulance.

"*My God*" I yelled.

Running in, I saw paramedics around her.

They were trying to get her to speak. "Mrs. Burge, we are going to take you in the ambulance."

In a slow, slurred tone she said, "No, you are not."

I spoke up. "Momma, Yes they are."

Her body appeared paralyzed. One side of her face was different and I knew the signs looked like a stroke. I was following the ambulance. I took my mobile phone and called my brother and sisters. We had no idea how bad she was. She was paralyzed and over the next two months she could not speak or move. Pam and I stood out in the hallway and held each other's hands while praying for God to heal her or take her without leaving her like that. Momma had always been strong minded and independent. She was the glue in our family. We could not bear to see her in this state. She had movement on one side of her body as she lay in the hospital, but she was not able to communicate. We were devastated.

She was never left alone. She was taken to another floor to begin rehabilitation. We were told if she didn't show signs that she could do certain things, she would be sent home and most likely not improve. They moved her from the wheelchair to a mat that was raised to chair height. They then sat her down to see if she could sit alone. She began to slump over, lying helplessly on her side.

I sat down beside her and whispered in her ear, "Momma, please try with everything in you."

I started to cry uncontrollably. She was put back in her hospital bed.

A nurse at the rehab center said to me, "I have worked in other states at other rehabilitation hospitals, but I have never seen so many stroke victims like you see in the South."

I asked her, "Is it because of our fried food, high fat diet?"

She said it was because of the Bible belt. "You know most Southern Christians think it's a sin to have a glass of alcohol."

She didn't know she was talking to a preacher's wife.

The Bible talks about not drinking to excess and drunkenness. I always told Steve I wish it wasn't a sin because I thought it looked so romantic seeing a man and woman at a restaurant having a glass of wine together. The doctor had tried to get Momma to have a glass of wine. Doctors were talking about the health benefits of red wine. I began to do my own research on the matter, spiritually and medically. I knew preachers who drank in the South, but only in the privacy of their homes, as to not offend other Christians. I also knew preachers in the Northern states which thought Southern preachers took the scriptures to extreme by saying it's a sin. I was going to be open to God to show me if it was going to separate me from Him. Steve grew up in a home that had wine at the dinner table. We had preached in other countries where the preachers drank alcohol, but thought caffeine was a sin. Steve and I loved our cup of coffee every morning.

My journey began. I began having a glass of wine with my evening meal. At first I felt I was sinning. I had to ask myself, "Is this conviction of the Holy Spirit or is it guilt from the way I was raised?" I realized it was my upbringing. I know this; the bible says if you drink to excess it makes you act like a fool, just like overeating is bad for your health. I have seen severely overweight Christians judge people for drinking. Isn't it funny when you think about a three hundred pound Christian sitting there, eating a bowl of ice cream piled on top of a piece of cake, judging a person for drinking a glass of wine? They point their finger judging while they have four more fingers pointing back at them and they don't even know it. Funny Huh.

Now, I was telling you about us at the hospital. Janice, Pam and I stood around Momma in the hospital room. She was staring straight at the ceiling not even blinking. Her breathing was slow to the point that we could not tell if she was breathing.

Pam said, "I want to be the one to get Momma's last breath. I want to be there when she takes it so she can breathe into me, her anointing."

Momma had been kind, loving and a wonderful person, a mother who loved her children with every breath she took. She was anointed by God to be a Godly woman. Pam wanted Momma's anointing.

Janice laughed as she said, "What gives you the right to get her last breath."

The two of them were having this conversation and looking down at Mom.

I spoke up, "Neither one of you are going to get her last breath. I will be the one, so you two might as well stop arguing over it."

We all laughed at each other.

Janice, being a character, leaned down into Momma's face, looked into her eyes and said, "Is anybody in there?'

Pam pulled Janice away from Momma's face, "Janice, quit it."

Janice said again, "Is anybody in there?"

Momma's strong voice was as clear as words can be spoken, "You girls quit it."

Janice said, in a voice like the Exorcist movie. *"She's back."*

We laughed.

Momma would never totally recover. She spent the next six years in a wheelchair with the use of one arm and in a diaper. She could speak but she was helpless and fragile from then on. We shed so many tears over this. She moved in with Charlie and Jimmy, who became her caregivers. To this day I do not see how they did it as long as they did. Momma grew to love Jimmy and treat him like a son. He could not have been better to her if he were her own son. Charlie and Jimmy spoiled her in every way. Charlie played her Christian worship music while she ate her breakfast and let her watch her Christian TV channels all day long. Jimmy took Momma in her wheelchair to a little Methodist church nearby on Sundays.

I asked Mom several times over the next six years, "How do you deal with being in a wheelchair?"

She lifted that one arm into the air and declared, "I trust God."

I asked, "Do you ever get depressed about it?"

"Yes, but then I just turn my trust toward Him."

I asked, "Momma do you really believe it is wrong to drink alcohol?"

She answered, "No."

I ask, "Why did you teach us it was a sin?"

"Because my Momma told me it was a sin." She said.

I heard a story once about a mother who was teaching her daughter how to cook a ham in the oven the Southern way. She showed her daughter that you take the whole ham, set it on the cutting board and chop both ends of the ham off before you put it in your pot to stick in the oven. The daughter asked, "Why do you cut the ends off?"

Her Momma said, "I don't know. That's the way my Momma taught me how to cook a ham."

Suzy said, let's call grandmother and ask her why. Suzy's Momma called her mother and said, "I'm teaching Suzy how to cook a ham in the oven and we have a question. Why did you always cut both ends off the ham before you cooked it?" She laughed and said, "Because my pot was too small."

Traditions are past down from generation to generation until someone begins asking questions, even in the church. Some preachers are afraid to search for the truth, for it could cost them in their community. I say, *"Let's give them something to talk about."*

~~ 18 ~~
JERK THIS CAR IN REVERSE

S UMMER 2004 WAS BUSY with a fast growing church and ministers all over the country were calling Steve for help.

The family remained very significant in our lives. Stacy and her husband, Brian, bought the home across the street from us and were on staff at the church. They had a daughter, Stacy, and two sons, Sterling and Dylan. Misty had three children. Her oldest was Misty; a son, Cruise; and a baby girl, Navy. Stephen and Hillary had two sons, Stephen and Roman. Denice was married, but had no children yet.

It was a hot, humid summer evening in Alabama. Charlie brought Momma to stay with me for ten days while he and Jimmy went on a cruise. They desperately needed a break and it was a well-deserved one, since they had been taking care of Momma. I wanted to see if I could take care of her. Lifting her from her wheelchair was going to be challenging. I was dealing with my own pain from rheumatoid arthritis.

I had it all planned out. Steve was in Africa, so for two weeks and I was going to give her my total attention. It was going to be, Nellie's ten days at the spa. Since my master bedroom was downstairs and knowing there was no way I could get Momma up stairs to one of the guest bedrooms, I ordered a blow up Aero Bed mattress which I put on the floor in my bedroom. I knew she could not sleep with me.

I had to use a step stool to get into my bed. A blow-up bed placed on the floor that rose to the height of the box springs and mattress would be perfect. If she needed me during the night, I would be right there.

Several days before, I had gone to Hobby Lobby and bought a beautiful brown wicker basket and two bleached pine eight by ten photo frames. I filled the basket with Bath & Body Works products. Moonlight Path Bubble Bath, True Blue Spa soap, a butter creamy cleansing bar, Aromatherapy Spearmint Massage oil, sugar scrub, Cherry Blossom Moisturizing Cream. Each item was tied with a tiny satin ribbon bow in pale colors of pink, blue, lavender and green wrapped in soft netting. A bottle of Michael Kors Island perfume, and two new face towels in mint green and lavender were rolled up. Beside the basket placed on my garden tub were the two photo frames. Beautifully boarded in a soft sage green was written:

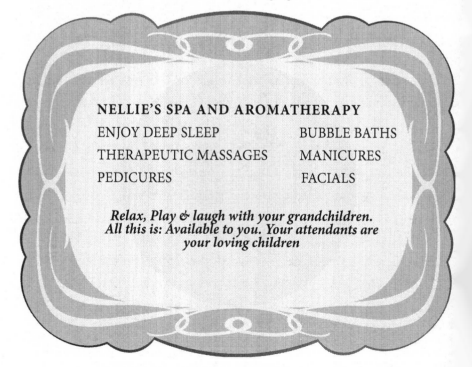

NELLIE'S SPA AND AROMATHERAPY

ENJOY DEEP SLEEP	BUBBLE BATHS
THERAPEUTIC MASSAGES	MANICURES
PEDICURES	FACIALS

Relax, Play & laugh with your grandchildren.
All this is: Available to you. Your attendants are
your loving children

The other 8X10 frame had this letter to Momma:

Dear Momma,

You are loved and adored. For the next ten days, I will bless you for all that you have done for me in my heart and my life. Every morning you will receive a full NELLIE'S SPA treatment. I will cook your favorite foods. We will watch your favorite movies together: Gone with the Wind, Titanic, and of course your boyfriend Mel Gibson's Man Without a Face are waiting for you. We will have a wonderful ten days together, and you will be reminded how much your children love you. No one has touched my life like you and now it is my time to be a blessing in your life. I love you, Momma.

With all my heart,
Love, Denice

CHARLIE AND JIMMY drove into the driveway that circles the front yard of my house. I ran out to greet them. I opened the backseat car door. Dancing and saying, "Where's my baby? Where's the Duchess?

Lifting her only good arm, she gave a queen's wave. The look on her face said it all. Her skin was soft, like a baby's. Her rosy, high cheekbones showed with a smile that lit up the world. She said, "Hey, Baby."

Charlie opened the trunk of the car, pulled out the wheelchair, snapped the footrest back on and threw the extra gel seat cushion into the chair.

I was busy kissing Momma all over her face as if she were a baby, while she laughed and said, "Oh, my girl."

I danced around as I sang, "Party, party. We are going to party."

Charlie was trying to get me to move out of the way so he could lift her out of the car and place her in a wheelchair. Jimmy pulled the luggage out of the back seat.

I said, "Y'all come on in."

Jimmy carried her luggage into my bedroom along with her portable potty-chair and large brown paper bag with extra diapers, bed pads, and her medications. Charlie wheeled Momma into the living room and began to explain her medications. He was very organized. He had written instructions on how to dispense her medications. He had also written how many and what to give her in case she was in pain.

I said, "Charlie, I've got it. Don't worry. We will be fine. We are going to have our own vacation while you and Jimmy are on yours."

Charlie looked at me and said, "I'm not going to think about anything but myself while I am gone."

I said, "Go have fun."

They left for their cruise. He and Jimmy were ready to vacation.

254

I was ready and willing to give Momma the works. We ate a snack and then it was time to put her to bed. I gave her the medicines for the evening and pulled the potty chair up side by side to the wheelchair.

"I'm going to stand you up and you lean toward me."

"Denice, are you sure you can do this?" She questioned.

I assured her that together we could do this, but her fear of falling made me scared. I moved her footrest back from the wheelchair and placed her tennis shoe enclosed feet firmly on the floor.

I said in a calm, loving voice. "Momma, put your good arm around my neck."

I began to lift her and pain shot up from my arthritic hands. Momma tensed up and screamed out in pain, scaring us both.

"You're killing me! God help me!" she screamed.

"Momma, try not to tense up. You're stiffening your legs and I don't want to drop you."

She yelled, "Lord, help us."

I felt helpless. But, bless her heart she was helpless. I could not let her fall. I had to take all the weight because she was unable to help. I twisted her dead weight over to the porta-potty and I tried to pull down her navy blue sweat pants and diaper at the same time.

"Thank you, Lord," she shouted out and gave her Queens wave to God. The sweat was pouring from my armpits as my heavy breathing was calmed down.

"Thank you, Lord" I gave my own shout out.

She responded with a gasp, "Yes, thank you Lord"

I said, "Momma, sit and do you're business while I take your pants, shoes and socks off."

She began to sing while she was on the potty. "Oh-s-a-ma-me-ah, how much I love you, how I adore you," smiling as she sang.

I told her, "Let's put your night shirt on you while you're on the potty."

It was a large man's T-shirt. I said, "Then we will get you into bed and I will put a fresh diaper on you."

I realized I was going to have to go through that ordeal to get her back into the wheelchair and then from the wheelchair to the Aero bed. I finally got Momma into bed and placed extra washrags in her diaper to help absorb the urine. I put on her white support stockings and her night leg braces, gave her pills, and slid her neck pillow under her neck. I kissed her face and said, "Now go to sleep, Creep."

She laughed as I pulled the top sheet up under her chin. I teased her and she loved it when I called her *"Creep"*.

I began to pray over her. "God, thank-you for blessing me with Momma. Give her good sleep tonight. Help her not to have pain so that she will wake-up rested in the morning, Amen."

She took over the prayer and prayed that Charlie and Jimmy would have a good time on their cruise. Momma prayed over all her children, grandchildren and great grandchildren. There were forty-five people she prayed for and that included Jimmy and Charlie's dogs, the boxers, Wes and Frankie. She finished with, "God bless my Denice for taking care of me. Amen."

I gave her one last kiss on the lips. "I love you, Momma. Good night."

I woke the next morning to the thought. I did not hear a sound out of her all night. I looked over to her to find that her aero bed had deflated. Her body was flat on the floor, her face covered by the sheet and the air that was left in the mattress had formed a taco around her. I leaped from my bed, panicked and thought, "Oh no, I have killed Momma."

Pulling the sheet back from her face, I shouted, "Momma, are you all right?"

Her eyes opened wide as she said, "I slept wonderfully!" Her skin was smooth and cheeks were rosy. Her smile lit up my heart.

I said, "Momma, your mattress deflated."

She laughed. My mind was racing. How was I going to lift dead-weight off the floor? I put my arms under her arms and lifted her into the wheelchair. I knew my back would hurt that night. The arthritis pain would go straight to my spine.

I said, "I am going to start a bubble bath and then we will get you into the tub."

She loved laying in a hot tub for as long as you would let her. Throwing her right arm up in the air with a smile as big as the world, she said, "Yes, yes, yes. Amen. Yea!"

I started the tub and then returned to wheel her into the bath-room to find that the wheelchair would not fit through the bathroom door.

"Don't worry, Momma. I have another plan." I said assuring her I could handle anything.

She waited until I returned from the storage room with a desk chair on wheels. It had a black leather seat and back with no armrest. I shifted her body from the wheelchair over to the office chair on wheels. I rolled her into the bathroom where the tub was filled with bubbles. For the next ten days, it was a constant effort to maneuver her from wheelchair to potty-chair to the Lazy Boy chair in my living room and into the tub or shower. She relaxed in her bath as I sat on the side of the tub to visit while she soaked in her bubbles. I began to show her all her beauty products in the basket I had made up for her. I read to her what the two picture frames said.

She made her declaration, giving her wave to God, smiling while enjoying all the pampering, "I am blessed, yes, I am blessed."

I said, "Momma, your skin is dry. Let's add oil to the water."

She said, "Denice, you are so good to me. All my children are. I am so blessed. Yes, I'm blessed. I'm blessed. Amen!"

I poured the oil into the bathtub and said to her, "You deserve to be blessed. You are a wonderful Momma."

She raised her hand in the air and said, "I love my children with every breath that is within me."

I smiled and said, "All right, you little brat. I am going to go start your breakfast. You lie here and relax."

She laughed at me for calling her a brat.

She said, "You're such a crazy girl Denice."

I returned telling her it was time to get out. "Let's drain the tub so that I can stand in it to lift you out." I began to lift her and realized she was slippery from the oil. I knew I would not be able to do this on my own.

I called Janice, "I have a problem."

Janice asked in a tone like, I told you so, "*What have you done to Momma?*"

I dreaded telling her, "I put oil in her bathwater and now she is too slippery for me to get her out of the tub."

Janice said, "I told you this was going to be too hard for you."

I firmly said, "Janice, let's don't go there." I was already having a bad start.

She said, "Don't move her. I will be there in a few minutes." Janice and I were able to get her out.

Every night for the next few nights, I cried myself to sleep, soaking the pillow with my silent tears. I was angry that taking care of her was so hard. I was angry that my body hurt and I felt sorry for myself. I was not physically able to do this. It was much harder than taking care of a baby. She would feel she needed to get on her potty chair, then after all the maneuvering, she'd find out she didn't need to go. This would occur every few minutes. Finally, she would end up going in her diaper.

I wanted this to work so that she could stay with me more often. She thanked me continually. Bless her heart, she was so grateful. The pain in my own body fought me every move I made.

By the time Charlie and Jimmy arrived from their trip, I was glad that day had come. I was going to miss her, but my body was in pain and I needed to crash and recover. Jimmy spent the night with his parents. Charlie slept upstairs in one of my guest rooms. My kids were older now and had their own places.

The next morning she was still sleeping when I went outside and found Charlie sitting by the pool having a cup of coffee and smoking a cigarette. I poured myself a cup of coffee and joined him. I told him all that had occurred while he was gone. We drank our coffee and laughed.

I said, "Charlie, I don't see how you do it."

He looked at me and said, "Sometimes I go out in the backyard and throw a fit and cry by myself, but I know I am doing the right thing. I will not regret taking care of Mom."

I looked at him and said, "If it ever gets to be too much, just let us know. We will put her in a nursing home and visit her every day."

"I cannot do that," he said.

Changing the subject, I said, "Charlie, I woke up with a thought. I read that at Office Depot you can get a will. As long as the person signs it, and it is notarized, it nullifies all other wills. I was thinking we could put Momma in the car, call Pam and Janice and all go see Daddy. We will get him to do a new will. I am sure he has left everything to some woman who doesn't even matter."

Charlie took a drag from his cigarette, looked over at me and said, "I don't want anything he has."

I looked at him and said, "All of us girls are taken care of by our spouses. We live in the finest neighborhoods and are so blessed. You deserve to inherit whatever he has. You are the only son. He never did anything good for any of us and he needs to make it right. We can at least try."

He agreed.

I called Pam and Janice. Leeann was working at her decorating business. I didn't call her. It was hard for her to take time off. Pam drove her Suburban, which accommodated all of us, including Momma's wheelchair. We headed toward Birmingham. It was about two hours away.

I called him, "Is this Charles Perkins?"

He said, "Yes, this is Charlie." He sounded very old.

I said, "This is Denice, your daughter. Momma, Charlie, Pam, Janice and I thought we would come visit you today."

He said, "Well y'all come on." He gave me directions to his house.

It was a small, red brick house with an attached rusty, metal carport and a small front porch that Daddy must have built with some old lumber. There were four steps leading up to the front door. There was neither stain nor paint on the wood. The house was dilapidated.

Sitting in white plastic chairs were two old looking men. I was not sure which one was Daddy. We pulled up in the dirt driveway and they stood up.

Immediately, I knew who Daddy was. The tall man bent over from years of back problems. The wrinkles on his face looked like a road map. His face said it all. He had been run over by life. The thing about life, nobody gets a free ride. I could see that he was balding, his hair had turned gray, and his body was thin and frail. His old shinny, worn, dress pants were gathered up. The belt kept them from falling down. He had on a white, baggy dress shirt with the sleeves rolled up. It appeared as if to be a hand-me-down.

A short, chubby, bald man walked down the steps to greet us with a big smile on his face. Charlie got Momma out of the car. Pam, Janice and I walked over to say hello.

I spoke up first. "Hello."

I walked towards him, extending my hand to shake his.

He said, "Hey, I am your Uncle Jeb."

"Uncle Jeb, it's, good to see yah."

Momma had always told us about Daddy's brother, Jeb. She said he was a kind Christian man.

I walked toward the steps and saw Daddy.

He smiled, "Y'all come on in." I noticed he did not have any teeth.

We got Momma's wheelchair situated in the living room. Daddy walked slowly, bent over. He moved toward his chair gasping for breath. He sat down in his recliner and put on his oxygen tube that was attached to an oxygen tank that had been placed next to his recliner.

He said, "I had open heart surgery a few weeks ago. "His black dog poodle jumped onto his lap as he continued talking about himself. "I can't breathe. I have to use this oxygen tank."

My eyes began to scan the room. I had a flashback, as a teenager. I had stopped by his house when he was living with his new bride, Marie. Their new furniture was still fresh in my memory. I am fifty-three, Pam fifty-five, Janice fifty-seven, Charlie forty-six, and Momma, wheelchair bound, was eighty years old. It has been over forty years and he still had the same furniture.

Daddy's brother was talking about a time when he and his wife were young. "Your Momma took my wife and me to a tent revival and we accepted Christ as our savior."

I glanced over at Uncle Jeb as he was talking about the tent revival and how it made the difference in his life. Momma smiled as she enjoyed the memory. She nodded as he talked.

I was still scanning the room. I was amazed to find that things that had seemed so beautiful and expensive were not at all what I had thought. The sofa was cheap, the shinny, two end tables and matching coffee table were shiny because they were Formica. They were not real wood. The two matching lamps were cheap metal. The oil painting on the wall was now just a faded print. There stood the same stereo cabinet that played old 45 records and a radio. The brass wall sconces were not brass they were plastic. They did not house silk flowers in them, they held plastic. He was sitting in the same green recliner that was not even leather. It was vinyl.

I no longer had the innocent eyes that I once had in my youth. I could now see things as they really were. Just like he had me as a child, planting plastic tulips in the winter, his house and life was all plastic. Fake, he always was the great pretender, not the real deal.

My brother Charlie and Uncle Jeb had pulled chairs up from the kitchen table next to Momma's wheelchair. I grabbed one and pulled it near Daddy. Janice and Pam were sitting on the sofa. After a few minutes of small talk, I spoke up.

"Daddy, since Momma and Charlie were in town visiting, I decided to get all of us together to talk to you about your will. All of us girls are very successful and blessed."

I looked over at Janice and pointed toward her, "That is Janice, your oldest child. She is married to a retired Colonel who worked at the Pentagon. Pam is married to a doctor and I am married to a successful minister. Leeann owns her own business but Charlie has had to stop working to take care of Momma and we send money every month to help with the expenses. We all agree that it is only right for you to leave everything to Charlie."

He looked at me and said, "I am not leaving you kids anything. You kids never came to see me. I put all y'all through college and you never did a thing for me. You kids were never any good. I tried my best with y'all but you were just no good."

I pulled my chair closer, right up in front of him to get in his face. I said, "First of all, you never paid your child support and you did not send us to college. We were all high school dropouts. You never came around to see us. It was not our responsibility to see you. You were an adult and we were the children. Only one time I remember you were going to take us for ice cream and you never showed up. I waited by the window all day. The only time we ever saw you was when you whipped in and out of town with a new woman in the car. You owe Charlie and you need to make up for your failure as a father."

He responded, "I'm not doing it. You kids were never any good."

Charlie spoke up, "Denice it doesn't matter," and then Charlie looked at Daddy and said, "Can I just ask you for something? Can you take your glasses off and let me see the color of your eyes?"

We were all brown eyed and Charlie had green eyes. Daddy removed his glasses.

Charlie said, "They're the same as mine—green." He then took Daddy's hands and compared the palms of their hands side by side and said, "We have the same hands."

I felt a moment of sadness. Charlie was looking for his identity in Daddy. He had been raised with girls. Charlie had never been around Daddy, yet he was built and looked so much like the younger version of his father. Charlie had all the charm that Daddy had had at one time, but he was not at all like Daddy. Charlie was an honest, loving, caring man, not at all like Daddy.

I didn't feel Daddy was even worthy of Charlie touching his hand

I stood and looked directly in his eyes and with firmness said, "Here is the will. Do one thing right in your life for you're children. Make everything right in the end of your life."

He responded, "No, I'm not doing anything for you kids." I bent down to make sure we looked eye to eye.

I said. "If you do not do what I am asking you to do, I will one day look down at you in your coffin and say, "You never made it right. You never did one good thing toward your children."

Then I stood up to leave. I turned and said, "I am going to leave this will on your table. If you change your mind, our phone numbers are on another paper there."

Pam spoke up as she was pulling out of her purse her Polaroid camera, "Daddy, can I get a picture of you?"

Pam flashed the image of him in his recliner with his oxygen tube in his nose. Then he stood as we were leaving. She shook his hand and said. "This is good-bye. I will never see you again."

At that moment, I felt something odd. It was like an electric current went through my body when she said that. I thought, how odd. I guess she just needed closure. Her words seemed so final and matter-of-fact. We all walked outside, as Charlie was busy putting Momma and her wheelchair in the car.

I took Uncle Jeb aside and told him, "I know you don't know us and I am sure we seem like horrible people, but Daddy molested Charlie when he was young and exposed himself to his daughters. He owes Charlie. He needs to do this one thing right."

Uncle Jeb shook his head as he made a groan like he wanted to spit at that news.

He said, "Denice I know y'all do not know this, but I have not been around your Daddy in years. I do not know him very well. He called me and said y'all were coming and bringing your Momma, so I wanted to see her. I do know this one thing. He will not be coming around my children and grandchildren."

I said, "Uncle Jeb, Momma always spoke highly of you."

I wish we had gotten to know him. I could tell he was a wonderful man. He spoke about his children and grandchildren in a loving way. We all loaded up in Pam's car to back out of the driveway.

Pam turned the ignition on and looked in her rearview mirror and said. "Daddy is standing behind the car. I can't back out of the driveway."

Charlie spoke-up, "Jerk this car in reverse and run over that ass-hole."

We all broke out into laughter. It needed to be said and Charlie needed to be the one to say it. It was as if he had said, "I am above you and you are beneath me, you're just a dirty spot under my shoe."

Daddy stood broken down from his self-absorbed life. Nothing ever came of that visit.

I went back to see him on my own one more time. I did not care about his will. I needed one last chance to see if there was anything about him that I could find that would change my opinion of him. One last chance on my own, to make sure I had given him every opportunity to show me the good side of himself. I packed my luggage and told Steve I might stay a few days if it went well.

Driving there, I pictured us spending a few days together laughing, me telling him about my life, the things I had seen and done. I'd tell him about my children and how much I love them. I would tell him about the foreign countries I have visited and the wells we put in for villages that needed water. I could tell him about writing my first novel. I thought about what it could be like to have a conversation with my daddy. The kind of things a dad should know about his daughter.

I arrived at his house. I went in leaving my luggage in the car. I sat with him and he said the same old things. He told lies about Momma and lies about the women in his life. He talked about how they all used him and left him for other men, how he worked so hard as a provider.

He said, "And you know, you' kids never were any good. I tried, but you kids were a disappointment."

I almost laughed out loud when he said that. It was like a skunk telling a bunny rabbit, *"You stink"*. Can you picture that? I asked him to tell me about his childhood and that's when he told me about the old fashioned hoedowns and leaving the country to go into the city. He seemed to enjoy talking about that. I heard he was performing abortions, pretending to be a doctor. How much of that was true I will never know.

I asked, "How did you become a doctor without getting an education?"

He said, "On the job training."

I asked him if he was ready to meet the Lord. His black poodle was in his lap as he was petting that dog. He said, "Wherever this dog goes is where I want to be." I think he loved that dog. He had never felt that way about me. Isn't that sad? I sat there thinking that if his lips are moving, he's lying. There is an old Indian Proverb, which states, "Listening to a liar is like drinking warm water."

We went down the road to a country store and got barbecue sandwiches. He introduced me to the woman behind the counter, "This is my daughter."

I had never been called that before. It felt strange. I dropped him off at his house and then drove the hundred miles home. It was settled. He could never be the Daddy I longed for and it was okay. He did not ever love me and I was ok with it. I was glad I went to see him. It was to be the last time I saw him alive.

~∾ 19 ∾~
SOUTHERN WOMEN AND
LITTLE WHITE LIES

A FEW WEEKS HAD PASSED. Momma was back in Atlanta with Charlie. Pam, Janice and I drove to Atlanta to spend the day with her, letting her pick where we were going to go eat. Sometimes we stayed overnight at a hotel near Charlie's house.

The three of us enjoyed the drive to Atlanta. We played a game we made up, which we called Southern Women and Little White Lies. We made up stories about a small little Southern town. It had an ice-cream parlor, beauty parlor, post office, and the corner drug store. There was a First Methodist Church that most people attended in the town, where they showed up in their Sunday best. We spoke very Southern, with a deep Southern lazy drawl, as we told our made up stories. There were the two old-maid sisters, retired schoolteachers. They were always serving Papa's recipe in their china teacups and talking about the Civil War and how they had hidden their silver trays and candlesticks under the front porch.

We had many Southern women in this made up town and told the latest gossip going on in their lives. We laughed so hard we cried. We interrupted each other to add our part of the gossip. I always brought the town slut in on the story. Being a pastor's wife, I just wasn't given to gossip and calling people sluts and whores. Every now and then, reiterating to my sisters, it was the town whore speaking.

I told them, "The men at the barbershop named her the town bicycle because everyone gets a ride." Pam and Janice screamed out in laughter when I talked about her entering the corner drug store or a beauty parlor. I understand that a preacher's wife should not talk like this, but it was just between us sisters. It was a fun time and a wonderful memory of our times together.

It was one of these trips when Pam told us something that really happened to her the week before. "I received a phone call from one of my friends. Her husband was the owner and CEO of a very large corporation," Pam said to us, "You know how Southern she is, very slow and soft spoken. She said to me, *I did something and I am so ashamed, Pam. I had to call you and tell you what I did.*"

Pam asked, "Savannah, what did you do?"

She said, "You know it's Christmas, and again it is time for our annual Christmas party for the company. My husband informed me I was not welcome this year, but that I had to prepare and send my special Christmas punch. My punch is always the hit of the party."

She went on, "Pam, I knew why I wasn't invited this year. My husband had an affair with that slut of a secretary in his office. He informed me he would take the Christmas punch to the party. Pam, I pulled out my fine crystal punch bowl that my grandmother left me. I began to mix my special recipe. I thought about not being included and that slut of a whore would be standing around my crystal punch bowl, drinking my punch. I just felt faint at the thought of it. I walked over to my cupboard and pulled out a teacup. You know my fine chine, the one my grandmother left me in her will. Well Pam, I hate to tell you, but I peed in that tea cup and added it to the punch."

Pam gasped, "Savannah you didn't?"

"Oh, yes I did. He left with the punch bowl and my special recipe and I went into my master bathroom, put on my beautiful long sexy nightgown, a black lace one he gave me for our anniversary. I fixed my

hair and makeup and put on my favorite perfume. I turned on romantic music, lit a fire in the fireplace, and poured a glass of red wine. Pam, as I relaxed in front of that fire, I pictured that party around my punch bowl with that slut drinking my Christmas punch. Pam, I could hardly contain the laughter. It was the most marvelous evening around the fire. I felt fabulous. My husband walked in after the party, carrying the empty bunch bowl." He said, "Well, Savannah, as usual, your punch was the hit of the Christmas Party." "He was grinning from ear to ear. You know that smirk smile of his". I smiled and said, "I am so glad they enjoyed it and did you have some yourself?" He said. "Of course I did. I love your punch recipe!" I smiled at him as I sipped on my wine and said, "Well, that's just marvelous." He went to go shower. I poured another glass of wine. I was very relaxed. I guess I was even a little tipsy. I kid you not, I felt powerful. It was most definitely a triumphant feeling!" "Do you think I'm a bad person, Pam? Do you think I'm bad to the bone?"

Janice and I were screaming with laughter while Pam was telling us about this true incident.

Southern women have a way about them that puts off an air that they are made of fine china. Though the surface may look like fine china underneath, there is a devil waiting to be released. When push comes to shove, a Southern woman will leave you scratched and bleeding.

We continued to make memories with Momma. Pam, Janice, Leeann and I took her to see New York. We all met at the airport in Montgomery. I got out of the car with a jam box playing a CD real loud so Momma could hear it. It was Frank Sinatra singing, "Start Spreading the News, New York, New York"

We rented a limo in New York and we had the limo driver play it for Momma. She wiggled in her seat, moving to the music. Pam and Janice also took her to Atlanta, Georgia, to hear Andrea Bocelli. She loved every minute of it.

MY MISTY WENT through a divorce. We stood beside our daughter to hold her up in her pain. I still find it peculiar how people are so quick to judge and whisper instead of praying. I learned that until you have walked in someone else's shoes, keep silent and pray. There were those people Steve and I over the years stood with, in their time of trouble, and they too whispered about my daughter. I cannot relate to that kind of friend but I forgave them, they never knew I heard their words.

Life is good. Life goes on. We always are looking forward to the future and not looking back. Life is Beautiful.

20
RUN TOWARD THE LIGHT, CROSS OVER

ONE EVENING, AS I was in the kitchen making a big pot of homemade chili for supper. I noticed Pam drive up. She pulled in around to the side and came in through my back door. It wasn't unusual for her to drop by, but the look on her face as she opened the door told me something was wrong. I turned the burner down low, so that we could talk. "What's up?"

I placed two glasses of sweet tea down on the table for us to drink. She sat down and took a sip of tea. Her bottom lip shook as she struggled to hold back her tears.

I asked again, "Pam, what's wrong?"

She paused, looked down at her glass of tea, giving much thought to her next words and she said, "Denice I think I am going to die."

"Pam, why do you feel this?" I asked in concern.

She said, "I don't know Denice. I just do." She began to cry.

I reached over to comfort her and I told her she might be having a hormone imbalance or depression. Maybe it was as simple as getting on hormone pills or an antidepressant.

She said, "It's just a feeling, a sense inside of me, that I'm going to die."

I began to rebuke her and tell her to stop confessing that. I reminded her of what the Bible says about the power of the tongue.

"Pam, you know the Bible says, *I set before you, Life and Death. Choose which way you will go.*"

She shook her head and said, "I know you're right."

Pam was a real intercessor. She could hear from God. It really bothered me. Pam did not live in fear, not at all. She was delivered. She totally trusted God.

I told her, "Now you go tomorrow and see your doctor. Get him to check your hormones and talk to him about putting you on an antidepressant. Do you hear me Pam?"

We prayed together and that was that.

She wiped away her tears with her Kleenex. She nodded her head in agreement.

She said, "Maybe you're right. It is my hormones."

"You're going to be all right Pam," I assured her.

It was a few months later that Pam started saying," I'm having trouble driving, staying in the lane."

She said her husband did not want her to drive anymore until she finds out what her problem was.

I told her, "Pam that sounds like you may be having inner ear problems, like vertigo. You need to go to an ENT doctor."

I was off my feet for five weeks. I had just had one of many foot surgeries. The rheumatoid arthritis had curled my toes and I had them straightened with pins that were sticking out of each toe. I had to keep my feet propped up as I watched TV all day.

Pam was able to get right in to see an ENT. Pam and Janice stopped by to see me after the appointment, informing me that he wanted Pam to go have a brain scan.

My response was. "That makes sense." No big deal to me, just good sense.

Later that evening, I had just finished my bath, when the bathroom phone rang.

It was Janice, "Denice, Pam has something seriously wrong."

I responded, "Why are you thinking that? It is going to be vertigo." Janice was always a drama queen, so I was not going to let her go there.

I was still on week four of staying off my foot, so Janice took Pam for the brain scan. They came by my house after they had gone to lunch and Pam still had no answers. That afternoon Pam's husband received a call from the doctor.

He said, "I need you and Pam at my office tomorrow morning."

The next day after they met with the doctor, Pam called me and told me there was a tumor on her brain and that the doctor wants her to get a full body PET scan. I immediately called Janice.

"Denice, I told you" she responded.

I then said back to her, "Everything is going to be all right, Janice."

My insides shook to the core as I realized Pam was in trouble. This can't be happening. Janice took Pam for her PET scan. The doctor called again, requesting Pam and her husband come to his office. That afternoon after the appointment, they came straight to my house. I had my foot propped up watching Ted Turner's old classics on the movie channel. Steve was out of town and I was alone.

Pam sat and pulled a Kleenex out of her purse. She began to fold it into that perfect square she always made and then a triangle to catch her tears. Her husband began to tell me that the cancer had started in her pancreas and had spread to her brain. She had pancreatic cancer and a brain tumor.

As those words came out of his mouth, I looked at Pam and watched her catching her tears from the corners of her eyes with her Kleenex. She looked helpless at that moment. Her husband was still talking while my mind was trying to take it all in. Pancreatic cancer and brain tumor were overwhelming words. I thought to myself, I'm not hearing this. This is not real. My mind screamed in silence, "MY GOD!"

He continued, "The doctor says the brain tumor will take her before the cancer in the pancreas. She has eight to twelve weeks to live if left untreated, if treated they might be able to give her a year to year and a half."

I was taken back. Was I really hearing this? Pam wiped her eyes as her bottom lip quivered. She cried quietly and then she was still.

She spoke in a weak, trembling voice, "If they can only give me a year I am not going to have treatment."

Fight rose up within me, so I looked at Pam and said, "We know how to fight this battle. We have been here before with Momma. God will do it again for us, Pam. We are not quitters. We are fighters. We know who our God is." She wept. She nodded her head agreeing with me, wiping away her tears.

I looked at her and said, "Pam, you will get treatment and you will live and not die. God will make a way of escape for you. We will beat this. You will fight and there will be no giving up. We will look the world over for a cure. We will beat this." I declared.

They both agreed. Pam and her husband went home. Steve was out of town and I was in shock. I had a gut feeling. It was a knowing that was settled in my soul. She was not going to beat this. This was a battle we were not going to win.

When Momma was told she was dying of cancer there was a gift of faith present, but this one was different. There was a knowing that the supernatural faith was not there. It's hard to explain until you have walked in it. I picked up the phone and called the church. My oldest daughter's spouse, Brian, was the assistant pastor. My son Stephen worked in our television ministry. Our youngest daughter Denice worked in the youth ministry. I called Brian.

"Brian, come home!" I screamed and hung up the phone. That's all I could say. Within minutes, my daughters Stacy, Misty, and Denice, with their spouses, along with Stephen and his wife Hillary, all drove up.

Stacy ran in and asked, "Momma what is wrong?"

I could see the look of fear on her face as she asked. They all thought that I was going to tell them their Daddy was dead. Steve was flying his own plane and their first thought was that I was going to say there had been a plane crash. My children had never seen me like this. I was doubled over in my chair screaming a blood-curdling scream until I thought my head was going to burst as I talked through the horror of the moment.

"Pam is dying." I said those words "dying" and hopelessness overcame me. I screamed and cried. I covered my face with my hands to muffle the scream. I had a flashback of her shaking Daddy's hand. "This is good-bye. I will never see you again." I remember when she came walking into my kitchen crying, "Denice, I think I am going to die." My kids were crying for Pam and they were crying because the mother who had always been so strong was folded over in despair. I cried from my gut.

I called Janice, "Janice, Pam is dying." I cried.

Janice said, "Denice I told you it was bad."

I said, "My God Janice, this can't be happening."

Janice said she would go by Leeann's store to tell her and I called Charlie. He began to sob over the phone.

"Charlie, I am coming to Atlanta in the morning to see my foot doctor and get these pins taken out so I can walk. Please do not tell Momma until I get there. I want to be there when she is told." I could not bear the thought of her being told her daughter was going to die before her.

I called Daddy to tell him the bad news. "Daddy, I called because, I felt you should know that one of your children has been told by the doctors she has cancer and is going to die."

"Which one?" he asked.

"It's Pam, Daddy," I said.

His response was, "Well I haven't been feeling very well lately myself."

I said, "Do you understand what I just told you? One of your children is going to die."

He answered me, "Ever since I had my heart bypass surgery I just haven't felt good either."

I then said, "You know, when I was a little girl I remember thinking you were a fool and now I am in my fifties and I realize you are still a fool, just an older fool. I will never call you again."

I hung up. I don't know why, but I still wanted to think he would care. It was just not in him to care. My mind could not comprehend a parent not feeling pain of the news their child is dying.

The next morning I explained to my foot doctor why he had to take the pins out. I wore a special shoe for a few more weeks. I went straight to Charlie's house. Momma was sitting in the living room. I wasn't sure if Charlie had already told her.

Pulling a footstool up close to her, I said, "Momma, Pam has some bad news." She looked at me.

I said, "Mom, the doctors found a brain tumor. It's cancer in Pam's brain and pancreas. They have given her eight to twelve weeks left to live."

Momma lifted her hand in the air with her face tilted upward as she said, "God, my baby, my baby. God, my baby," she moaned a moan so deep and agonizing I could feel it inside my soul.

She made her declaration, "God I trust you. I trust you God." She made her hand into a fist toward heaven saying again, "I trust you God."

I knew Pam was not going to make it.

I said, "Momma, if Pam goes before you, Pam will be there waiting for you, to show you heaven."

She nodded, "Yes." She was trembling in her wheelchair, like the wind had been knocked out of her. We held hands as we prayed together and then I grabbed her face between my hands, kissing it all over.

"I love you, Momma."

I said," Janice, Pam and I will not be coming to Atlanta. We will be busy taking Pam to her treatments."

She said, "I will come see y'all."

On my drive back to Montgomery, I called Janice on my cell phone. We agreed that together we would take Pam for her chemo and brain radiation treatments. We agreed she would not be allowed to be alone for one moment. I could not stand the idea of her being awake, alone in the house with her thoughts. Janice and I agreed that together we would walk this journey with Pam.

Steve and I hired a contractor to remodel our house, a total facelift on the inside and outside. The outside would go from looking like a two story brick house to a two-story stucco and stone. We added a slate walkway going up to the front porch that was all stone and slate. Inside, the floors would be travertine on the main floor with hardwood floors upstairs. The house would look brand-new, even the landscaping in the front and back and around the pool.

To do all this work Steve and I had to move out, so we rented a house at Lake Martin. We knew it would be peaceful on the lake. Every day Steve and I drove to Montgomery, dealing with the contractor and the church. I would go to Pam's to meet up with Janice.

I arrived at Pam's. The housekeeper was working in the kitchen. Pam was either soaking in her garden tub, or putting on makeup, getting herself ready to go out for the day.

Her doctor had said the brain tumor would take Pam before the cancer in the pancreas. He said pancreatic cancer is the most painful death and that the tumor in the brain could be a blessing.

Pam decided to fight. She began treatment, attempting to shrink the tumor on the brain with radiation therapy followed by intravenous (IV) Chemo Therapy to attack the cancer in the rest of her body. We all understood these treatments would only give her months to a year to live. It was not going to be a cure. I spent most of my nights awake praying for God to give us a miracle, trying to connect with faith. Faith that had a knowing God was going to pull this off, a miracle. I just couldn't get it. I would fall asleep at night and after only a few hours of sleep, I would awake with the horrible thought that Pam's dying. This can't be real. It was a hopeless feeling. I searched the worldwide web looking for a cure. I knew she was dying, but she was not dead yet.

Every day Janice, Pam and I drove to the cancer treatment center for Pam's treatment or to see her doctor. There were times she was so weak she had to walk arm in arm between us, prompting the memory of us, as we slept as children. Pam asking to wrap her arms and legs over and around us, so she could sleep without fear. Here we were again. This time the boogeyman was going to get her and we knew it. My God help us, we are fragile. I felt her slipping out of our hands. Life was so fragile. I was smothering, I could not show it, she was my sister and she needed me to be strong.

One morning, as I was sitting on the side of the garden tub talking to Pam while she shampooed her hair, she began to pour the fresh water over her head with a plastic container. Loose hair fell into the tub. Pam touched her head and a hand full of hair came out into her hand. She started crying, holding her hair in her hand.

I said, "Pam, you're so beautiful. Just put on some big earrings and strut your stuff."

She said, "I guess I should go to my hair dresser and get her to shave the rest off."

I said, "I will get her to shave me, too."

"Oh no, you won't," she responded firmly. "If you shave your head you will be the only bald one. I'm going to get me a wig."

I laughed. "Let's do that, today." We walked into the salon Pam had used for years. We saw the same hairdresser who for years had adored Pam. Pam's hairdresser was busy blow-drying a client's hair. She saw us walk in.

I said, "Peggy, does Jennifer have time to shave Pam's head?"

Jennifer walked in to the back room. Peggy walked back to talk to Jennifer and then came back to the counter and said, "Jennifer doesn't have time, but I will be glad to do it for you and it will be free."

I knew Jennifer had already heard Pam's prognosis and I could tell Pam knew Jennifer went to the back to cry. Pam had come prepared with a silk scarf to tie on her baldhead. We found a blonde wig that looked just like Pam's hair. I always joked about her hair. She kept the same hairstyle for years. It looked like a football helmet with bangs, always perfect.

We found a second wig that was far from who she was. It was a long blonde straight wig that fell to the middle of her back. It was very sexy, not at all Pam's usual classy style. She was fifty-five years old, but she wore it out in public anyway. She got a kick out of it. It was if to say, "What does it matter anymore? I'll just have fun with it. Who cares what people think?" I knew people in the city would find Pam's choice in wigs a little daring, but Janice and I enjoyed every moment of her wearing it.

Every day the same conversation came up between Janice and Pam. Janice would say, "Now, Pam, if you don't get your miracle and you take your last breath, when you start going toward the light, I want you to choose to come back because we will be standing over you asking God to give you back, to put you back into your body."

Pam agreed to make a decision, not to go toward the light.

She always said, "I'm not going to have to do that because I'm not going to die Janice."

Janice brought that up and sometimes Pam would stop her in the middle of the conversation and say, "I know, don't run toward the light."

We all laughed because this was a conversation, in the middle of our lunch or while shopping at the mall and as we looked through racks of clothes, pointing out cute tops or pants.

Again Janice would ask her, "Now what do you do as you feel yourself going toward the light?"

Pam would respond, "I don't go to the light."

We spent the days getting her treatment and then shopping until we dropped. We returned to Pam's house in time to watch TV until her husband came home from his office. Sometimes Pam would feel weak and she would go to bed. She always wanted Janice to come tuck her in. Pam would be in her pretty pajamas and a pair of white socks to keep her feet warm. She would go over to the bed that was already made up. Carefully, in a very neat manner, she would perform the same routine, pull the corner of her bed spread back and then take the corner of her sheet pulling it back even with the spread, smoothing the sheet with her hand, the way hotels do when they fix your bed for you in the evenings. This particular day, as Pam lay down on the bed, she waited for Janice to pull the cover over her. I think Pam didn't want to do it because she might get her pajamas wrinkled and Pam liked Janice babying her anyway. Janice pulled the sheet up under Pam's chin and then the bedspread just like Pam liked it.

This time Janice grabbed a pillow and started going with it toward her face saying, "Now I'm going to send you to Jesus, close your eyes," she said laughing.

Pam pushed it away from her face laughing, "Quit it, Janice." The three of us laughed. Janice was always joking with Pam and Pam was always tickled at Janice. We would be sitting in a restaurant and a beautiful young girl would walk by, Janice would look her up and down and say, "She makes me sick." We cracked up laughing.

Janice didn't wear makeup and kept her hair gray and short because it was easy to take care of. Pam and I did not intend on letting our gray show and we were both into makeup. Pam wore her linen pants while I wore my blue jeans.

Janice always said, "Why go to the trouble? Tom loves me already." She also told me Steve was too obsessed with me. I always laughed at her and responded, "I like him to be obsessed with me."

While Janice tucked Pam in, I noticed Pam had an eight by ten photo frame of Momma on her nightstand and sitting on top of it in the left hand corner of the frame was the four by six black white Polaroid photo she took of Daddy the last time she saw him.

I asked her, "Why do you have his picture by your bed?"

She looked at it and said, "So I will remember to pray for him. I wonder if he knows I'm sick."

I looked at her and was honest with her. "I called and told him, Pam"

"What did he say?" She looked at me with a look of hope that maybe he cared.

"He said he had not been feeling well himself. It was about him. He will never change Pam." Her mouth turned down.

She rolled her eyes and, said, "It doesn't matter."

I said, "Nope, he doesn't matter. He doesn't care about us and we sure don't need him."

Janice and I went into her living room to watch TV while she rested.

That night while I was up late searching the Internet for a cure for Pam, God spoke to me to tell Pam something, so I did the next morning.

"Pam, the Lord told me to tell you not to allow yourself go into dark places in your mind."

She began to cry as she sat in the tub.

She said, "That helps me so much. From this day forward I will not think of dying. I trust God. If he chooses to take me, I am at peace. I am ready to meet Him face to face, but I do not believe I am going to die. I am not afraid to die. I know I will be with the Lord. I will not go into dark places in my mind."

Pam walked this final chapter in her life as brave as anyone could have. There was no fear. She was at total peace with God. As a child she had feared the grave but now she walked this last walk with no fear, in total peace, resting in the arms of God.

Steve came by many times to take communion and pray with her. He gave her a CD by Sarah McLachlan "*In The Arms Of The Angel*". She would stand as he gave her communion as she silently cried. Steve laid his hands on top of her head and prayed over her. Pam's five children were all grown. Four were married with children of their own and her youngest was at college in Savannah, Georgia. Pam did not want her to quit school, but it was hard on her daughter. She called her mother three and four times a day. All Pam's kids would check on her during the day and her oldest son, while on his lunch break, would find us wherever we were.

We called Leeann to meet us for lunch at least every other day. She always came even though she was busy with her business.

The holidays were here. Janice had a large home on six acres of land with an indoor pool, a round game room, with two juke boxes she called her 50s room. It had a pool table and a couple of arcade machines, a bar and an antique booth. There was an antique cash register on the bar.

Her open family room and kitchen had a stone fireplace. She and Tom set up tables to hold all our kids and us. The number varied between forty-five and fifty-five, which included Momma's grandkids and even great grandkids. Babies were crying, toddlers were running around and the teens were enjoying the 50s room. The men would go outside and shoot Tom's gun collection while the women were all getting the food ready. There was always plenty of food and deserts for everybody. Usually one of the teens had invited a boyfriend or girlfriend to join us. This Thanksgiving there was the unspoken reality that Pam may not be at the table with us next year. She chose not to wear her wig that day because it would feel hot and tight on her head. She had a beautiful silk scarf wrapped around her head tied in the back. Her makeup was perfect and she had on her two diamond rings and diamond stud earrings.

After we finished our meal, we sat with our coffee and dessert, talking for hours. Pam did the unveiling of her scarf to show anyone who had not seen her baldhead. We laughed, not at her, but with her. We looked at her beautiful face as she laughed with us.

I heard my soul say to me, "Remember this moment, she won't be with us next Thanksgiving."

I knew we all were thinking the same thing and we knew Pam was having the same thoughts. Family, what a powerful army it can be, united in our love for each other. Breathe in this moment. I am going to miss her.

New Year's was around the corner and church always put on a big celebration with skits, balloons and noisemakers. Our church congregation was large and it had a huge African American population. I always joked with them to wear their favorite hat, what I called their "Sister-Hats."

I had a jacket made of ribbons that looked expensive. It was every bright color you can imagine and I always got compliments on it. It was wired with tiny Christmas lights powered by batteries. You could not see the wires on the lights. I just pushed the button and I lit up. I added battery-operated lights to my "Sister-Hat." It always made the congregation laugh when I walked up on the platform. We went shopping for hats and we took Momma with us to the Burlington Coat factory. We walked in, Mom in her wheelchair.

I said, "Let's go to the hats. I've got to get a new "Sister-Hat" for New Year's Eve Celebration."

We wheeled Momma over to the hats. I grabbed a candy apple red hat that looked like it had a roller coaster on top of it with a red satin bow on the side. It was perfect for New Year's Eve. I placed it on Mom's head as Janice wrapped a cobalt blue long string of feathers around momma's neck. Pam grabbed elbow-length black gloves and put them on her. The background music playing in the store was perfect for this moment of joy. People walked by, looking at us dressing this little old lady in a wheelchair as we danced around her laughing. I began to spin her wheelchair around, moving to the beat of the music as she laughed and gave her queens wave in the air. She loved all the attention we gave her. People passing in the store stopped to watch. We had fun that day. It made a great memory. Memories must be made. They take only seconds of your day but last for a lifetime.

The holidays came and went. It was March. Every summer Pam and her husband took all their married children and grandchildren to their beach house in Destin, Florida where Janice and Leeann also owned beach homes. It was a family time every summer in June, just for them.

We had just taken Pam for her treatment and had grabbed a bite to eat at one of Pam's favorite restaurants next door to the Burlington Coat Factory. Pam had mentioned she needed to go there to find some new summer sandals for their vacation in June. Janice and I knew Pam was not going to be going on that family vacation. Pam loved shoes—high heels, flats, and sandals. She had tiny feet and always kept them manicured.

Pam had times when she became confused and this was one of those days. She began to try on shoes. She got excited and went up and down the aisles trying on shoes and then placing them in her buggy. Janice and I pulled them out and put them back on the shelves. We expressed excitement over each pair she tried on. Janice and I laughed as we pulled them out of the buggy.

Pam kept asking; "What are y'all laughing about?"

Janice said, "Oh, nothing, Denice is crazy. I'm laughing at her."

Pam said, "You know I need to go look for a bathing suit to take on vacation."

I said, "Let's go to that department, you already have plenty of shoes." She found two bathing suits and a pair of shorts.

I said, "Pam, it's getting late. Let's go pay for this and get back to your house so you can rest." Unloading her buggy at the register, she found only two pairs of sandals.

She said, "Hum, that's strange, I could have sworn I found more than two pair."

I said, "Remember, you put them back, those are the ones you wanted."

She nodded, "That's right."

We took Pam home. Her housekeeper informed her that Walt, her son, had called and would come by to see her later. Pam smiled. She loved seeing her son. Her younger son, Cameron, would come by in the mornings and make her some hot tea. They loved their mother.

Pam headed toward her bedroom and said, "Janice, come tuck me in bed."

Janice said, "Come on let me tuck my baby in bed."

Janice loved every minute of it. She took Pam through her routine and then she walked back into the living room where I was having a glass of sweet tea.

Janice sat down on the sofa, looked over at me and said, "I am studying every little thing about her. I observe her every minute of the day. When we sit across from each other, I study her face, her expressions, the way she holds her teacup as she sips her hot tea, the way she takes little bites and chews forever before she swallows. Every move is so dainty, feminine, and full of grace. I will remember everything about her. I am taking in every moment."

I listened to Janice and responded, "I know." That's all I could say.

What I did not say to Janice was that I wanted to fall on the floor, curl up like a baby, and scream out, "No, no, no!" I wanted to yell at the heavens and make the earth shake with my cry to God. My sister was dying. I couldn't believe life was dealing us these cards. I cannot save her. Life isn't fair. My God, I wanted to fall apart. I kept calm for Pam and Janice.

Janice caught a bad cold and was going to stay home a few days to get well. We knew she didn't need to be around Pam. Pam and I went to eat lunch. I decided to talk to Pam about things she should take care of.

"Pam, I was thinking about myself and how important it is to update wills and what things I would leave to each of my children. This is not to say you are going to die, but don't you think this is something you should do?"

She responded, "I don't want to think about it."

I accepted that as her answer and was going to leave it alone. The next afternoon her oldest daughter Melissa came by. Pam had just taken a bath and was putting her pajamas on. Melissa and I were sitting on the bed talking as Pam took off her wig and tied her silk scarf around her head.

"Melissa," Pam said, "I want to show you these diamond earrings I am going to leave you one day."

Pam went over to her jewelry box, pulled out a tiny white box and reached in to pull out her long string of diamond earrings she had worn to a southern ball. After Pam showed them to her, she went back into her bathroom to put on face cream.

Melissa and I were still sitting on the bed and I whispered to her, "Go find a pen and some paper."

Pam walked back into the bedroom.

I asked, "What about all of your diamond rings and your minks? Which daughter gets which mink?"

She went over to her closet and pulled her mink coats out and said, "Melissa, you can have this full length black sable and then she pulled out two more minks for the other two daughters."

I said, "Pam, Melissa is going to write all this down."

Pam knew what I was up to. She calmly began to pull out all her expensive jewelry, showing Melissa, and telling her which child it was to be left to. She wanted her two son's spouses to receive a piece of jewelry, too. Melissa wrote it all down. Pam told Melissa of a savings account she wanted all five children to split.

I was so proud of Melissa. She was not crying as Pam pulled the items out. She took notes as if she was a secretary. Pam told Melissa that if she went on to be with the Lord, she wanted Melissa to see to it that when her little sister falls in love and marries that she take Pam's place to help her plan the wedding of her dreams. Pam's other two daughters had beautiful Southern weddings. I could tell Pam was glad she and Melissa took care of that.

The next morning, I was driving Pam to the Cancer Center for her IV treatment. She was weak, thin, and the color of her skin looked yellow. She didn't bother to put on any makeup and she had her silk scarf tied on her head. As we walked to the car she was weak, walking slumped over and slow. As I put the car in drive, pulling away from her house, she said, "Denice tell me about God." I began to remind her of what a big God we serve. As I was listening to myself talk to her, I was thinking how tired I was, emotionally drained. But, I kept talking to her.

I said, "Remember years ago when we went to hear Betty Baxter share the miracle she received in her body?"

She answered in a weak voice, "Tell me again about her miracle."

I began to tell Pam the story, "Betty was born with a disease that had made her an invalid, and her body was all twisted. God told her and her mother that he was going to come and perform a miracle on a particular day at three o'clock. They knew the date and time that he was going to do this. The day came, and her mother propped Betty on pillows by the window in a big chair. Betty had on a new pair of shoes her daddy bought her. She'd never worn shoes before. A few family friends from church and her pastor were there along with her momma, daddy and baby brother. They waited for God to come at three o'clock."

Pam opened her purse and pulled out a Kleenex, laying it flat on one of her legs, she began to fold it into a perfect square and then a triangle. I had seen her do that so many times in an organized manner. She took one corner of the triangle to wipe away the tears as they ran down her cheek.

She sobbed as I continued talking. "The curtains began to blow through the open window. Betty said to her Momma, "He is here." Every bone in her body began to snap into place. I said to Pam, "Pam, God can heal you."

She nodded "Tell me more, Denice, about God."

As I drove I continued telling her about the love of God and how he cares for her, but I was weak. Every emotion inside of me was stirring in agony and I wanted to scream my head off. I wanted to scream and throw a fit. I wanted to yell to the heavens that this isn't fair. I remained calm. I continued telling her about the love of God.

We finished at the treatment center and as usual, we went to eat. She was quiet, so I carried the conversation at the table. I told her that she seemed tired today and we shouldn't go shopping.

"No," she said. "I want to go to Dillard's Department store."

I told her she needed to lie down, but she was determined that I take her there. She said there was something she needed to get. Pam usually wanted make-up or perfume. We got out of the car but she was so weak I put my arm through hers to help her walk. We stood in the cosmetic department, and I asked her whether it was lipstick, blush or eyeliner.

"I think it is upstairs," she said. We took the escalator up.

"Let's go over to the linen department," she said.

We stood in the department, but she could not get her thoughts together.

The sales woman walked up "May I help you?"

"Yes, my sister wants to buy something." I said.

The sales woman said, "Ma'am, is it bed sheets you want?" I looked at the woman and could see she was quickly assessing that maybe Pam was a drunk or possibly a drug addict.

So to protect my sister I said, "Pam, the chemo has made you tired." Then I saw a look of understanding on the women's face.

Pam said she would not leave until she found what she has come for. The woman began to show her towels and bath rugs.

Pam said, "I think it's made of marble.

The sales women said, "I know what it is." I immediately knew myself. Over the ten months of us shopping Pam had seen me look at the toothbrush holder, cup holder, hand pump and soap dish, all in red onyx marble that matched the red onyx marble I was having installed on my new master bathroom counter tops. The marble trashcan alone cost ninety dollars, and one toothbrush holder was around thirty dollars, and I needed two for two sinks. The sales person showed it to her.

Pam said, "That's it."

I said, "I'm not going to let you buy that."

She said, "I want the whole set, with two toothbrush holders. This is for you, Denice."

I decided to just let her buy me the trashcan for my own memory with her. I took her home and put her to bed.

The next morning I went over to Pam's but that morning she was still in bed and we could not wake her. Her housekeeper just let her sleep. We spent all day going into her room checking on her, but we could not wake her. We called her name, but nothing woke her.

The next morning, Janice was still sick. I would be taking Pam to her doctor's appointment without Janice. I was able to wake Pam and I told her to get dressed. She got dressed in her beige linen pants and her linen, short sleeve, mint green blouse. As we walked towards the car, I noticed she was thinner and the color of her skin was turning yellower. The whites of her eyes were no longer white. They were yellow. She didn't bother to put her blonde wig on. She tied her silk scarf on her head, no make-up on and no jewelry. She walked slumped forward instead of walking with the perfect posture I was use to seeing. To my horror I noticed her pants were wet. I wanted to weep.

I said, "Pam, your slacks are wet. Let's go back inside and change clothes." She mumbled, "No, let's just go. I don't care." It hurt to see her perfectly pressed slacks with a big wet spot on the seat. At any other time in her life, she would not have anyone see her like this. She would have gone back into the house to change.

The nurse saw Pam as we walked in. She took us to a room. Pam sat on the patient table and didn't say a word. I told the doctor about the changes I was observing in Pam. Pam didn't speak. She seemed very cloudy in her ability to focus her eyes and think.

I said, "Doctor, she did not wake up yesterday. We tried to wake her, but there was no response. Now she is awake, her bowels have not moved in days and she doesn't want to drink anything because she chokes. I tried to make her drink some water, but she could not swallow, so she spit it out in a bowl."

He looked at Pam as he put out his hand to take her hand in his. He said, "I am so sorry. This is the beginning of the end." He shook her hand and walked out of the room.

I was stunned. I wanted more from him, but I realized he dealt with cancer patients every day and this was his own way of dealing with it. I lifted Pam up off the table and grabbed her purse. I wrapped my arm through her arm to support her. She was weak and confused.

I said, "Pam, come on." We walked slowly to the car, arm in arm.

As I drove away, she turned to me and asked in a weak voice, "What did he mean by that?" I just could not say it. I couldn't tell her what he meant.

I just said, "I don't know. That was strange wasn't it?" I took her home and put her to bed.

That evening Steve could tell I was down. He suggested we get in the boat and go for a ride on the lake. He drove, sitting in one of the bucket seats. I went to the back of the boat to sit on the bench. I began to cry. I began to scream. It echoed across the lake.

Steve asked, "Are you okay?" He drove fast across the lake, so I could to cry and scream, where no one could hear me. He knew I needed a release. I grabbed a green towel to muffle the sound of my screams. I wept and screamed until I could weep no more. Steve took me back to the cabin and put me to bed.

The next morning, driving back into town, I began to cry again. Doubled over in my seat, I walled in agony. I could not control my emotions at all. The crying from my gut was so painful. Through my tears I said, "Take me to the emergency room. I think I'm having a break down. I can't stop crying."

He drove as fast as he could; he just kept looking over at me as I cried out loud in my pain. He was praying.

It was a forty-five minute drive from the lake to Montgomery. By the time we got into town, I had taken control of myself and had him drop me off at Pam's. She was still asleep.

Janice was better from having the flu and already there. I sat in Pam's den and watched television. Pam's housekeeper was in the kitchen cleaning. Janice went back to Pam's room to check on her.

She woke up and in a weak whisper said, "I need to tell Denice something."

Janice came into the den. "Denice, Pam wants to talk to you."

I sat on the side of the bed next to her. "Pam, what is it?"

Her voice was thick because she could no longer swallow fluids. "I need to tell you something."

I leaned in closer with the fear she would not be able to finish and I would never know what she wanted to tell me. I ask, "Pam, what is it?"

"I need to tell you something. I need to tell you something." she kept saying that. It was as if she had been lying there, thinking she needed to wake up to tell me what she was thinking.

I said, "Pam try to tell me."

Very slowly she pushed the air out with her words, "I don't want to leave my body."

She could feel her soul being pulled, separating from her body. She was asking me to keep her in her here. I felt helpless.

"Do you want me to pray Pam?"

Struggling to push out her words, she said, "Yes."

I laid my hands on her chest and began to pray out loud. "God, please God, please, God, please," I begged.

I prayed. "Let Pam stay, God. You are a mighty and powerful God. You, God, changed all our lives. We know you, and we know your power. You have control of this. You are a healer. You are Pam's savior. I am asking you to leave Pam with us and let her be healed. Change your mind about this, God. You are our only hope. You are our only answer. You are mighty and powerful. You are God."

I leaned close to Pam and asked, "Pam can you hear me? Did you hear me praying?"

She whispered, "Yes, pray louder." I prayed again, pleading my case with God. She drifted off into a deep sleep again. I went back into the living room to let her sleep. For two more days, she was in and out of sleep. At one point, Janice and I walked in and sat on the bed looking at her.

She opened her eyes, looked at Janice and me then smiled as she said, "If you could see what I am seeing, you would be jealous."

I asked, "Are you seeing angels?"

She replied. "Yes"

We called Hospice and they came. Janice and I explained to the two nurses that Pam had been active until a few days ago. "This is the process of her shutting down," they explained."

While we were talking, Pam walked into the room with her eyes wide open and alert. She sat down on the sofa next to me. My mouth fell open for a moment to see that kind of strength after Pam had been weak and asleep for days.

We explained to Pam, who the nurses were. "Pam they are from Hospice."

She said, "I know."

She sat proper, as she always did as they began to ask her questions. Answering them as calmly and lady-like as if she were on a job interview.

"Mrs. Pam, are you fine with us checking in on you every day?" the nurse asked.

"Yes", Pam answered. I saw them to the door and walked over to Pam, who was still sitting on the sofa. I sat down on the edge of the coffee table in front of her.

I took her by the hands and said, "I don't want you to die." I fell to my knees, burying my head in her lap. I sobbed, tears falling from my cheeks onto her pajamas. Pam placed her hands on top of my head.

She said, "Denice, I'm not going to die." She said it slow and distinct.

I looked up at her face and said, "Pam, you are and if we don't get a miracle, you are going to die soon. You are going to be with the Lord, Pam." I didn't want her to leave without us saying goodbye.

"Denice, I am not going to die," she said in a whisper. I knew she knew she was dying, but she was seeing it as stepping over to a life in heaven. Pam had peace. I sobbed with my head in her lap. She caressed the back of my head to comfort me, rubbing the back of my head. I then put her to bed.

That weekend was Mother's Day. Pam's family spent that day alone. Pam was in and out of consciousness. Charlie brought Momma so that we all could spend Mother's Day with her. We gathered at Janice's. We brought covered dishes. All of Momma's children and grandchildren were there.

Monday morning Charlie came over to Pam's house before they left to go back to Atlanta. We had already informed Momma that Pam might not wake up to talk to her, since she was in and out of consciousness. We gathered around the bed.

Janice said, "Pam, Momma is here."

She opened her eyes and tried to lift herself, reaching her arms out toward Momma like a little girl reaching for her Mommy.

She said, "Momma."

Pam's daughters got in the bed with her and sat behind her. They lifted her from behind so she could sit. Pam wanted to touch

Momma. Charlie pushed Momma's wheelchair over to the side of the bed. He pushed her footrest to the side placing her feet on the floor and stood Momma straight up. Her full body weight was against him as he stood behind her.

Jimmy moved the wheelchair out of the way. We moved Pam's legs off to the side of the bed and held Mom's back to support her so she could face each other. Pam reached out toward Momma and wrapped her arms around Momma's neck.

She whispered, "Momma, I don't want this to hurt you."

Momma cried out, "My baby, my baby, my baby."

Momma wept, holding on tightly to her.

Pam whispered, "Momma I love you." She laid her face against Momma's neck the way a baby does its mother.

"I love you! I love you!" Momma cried out.

Pam whispered, "I love you momma."

We laid Pam back down and she fell asleep. Charlie sat Momma back into her wheelchair. We went into the living room and decided it would be better for Charlie to take Momma back to Atlanta where she had all her necessities. We told him we'd keep him informed and would call if we saw a turning towards the end. Momma must rest for the days that lay ahead.

Hospice told us that she would be in and out of consciousness. Even as a little girl she loved to be held. She would say, "Hold me, Daddy, hold me." His black and white picture was still next to her bed on her nightstand. He never called to check on her during the ten months she was getting chemo.

The next day all of Pam's family was in and out of the bedroom, taking turns sitting with her.

Janice crawled up into the bed with her, loved on her, saying, "You have been the most wonderful sister to me. You have loved me so beautifully. I always knew you loved me, Pam."

Leeann was holding her feet, saying, "My darling Angel." Tears ran down her cheek.

I took my turn with her. I lay across her body and cried. Her eyes were now open but she was not blinking and her breathing had slowed. Pam's breathing was slow and shallow. Her eyes were fixed and we knew today would be the day. All of the family, except the youngest grandchildren, stood around Pam's bed. Janice and I were at the foot of the bed. Janice was on her knees and I was standing next to her. Pam's children and their spouses were on each side of the bed; my children and their spouses were in the room, also. Steve was standing next to me.

It would take Charlie about two hours to get Momma fed, bathed, dressed, and on the road. We told him to go ahead and get on the interstate and come. Her breathing was changing. It was slow as she gasped for air. We did not want to see her struggle for air. I felt she was waiting for us to release her and let her go. I knew Momma wasn't there, but also knew Momma would not want her baby struggling for air.

I looked down at Janice and said, "Janice, tell Pam to run toward the light."

Janice cut her eyes toward me and said, "No."

Holding back tears, I said again in a firm tone, "Janice, you tell Pam to run toward the light."

Janice looked at me, paused and took a deep breath as she gave the command, "Pam, run toward the light. Run Pam. Run to the light.

I then yelled, "Go Pam, run. Pam, run to the light. Go to Jesus. Go into His arms. Cross over." Everyone in the room began to say, "Go to Jesus, run to His arms."

I yelled again. "Pam, cross over. Run Pam. Run toward the light."

Pam took three deep breaths. Chill bumps appeared all over her arms and then she was gone. She exhaled her last breath and we literally could see her spirit leave her body. It was the most beautiful sight I have ever seen. It was powerful, it was mighty, it was holy and the holiness of holies was in the room. It was more beautiful than the birth of a newborn baby.

The Hospice nurses waited in the other room, allowing us to have these last moments with our precious sister. We asked them not to take her until our mother arrived. They waited three hours. The hearse was out front waiting and a police officer came and stood in the corner of the bedroom by the fireplace, very respectfully, almost like a soldier protecting a royalty.

The phone rang in the kitchen and Leeann answered it. It was Daddy.

"This is Charles Perkins. How is Pam doing?"

Ten months and he had finally called and wanted to know about his child.

Leeann said, "Well, Daddy, it's odd you called. She passed away an hour ago."

"She did?" He said, and then his song and dance routine began. "Well, I'm not going to be able to come to the funeral. I haven't been feeling well." He did not skip a beat and immediately gave his excuse as to why he would not show up for his own child's funeral.

Leeann said, "You son-of-a- bitch" and hung up. I thought how strange he called right after she took her last breath. We went into the living room and waited for Momma to arrive.

I called Charlie on his cell phone and said. "Charlie, Pam just passed away."

The words were hard to say. "She's gone."

He, Jimmy, and Momma were already in the car driving on the interstate heading toward Montgomery. I heard him say, "Momma, Pam is gone."

Momma sobbed.

I heard her say, "I want to stop all these cars and tell them, my baby just passed away, that my baby is in the presence of God. They don't know what just happened to my baby. These people don't realize today is not just a regular day. My baby, my baby, Oh, my baby," she cried.

I hung the phone up, looked at Janice and said, "We did good."

She nodded and said back to me, "We did good."

We knew what we were referring to. We were remembering how as little girls laying in the dark; we let Pam wrap her arms and legs around us so she would feel safe. We did that for her again as she took her final journey. We did good.

Charlie arrived with Momma. He brought her into the room in her wheelchair to see her baby one last time before they took her body away.

Momma's body was slumped forward in her wheelchair as if she could hardly breathe. Her eyes looked at her child with such sadness and pain. I wondered how her body could hold up under such pain in her soul. She raised her hand toward God, and for the second time in my life I saw her ball her fist up in the air and say, "My baby." Momma wept.

Pam's body was wheeled outside on a gurney with a sheet covering her. I stood on the front porch of Pam's house. They placed her in the hearse and shut the doors on the hearse. They took a right turn out of the driveway. It was a dead-end street. The hearse turned and passed by the house again before leaving the neighborhood. I didn't like the thought of her body being in the back of that hearse alone.

I whispered under my breath, "Bye Pam, I love you. I will miss you."

I watched as the hearse left her street, it disappeared.

My sister had died and it was time for Steve and me to be her pastor. We prepared for the funeral. The church was packed. Pam's children each shared stories about their mother. She would have been so proud of them.

I shared events about Pam's life—the eight boxes of Valentine candy, the day she defended me and I fought Fat Henrietta with my frog.

I told them, "Pam is looking down at me right now, laughing. I feel her."

I told them she was my biggest cheerleader in life, always bragging about me to others and telling me the message I preached really helped her. I told them that every time I preached at the church, Pam ordered at least eight tapes of my sermon and passed them around town. I told them how Pam and I had lived together while our spouses were in the Navy. Pam and I ran after God together. I told them how I tried to get Pam to flirt with her boss to get him to notice her. The congregation laughed and cried. I told them what an honor it was to have been blessed with my sister. I have been lucky in life to love her the way I did and to be loved by her.

I said, "She is not in my past. She is in my future and I will see her again."

Her death was beautiful—it was personal, painful and empty, and I miss her. Pam passed away Wednesday, May 11, 2005. She was fifty-six years old. After everything was over, I crashed. The grief was unbearable. I woke up and my first thought was, this can't be true. She came to me always smiling and I would ask, "Why are you here? You died." She would just continue smiling at me.

Janice started staying at her beach house in Destin, Florida. She just didn't want to be in Montgomery with all the reminders of Pam. We tried going into department stores and the sales people would ask, "Where is the other sister?" It was too painful to say she passed away. Janice just couldn't do it any longer.

I told Steve I needed a break from the ministry. I felt I had nothing to give. The separation between earth and heaven at first was unbelievable pain.

Top photo: Pam and Mom the year before Pam passed.
Bottom photos: Mom and Pam, one year before she passed away.

WHEN I ACCEPTED *the fact that I missed Pam, but she did* *not miss me, I began to heal.* I know for Pam, it will be as if it was a few seconds ago, when we last saw each other. They do not experience separation in heaven. If they did, there would be pain and there is no pain in heaven. This is a part of life for everyone and we do not learn this through books but through experience. Life is a teacher, isn't it?

Little Denice's marriage ended in divorce with no children after four years. Our son Stephen and his wife Hillary were moving to Los Angeles to pursue his career as a singer and songwriter. We decided to go too. After twenty-six years of pastoring, we turned the church over to our oldest daughter and her husband.

We kept our home in Montgomery and leased a beautiful home in the hills of LA. I could see the Hollywood sign from my back yard. Little Denice moved to California with us. Misty was living in Niceville, Florida, near Destin.

We left our home in Montgomery furnished so that we could come back and forth from LA. That way we could see our children and grandchildren and spend time with Momma, who was still with Charlie and Jimmy.

On one visit to Atlanta to see Momma, she told me, "Denice, something happened last night. I don't know if I saw it or if it was a dream. It seemed so real." I told her to tell me about it.

She said, "I stepped into this room in heaven and I saw a beautiful banquette table with people sitting at it. Pam was sitting there, talking and laughing. When she saw me, she waved for me to come and sit across from her. She saved me a seat. Pam was smiling. She was so excited to see me and it was as if she heard I was coming and they were all waiting for me."

I said, "Momma, I believe that was from God. Maybe you are fixing to go and join Pam."

"That would be wonderful, perhaps so," she said with serenity.

I told her, "I believe she is saving you a seat, Momma."

"I do too," She said in such a tender voice and a look of excitement in her eyes.

It was getting harder for Charlie to take care of Momma and we all agreed she should be in a nursing home in Montgomery. I stayed to help Charlie get her settled in a nursing home near my home. I spent every day with her and even became the official bingo caller. I ate lunch with her and got to know each person at her table. She and two others in their wheelchairs became buddies. Every day I took them outside to the gazebo and read a book to them.

Leeann told the owner that she would give the cafeteria a full face-lift—a total make over at no expense to the nursing home. Momma was so proud of Leeann and how talented she was.

Isn't it something how life makes a complete circle? It was the same nursing home I had danced at when I was a child and here I am with my Momma in that very nursing home. I ate lunch with her in the very room I had once danced in to entertain the patients of the home.

She lived five weeks. It was a blessing I got to be with her during those weeks. It was Easter Sunday weekend. The nurse in the nursing home tried to wake mom and she had had another stroke. We filled the hospital room with family, taking turns loving on Momma, singing all the church songs that had meant so much to her.

Realizing Pam wasn't there to take Momma's last breath. I sat on the edge of her bed lying over her as I pressed my lips against her lips, letting her breath into my mouth. I breathed in her breath. I looked over at Janice.

She smiled and said. "I know what you are doing."

I smiled at her with a twinkle in my eye and said, "I told you and Pam, I would be the one." I kissed her face and told her I loved her.

"Momma," I repeated to her over and over again, "Momma"

It was a beautiful word to me. She passed away April 9th, 2007. I know Pam was sitting at that banquet table in heaven—having gotten word that Momma was coming. She was smiling, waving for Momma to join her. Pam had saved Momma a seat!

W E RECEIVED WORD DADDY was in a nursing home in Birmingham, Alabama. Charlie and Leeann went to see him twice. Daddy had always said he wasn't Charlie's Daddy. Charlie wanted to know, one way or another. Charlie and Leeann told Daddy they were going to check his dentures. Charlie ordered a DNA test kit. He swabbed Daddy's mouth, sent the kit off and got the results a few days later. The test came back 99 percent positive, Daddy was Charlie's father. We knew he was, but Charlie wanted to have it settled.

One afternoon I stopped by Leeann's new building.

She said, "I received a phone call this morning from a funeral director at Green Valley Funeral Home near Birmingham. He said he had Daddy's body and asked if we wanted to view it. The director felt someone should view it before he was lowered into the ground." I knew this day would come.

I told Lee, "I will go if you are busy with your store's grand opening. Don't feel guilty for not going. You know Leeann, if you had died, he would not have bothered coming."

She said, "Let me think about it overnight. I'll call you in the morning."

Charlie and Jimmy were out of the country for a month traveling around Morocco. They were to arrive home that Wednesday. I called

Janice and told her. She decided to go. Janice, Leeann, Steve and I went together. We arrived at the funeral home. The director walked us into a conference room. We sat down and he opened a folder.

"Your father had come by a few years ago to take care of the arrangements. He did not want a service or a viewing, just to be put in the ground. Two women dropped by with a death certificate, but they did not want to view him. What are your wishes?"

We all agreed we needed a moment with Daddy. The director said that Daddy was not in a coffin, but would be on a table with a sheet covering all but his neck and head.

He led us into a room and there he lay. Daddy looked as he did the last time I saw him alive, old and frail. He looked like an old man that could have been a loving father, maybe a man who loved his children and grandchildren. He could have been a man that could have been successful in his life—one who's loved ones wept at his passing. The reality was no one was weeping and no one came but the children he had left behind. We stood silently looking down at his lifeless body on the table. The director stood in the back of the room as he heard me speak up.

"Well, Daddy, here we are. You know, you never did right with your children. You never loved us. You were the one who missed out. We were great kids. We are good people. Your life was a sad life. You know Daddy, everyone liked you but nobody loved you except those you walked away from, Momma and your kids. It was all about money and what your flesh wanted. Now you're gone. You are dead and none of those things you loved more than family are with you. I choose to close the last page of this chapter in my life. I do not need you. I have all I need in this life to make me complete. Your children are blessed. We have found love without you." Janice was standing to the right of me.

She spoke sincerely and with mercy. "I don't know if you are in heaven or hell, but I believe you can hear me wherever you are. I know you had mental problems, so I forgive you for being a child molester." She took a few steps back.

Leeann began to sob. I pulled her close to me and held her.

She said, "I have no childhood memory of Daddy."

THE NEXT MORNING, I called the woman who had his death certificate.

She said, "Your Daddy always said you kids didn't belong to him."

"Yeah, it was his way of not having any guilt about abandoning us." I said.

She said, "Well, in his will he did leave you kids something."

She said it in a way, which told me dad had told her, all we wanted was his money. She said, "He left each child a one dollar bill." That was a slap in the face from Daddy.

"Of course, he did. That was Daddy." I said.

She continued, "Your Daddy always went to the nursing home chapel service and he loved his gospel singing."

"Yeah, he always did love those quartets," I said.

All my life, I felt that in the end, Daddy would make it into heaven, not by his own right, but by the mercy of God and the prayers of Momma and his children. Who knows the thoughts of a person taking his last breath? If he did make it into heaven, I am sure the gates of pearl kicked him in the butt as he entered.

I called Leeann and Janice to tell them of their one-dollar inheritance. The two women got his home and everything in it, including his car.

Janice answered, "Well, he can take it to his grave because that is the only thing he loved in his life—money."

We were still waiting for Charlie to arrive back to the States. Charlie arrived and called from Atlanta. We agreed that Janice and I would meet him and Jimmy at the funeral home the next morning so Charlie could have closure.

Janice and I sat in the waiting room finishing our Starbucks before they arrived.

Charlie and Jimmy walked in and we hugged each other. We asked about their overseas trip. The director walked up to us to see if we were ready to view Daddy's body. We entered the room. This time he was in a baby blue coffin, a beige suit, starched cream dress shirt and a baby blue tie. Jimmy took a seat as Charlie, Janice, and I stood looking down at Daddy.

Charlie spoke up in a trembling voice, "Daddy, I forgive you for molesting me, for grooming me to be molested. I was young and wanted so badly to have a Daddy. I wanted you to love me. You told me that you wanted to show me a gun you had in your suitcase. You held it in your hand. You said for me not to tell Momma about the gun. You said it was a secret between us, between buddies, that men have secrets together. Then you took advantage of me, a child. I realize now that you didn't have it in you to love me. I truly forgive you. I hope you're at peace and I hope God had mercy on your soul. The times that I did see you, I thought you had a good personality. You were funny in a strange kind of way. Everybody around you seemed to like you. I would have liked you, if I hadn't known what I knew about you."

Charlie laughed as he looked down at Daddy. "Your dick and money are all you cared about."

I laughed and said. "On that note, Daddy, you left each of your children one dollar. We do not want to inherit anything from you. So here are five one-dollar bills from all of us. One is from Pam. We want you to take it with you to your grave. We do not need anything from you."

Charlie tucked the five one-dollar bills into Daddy's suit.

Janice and I walked over to sit down with Jimmy and left Charlie looking down at Daddy.

Charlie said to Dad, "Well, speak up, don't you have anything to say for yourself?"

We all laughed. Charlie walked over to us, lit a cigarette, smoked a few puffs off it and threw the butt in the coffin with Daddy.

I said, "Charlie, he is embalmed. His body could explode with fire."

We burst out in laughter. I know it sounds disrespectful, the way we laughed and joked, but I also realized it was because we were truly free from the pain he caused in our lives. We were not his victims.

Charlie lifted up the lid of the coffin that was closed over his legs and feet. There was a plastic bag, between his legs, that held his false teeth, his wallet, a paperback Gideon Bible, and his cheap watch. Charlie opened the wallet. There was a one-dollar bill in it.

Charlie asked, "I wonder why he had a one dollar bill in his wallet?"

I said, "Maybe he wanted to give it to Pam when he got to heaven." We laughed.

The director walked in to say they were ready to put him in the ground. We drove our cars to the gravesite. We arrived just as the hearse pulled up. It was the dead of winter, and the sky was overcast. A damp cold breeze was blowing. We bundled up with our sweaters and coats to get warm. The director, two elderly men, and a young man in his twenties set the coffin down onto the belts to lower it into the ground. No one else was there to testify to a life lived, only the children that he said were no good and did not belong to him.

Charlie walked over and lifted the lid of the coffin to look one last time. In all my years in the ministry, I have never seen anyone open the coffin at the gravesite.

I looked at the director to see his response to Charlie opening the lid. He seemed to make a quick decision, allowing him to do what he needed for closure. The director had overheard everything we said to Daddy. Charlie began to lower the lid and the director reached to give a helping hand. Charlie pushed his hand away as if to say, I need to be the one to slam this coffin shut. He then walked around to the other side of the coffin. They began to lower it into the ground and Charlie then kicked the coffin as hard as he could.

A feeling of victory swept over me. I no longer saw a passive boy. I saw a strong man. The young boy became a man and kicked the loser's coffin. He then walked over to stand by Janice and me.

"Charlie," I said, "You have the right to do and say anything you feel at this moment. This is our closure. I am proud of you as a man. I like who you are. I am proud of all Mommas' kids. We are good people. We were loved by our Momma and her love was enough."

We watched his coffin as it was lowered into the ground. Janice, Charlie, Jimmy and I gave a group hug to say goodbye, then turned and got into our cars.

I opened the car door to my red convertible, paused for one last look toward his grave. How strange, I thought. Daddy was buried among all the plastic flowers. One day I might come by and put some plastic tulips on his grave. I'll plant plastic tulips in the winter. He would like that, just as he said, "When people drive by and see his tulips, they will wonder how tulips can grow in the winter." His grave will be the only one that can grow tulips in the winter.

~∾ 22 ∾~
ASHES TO ASHES, DUST TO DUST

SUMMER 2007

ASHES TO ASHES, DUST to dust. Momma always said she
wanted a marching band with a choir singing When the Saints
Go Marching In. She wanted it to be a time of celebration. There
Janice and I stood. She was sixty, and I was not far behind. How did
the years pass so fast?

As Janice and I looked out over the ocean, the setting sun cast
an orange hue across the water. All the sunbathers and the children
playing had gone in for the evening. Our toes were dug deeply into
the wet sand as the waves rushed over our feet. The breeze, filled with
the salty air, blew against our face. We stood side by side, looking in
deep silence... and from the depths of my being I heard my soul cry,
"Momma, are we there yet?"

Our eyes were fixed on Steve and Tom as they stood waist deep,
slowly sprinkling from two clear plastic bags Momma's ashes. Steve
was now in his sixties, still very handsome and distinguished looking, with white hair and mustache. I thought of all the people who
enjoyed the beach that day, who had no idea someone's ashes, someone whose life counted so much, were being emptied into the sea. I
wondered how Steve felt as he scattered Momma's ashes. He loved

her. There was no choir or marching band, no celebration. The breeze blew Momma's ashes as they skipped across the top of the blue water.

I whispered, "Momma."

I gave her a queen's wave and said, "Bye Momma, go into the ocean that you loved. It always brought you such peace."

"Momma, I *now* understand the journey through life was the destination. We were always there. Momma, you taught me that life is more than plastic tulips. When the storms came with all its sorrow and tears, we hunkered down and trusted God, knowing the sun would shine again. We laughed and danced for joy with the taste of victory in our mouths. It was part of our journey through this life. You taught me to hope in God. God was the answer, Momma."

"I now know that the test of life comes. Bad things happen to good people. The powerful weapon of choice that has been given to us all, determines how we go through this life."

"Mom, I will dance in the sun. I will dance in the rain. I realize money will be made and money will be lost. Children and grandchildren will marry and divorce. Babies will be born and loved ones will die. You have taught me how to live and love life with all its obstacles. Life happens to us and we determine the journey.

Life at its best is beautiful—full of love and laughter. Life's lowest moments are still worth living. God, laughter and tears joined you and your children's hearts and souls through this glorious journey called Life."

"God and the love we had for each other, gave us the strength to fight life through."

"I will find, with the help of God, a new normal in life's journey without you and Pam until I see you, both, again at the banquet table. *Save me a seat!*"

THE END

A NOTE FROM THE AUTHOR

*I*N WRITING MY story I attempted to tell you about my life, the way I saw it. If I had written about all the challenges I faced and miracles in my life, this book would not have been able to contain the pages. I fought back and forth on some of the things I told you about God and me. This was to be a story about three sisters and their two young siblings. I saw there was no way I could leave Him out. He was the driving force, the common thread that ran through all our lives.

If you received anything after reading my story, please share it with someone. I would love to hear from you. Help "Plastic Tulips in the Winter" become a best seller. Pass it on.

Denice Vickers

www.plastictulipsinthewinter.com

Made in the USA
Lexington, KY
30 November 2015